misogyny

misogyny
the male malady

david d. gilmore

PENN

university of pennsylvania press

philadelphia

10 9 8 7 6 5 4 3 2 1

Published by
University of Pennsylvania Press
Philadelphia, Pennsylvania 19104-4011

Library of Congress Cataloging-in-Publication Data

Gilmore, David D., 1943–
   Misogyny : the male malady / David Gilmore.
     p.   cm.
   Includes bibliographical references and index.
   ISBN 0-8122-3589-4 (cloth : alk. paper)
    1. Misogyny. I. Title.
HQ1233 .G55 2001
305.42 — dc21   2001027131

To Aggie and Julian

Contents

"God became man, granted. The devil became a woman."

— Victor Hugo, *Ruy Blas*

"Woman to man
Is either a god or a wolf."

— John Webster, *The Duchess of Malfi*

"Man's imaginative recognition of feminine charm, man's greedy lust, man's pride in possession, man's tremulous sense of the pathos of femininity, man's awe in the presence of an abysmal mystery — all these feelings exist in a curious detachment in his consciousness."

— John Cowper Powys, *A Glastonbury Romance*

Preface

Since I am a man writing a book about man's inhumanity toward woman, I feel I should explain my motives, if only by way of exculpation. Like most baby-boom males, I consider myself a tolerant and enlightened man, and I harbor a sincere fondness for women as friends, lovers, colleagues, workmates, and, of course, paragons of physical beauty. However, I do recognize occasional negative stirrings in myself, feelings that certainly exist in most of my male friends whether they will admit to it or not: these include impatience, peevishness, a tendency to scapegoat females, atavistic impulses (usually erotic), fustrations in trying to communicate, and anger over inherent differences. Most men who are honest with themselves will admit to such uncharitable feelings, no matter how incompatible they are with an enlightened self-image. Perhaps this book is an attempt to help combat masculine obtuseness on the subject of relations with women, but I also think that its writing was part of a detour toward self-improvement.

At an intellectual level, my curiosity about misogyny was aroused when I was a graduate student in anthropology at the University of Pennsylvania back in the 1970s. Reading the classic ethnographic monographs for the first time, I was struck again and again by the pervasiveness and intensity of misogynist institutions: rituals of mockery directed against unoffending women, hostile folklore and jokes, domestic despotism, demonization of women in magical beliefs, terror over female witches, a truly visceral horror about female glandular secretions, menstrual phobias and taboos, and so on.

I was also struck by a paradox that made misogyny far more interesting than a simple phobia because, wherever these rituals and misogynist beliefs were the most sordid and flamboyant, one also found their exact opposite: histrionic rituals of female imitation or glorification. This dualism clearly pointed to some deeper social and psychic dynamic concerning sex and gender that got me thinking.

Underlying my curiosity was the vague memory of misogynist themes in the Western canon that I had read and admired in college, especially in the works of the ancients, Strindberg, D. H. Lawrence, Swift, Pope, the Jacobean dramatists, Restoration dramatists like Wycherley, Ezra Pound, and so many others. Some of my favorite writers — Hemingway, Cowper Powys, Keats, even

Shakespeare — also expressed gratuitous antiwoman attitudes, likening women to inimical natural forces and taking an adversarial position toward them that sometimes seemed incongruous in their noble fiction. So the literary experience dovetailed with and abetted the anthropological, and this thematic congruence made a study of misogyny more urgent.

The current study was also motivated by what I have to call a negative phenomenon: the utter lack of interest in this subject among my (all-male) former anthropology professors. I brought up my observations with them time and again, only to be met with shrugs, smirks, and mumbled pronouncements about eternal verities and timeless commonplaces. One profesor, by way of dismissing my nettlesome queries, alluded to the universality of mother-in-law jokes. "Needs no explanation," he muttered, "just wait until you get married." While there was something to this, I thought then, and I still think now, that it does need an explanation.

My interest was further piqued when I spent a year in Spain during my dissertation research. Subscribing to a rather strict macho code, most men in my village (near Seville) were nevertheless alternately hostile and worshipful about women. Sometimes, in the all-male sanctuary of the bar, they tipsily denounced females as deceivers and cheats, valuable only as sex objects, ready to cuckold their men. Their wives and mothers-in-law were the butt of endless bar-room jokes and jibes. But sometimes the same men would just as vociferously idolize women, especially their own mothers and sisters, praising them as saintly, sacrificing, and pure, in fact as close to moral perfection as a human being can come.

My goal in this book is to provide an anthropological and especially cross-cultural view of misogyny as a global phenomenon. In this way I hope to broaden the scope of the inquiry, which so far has been largely limited to the West. Part of the objective is to show that misogyny is not a Western invention, nor is it confined to modern capitalist societies, as many feminists and Marxists have argued for many years. Thus the book widens into a general disputation against reductionistic politically charged explanations of human frailty and error. But in another sense my focus is narrower than previous studies. I want to emphasize the social-psychological aspect of woman-bashing around the world, the deeper affective meanings and fears that trouble the male psyche in so many disparate places. This book is partly intended as a step toward the discovery of antidotes to an irrational but ubiquitous prejudice.

None of what I say here is all that new; some (not all) of the anthropological data are old hat. The masculine turmoil I write about here is well known in history, literature, art, and anthropology. What is needed, however, is a comparative focus, one that considers all aspects of male-female relations, not just sex and marriage but also the regressive, alimentary, and gender-identity conflicts that all men face and that trouble their views of and relations with women. Such a synoptic view will show that misogyny is so widespread and so pervasive among men everywhere that it must be least partly psychogenic in origin, a result of identical experiences in the male developmental cycle, rather than caused by the environment alone.

Many people have helped me hone my ideas and have encouraged me to undertake and complete this project. I first want to thank a skilled editor, Anne J. Weitzer, who once again has turned my jargon-ridden academese into readable English prose. Gladys Topkis did likewise. Also due a word of thanks are Dan Bates, Judith Tucker, Tim Mitchell, Terry Hays, Alan Duben, James Taggart, R. Howard Bloch, Ulku Bates, Daniel M. Varisco, and Lisa Vergara, all of whom gave me valuable directions for research. My mentor and friend Ruben E. Reina, now retired from the University of Pennsylvania, pointed me in the right direction thirty years ago, and his gentle acumen remains a constant inspiration. He told me then that the worst sin in writing — scholarly or otherwise — is pedantry, and I hope I have honored his injunction. Patricia Smith of the University of Pennsylvania Press guided the work into the publication process with an alacrity and competence that amazed me.

A special word of appreciation is due my daughter, Aggie Gilmore, whose expert knowledge of Latin pulled me through some difficult translations and who remains a constant source of pride and inspiration. My twelve-year-old son Julian inspired me also when, hearing of this project, he confided that, despite the disparagement of some of his classmates, "girls are not all *that* yucky." These words of precocious wisdom encouraged me no end and gave me hope for the future of males everywhere.

Yes, women are the greatest evil Zeus has made, and men are bound to them hand and foot, with impossible knots by god.

—Semonides, *Woman*

Introduction

ONE AFTERNOON in the early fifteenth century, the Italian woman of letters Christine de Pizan writes, she was browsing through her library for something light to read and discovered Jean Le Fèvre's *Lamentation of Maltheolus* (ca. 1275), which enumerated in scabrous detail the wickedness of all womankind through the ages. So appalled was she by Le Fèvre's polemics that she countered with a book of her own, *The Book of the City of Ladies* (1405), which may be the world's first feminist tract.

Christine claimed that the *Lamentations* was an unscholarly treatise and full of lies and distortions (see Solomon 1997:1). She was deeply offended and disturbed by the fact that it was only one in a long line of antifeminist literature. In her own book she bemoaned the age-old tendency among male thinkers to malign women. "How [has] it happened," she demanded, "that so many different men — and learned men among them — have been and are so inclined to express both in speaking and in their treatises and writings so many wicked insults about women and their behavior?" (cited in Bloch 1991:4).

Men (learned and not) continue to heap scathing insults upon women. And these men can be found not only in the world that Christine de Pizan knew (little more than western Europe and the Middle East), but in every nook and cranny of the globe, from the jungles of South America to the remote uplands of New Guinea, and in every age from the ancients to the present moment, and in every form of society from primitive stone age hunters to enlightened modern urban intellectuals.

The Ubiquity of Misogyny

Before I begin to formulate what questions to ask about woman-hating, I will give a brief preview of misogyny around the world. I begin with a so-called primitive people, one of the last stone age groups to be contacted by the modern world: the highlanders of New Guinea in the South Pacific, known to the outside world only since the 1950s when the first Europeans wandered into their mountain aeries.

These men believe not only that women are inferior to men — a view that would not have surprised Christine de Pizan — but that women are also polluting to men, actually dangerous to men's health, both physical and moral. Prolonged physical contact with women's bodies can, they say, be sickening to a man and, if untreated with magical cures, will cause his skin to wither and his organs to waste away, until eventually he dies, his body full of pustules (Meggitt 1964; Langness 1976). The men declare that women's monthly menstrual flow in particular is the most powerful and deadly poison on earth; one drop is absolutely lethal to men, boys, and male animals. To protect themselves against such contagion, the men barricade themselves in isolated men's houses, which are barred to females on pain of beatings, gang rape, or even death; they hide their few possessions high in the rafters so that menstruating women will not touch them and thereby contaminate them; they watch their food carefully to make sure that no woman has stepped over it, exposing the edibles to her noxious vagina. Fathers subject their sons to elaborate prophylactic rituals to counteract their mothers' odious influences. Nervous and irritable, the husbands sleep apart from their wives, severely limiting unhealthful sexual contact, afraid that too much sex (more than once or twice a month) will deplete, sicken, or even kill them (Langness 1967).

Far away, in the rainforests of South America's Amazon Basin, many Indian peoples who have never heard of New Guinea regard women as the work of the devil — not only inferior to men (again), but also destructive, polluting, even demonic (Jackson 1996). Many Amazonian aborigines are revolted by women's bodies, especially their genitals, which they liken to dirt and animal feces, and, like so many of their New Guinea counterparts, fear the vagina's terrible emanations (Gregor 1985:140). Terrorized by their own premonitions, these Amazonians keep the female sources of their torment at bay through a brutal form of gang rape inflicted on any woman who so much as dares to venture into the forbidden men's areas. A woman can be raped for as little as approaching the men's preserves or even for viewing — if only by accident and from afar — the carefully guarded male religious rituals and paraphernalia (Lévi-Strauss 1961).

Lest the reader think such things are confined to the so-called primitive world, let me point out that a form of culturally approved, punitive gang rape used to occur commonly in one of the bastions of civilized Europe, Renaissance France. Historian Edward Muir (1997:28–29) writes that this practice was well documented for France between 1300 and 1500. Muir cites estimates showing that in the city of Dijon about half of the youths participated at least once in the gang rape of a young woman.

Like their "primitive" counterparts, these French rapists usually chose a woman who broke the rules of sexual behavior, even in the most minimal way, for example, by appearing outside unchaperoned. In violating wayward women, the French youths, like their stone age peers, acted as enforcers of the habitual misogyny of the community by rape-lynching transgressors. As in New Guinea, the rest of the people always considered the victim to be the guilty party (Muir 1997:28).

Nor have ritualized forms of misogyny disappeared from western Europe, though they may be less violent today. Even as I write, in Latin southern Europe, including Italy, France, Spain, and Portugal, the annual pre-Lenten carnivals feature stinging burlesques of women in which transvestite clowns parade in villages and towns, mocking females in the crudest pantomimes (Muir 1997). In contemporary Sardinia, for example, men in costume portray women as the source of sexual pollution and contagion (Counihan 1985:17). Wearing grotesque female clothing and disguises, the Sardinians portray women as irresponsible, wanton, and "morally and sexually loose." The carnival clowns wear ugly bloodstains on their genital region and carry mutilated effigies that symbolize the dangers of female sexuality. During carnival in nearby Spain, village men masquerade as witches and wantons, threatening passersby, wielding grotesquely enlarged breasts and vulvas like weapons, and singing satirical songs denouncing women as lewd, destructive, and dangerous (Gilmore 1998:chap. 4).

Like the Dijonnais rapists, the Italian and Spanish carnival transvestites, the New Guinea highlanders, and the Amazonian aborigines, the ancient Greeks (e.g., Semonides, quoted at the beginning of this chapter), often displayed a fierce misogyny, putting woman in the category of the god-given ills. The early Attic poets charged that women were the original source of *kakon,* or evil, in the world, which was created by the capricious gods to torture men (Meagher 1995). The ancients populated their cosmos with she-demons and sorceresses such as Pandora, who brought all trouble into the world, and the sinister island-dwelling Circe, a witch who turned men into pigs, not to mention the Furies and the Harpies, foul-smelling hags who arbitrarily persecuted men. Many other female monsters animated the classical world, inhabiting the dark places like forests and seas: sirens, nymphs, lamias, and the female sea monsters Scylla and Charybdis — one a devouring six-headed creature, the other a cruel whirlpool sucking men down to watery oblivion (Kestner 1989). The snake-haired female demon Medusa turned men to stone with a look.

Later, following the Greek tradition of blaming women for the world's ills, Roman poets like Ovid, Hesiod, and Juvenal wrote long treatises heaping scorn and abuse upon women and everything pertaining to them and urging men to avoid sex and marriage completely (Coole 1988). Such misogynistic ideas still circulate among many Greek and Middle Eastern men. Today, in northern Greece, for example, the Sarakatsani shepherds in the Mount Epirus area say that women are creatures of the devil, vixens and liars who challenge the honor and integrity of every decent boy and man, who threaten family honor because of their unconscionable lusts (Campbell 1964:31).

The myth of Pandora, who opens a box and admits evil into an innocent world presages, in equally gynophobic terms, the Christian parable of the Fall. Both myths, of course, provide pertinent scriptural justification for centuries of sexist reproach leveled at women who let in iniquity through their sex. Although they originate in classical antiquity, such reactive beliefs about the defining feature of femininity itself, the sex organ, are confined by no means to Europe or to the literate cultures, once again showing a pan-cultural thread. Many preliterate peoples also speak of the vagina as a gateway through which evil enters the world, as something "uncanny," the portal to a dark and menacing underworld. The gentle Yurok Indians of northwestern California, like the Greeks, speak of "a woman's inside," the vagina and uterus, as the doorway through which sin and social disorder entered the world. As do many preliterate peoples, the Yurok populate their folklore with frightening tales of mythical skate women (they say the vagina resembles a big skate), half human, half fish, who, like the sirens and lamias, lure boys and men, imprison them in their trap-like orifices, and drag them down to a watery death (Erikson 1950:179–80).

The Christian Bible, the Muslim Qur'an, the Hebrew Torah, and Buddhist and Hindu scriptures condemn woman, not only for her spiritual defects, but also for her body, which they deride in the crudest terms. All these great religions blame woman for the lust, licentiousness, and depravity that men are prone to, and for committing the original sin or its theological equivalent. It is Eve, not Adam, who brings about the expulsion from Eden. It is Eve who allows herself to be seduced by the serpent. Weak and gullible, it is Eve, like Pandora, who introduces sin and sorrow into the world.

The most influential of the Church fathers — St. Augustine, St. Thomas Aquinas, Tertullian, St. Jerome, clerics who virtually founded Christianity as we know it today — heaped scorn on Eve and her descendants, calling woman "the devil's gateway" and worse, and bemoaning her inherent tendency to gossip, to "dance with the devil," to sway man from righteousness, to do all manner of evil (Blamires 1992). Across the Mediterranean Sea, North African Muslims, with the justification of the Qur'an and other holy texts, excoriate women as "the devil's nets," human traps designed, like the Yurok skate woman's vulva, by demonic forces to drag men down into soul-destroying licentiousness (Dwyer 1978).

In many holy texts of classical Buddhism, too, woman is condemned as the sinful sex, the polluted sex, the licentious sex whose body hosts innumerable dangers (Sponberg 1992; Spiro 1997). An Orthodox Jewish man gives thanks to God every day that he was not born female and bemoans the fact that a good woman is so rare that she is worth her weight in rubies. Much of this gender hatred, as can be seen from the fantasies above, centers upon the vagina, the devil's entranceway in so many cultures. All religions abominate the monthly vaginal discharge (Delaney 1988). And wherever in the world men believe in them, witches are primarily women; thousands of innocent women and girls have been hanged and burned as a result of this myth (Brain 1996).

With their biological cycles and mysteries, women are seen as less human than men, allied somehow to the dark side of nature, party to all that which is uncontrollable by men. It is women who are born with the supernatural powers of witchery that poison, sicken, and kill; it is women who provide the devil entrance into the world, who "entertain Satan" (Demos 1982). As well as the monthly pollution they discharge between their legs, women are guilty of having evil tongues in their heads; it is women who are the malicious gossips, who wreak havoc on the innocent through their inability to keep secrets, who debase man's purest instrument, language, by turning words into deadly weapons (S. Harding 1975; Spacks 1985). In many cultures, women are even said to wear sharp teeth or knives in their vaginas, giving rise to the widespread motif of *vagina dentata,* the gnashing vulva.

In the late medieval and early modern periods, this deep-rooted misogyny reached a fever pitch. The witchcraft craze was only part of the problem (Bloch 1991; Blamires 1992). For instance, medieval scholar R. Howard Bloch (1991:1) notes that misogyny "runs like a rich vein" throughout the entire corpus of the Middle Ages, especially in French and Italian theology and ecclesiastical literature. It is this fact that so appalled Christine de Pizan, especially since, as she knew, woman-hating had the ex cathedra stamp of Church approval. But Bloch also observes that this rich vein continued unabated right up to the modern period of Western writing and philosophy, long after the ebb of religious faith. It is indeed apparent in writings of just about anyone who has touched the subject, from Tertullian to Nietzsche.

Having conducted one of the first panoramic surveys of misogyny from a historical perspective, Bloch argues that women-bashing is a *topos* (a "place of thought"), one of those enduring threads that connects one age to another in the Western intellectual experience. He suggests that misogyny is not only a unifying discourse of Western thought, but one of the most enduring: "So persistent is the discourse of misogyny — from the earliest church fathers to Chaucer — that the conformity of its terms furnishes an important link between the Middle Ages and the present and renders the topic compelling because such terms still govern (consciously or not) the ways in which the question of woman is conceived" (1991:1).

Another medievalist, Michael Solomon (1997), sees this mordant theme running through, and in fact dominating, early modern Spanish literature, a tradition in which women were defamed as constituting a kind of disease. Learned and highly respected Spanish doctors of the fifteenth century, for example, thought that woman was literally a "contagion" and an "epidemic," and was responsible for both the physical epidemics and the moral plagues that swept through Europe. Such sexist beliefs still seem to trouble some men in contemporary rural Spain, who fear that close contact with women will weaken them, make them deathly sick, and drive them to an early death (Brandes 1980:86).

Fear of women's evil and their destructiveness is found everywhere, even among the most sophisticated men. In her study of misogyny and other modern prejudices in western Europe, the social historian Nancy Harrowitz (1994) finds an emphasis on a "base of evil" in women in the work of such diverse eighteenth- and nineteenth-century writers as the Italian criminologist Cesare Lombroso and the French men of letters Flaubert, Zola, and Stendhal.

Indeed, a number of feminist writers have called attention to the misogynist tendencies running throughout all Western literature, not only in the early modern period, but from Chaucer through D. H. Lawrence to Norman Mailer and the present (Rogers 1966; Noddings 1989; Wilson and Makowski 1990). The same curious revulsion and fear are found in the work of innumerable English poets, from Swift and Pope to Milton and Pound (Rogers 1966:166–74; Glenn 1992:373), and strongly antiwoman rancor mars the work of Nordic dramatists Frank Wedekind and August Strindberg. Wedekind's bitter "Lulu" dramas and Strindberg's morbid plays *The Father* and *Miss Julie* feature the most destructive, murderous, demonic villainesses imaginable: female devils who destroy innocent men not only efficiently but, like the Greek she-demons, with evident perverse pleasure.

Loathing of women also mars the otherwise noble work of continental writers like La Rochefoucauld, Montaigne, Schopenhauer, Montherlant, and Sartre (Noddings 1989:39) and in the writings of psychiatrists and psychoanalysts starting with Freud, who, despite his efforts to understand women, wrote blithely about their natural inferiority as evidenced by their "penis envy" and innate sexual "masochism" (Slipp 1993). Freud (1931b:58) even argued that women were morally deficient, had weaker superegos than men, were less high-minded, less able to defer gratification, and were controlled by a cruder and more primitive biology that made them overtly "hostile" to the constraints of civilization, rather like mischievous children or dumb animals.

Similarly contemptuous attitudes show up in the European visual arts, which, despite their emphasis on the beauty of the female form, are nevertheless replete with icons of woman as snake, devil, vampire, monster, siren, and vixen (Dijkstra 1986, 1996; Kestner 1989). European aesthetic misogyny reappears in Wagner's operas, in the form of seductive sorceresses, like the Venus in *Tannhäuser* who enslaves men in subterranean caves of voluptuousness, subverting their manly quest for salvation. Misogyny also appears in Western folklore and children's folktales, especially in stories featuring the perennial stereotypes: nagging wife, abusive mother-in-law, and wicked-witch stepmother, as in the familiar Snow White genre (Watson 1995). Other examples populate the *Grimms' Fairy Tales,* where the wanton boys are portrayed as heroic and "bold" but the wayward girls are always "bad" and in need of punishment (Bottigheimer 1987).

Misogyny even shows up in the earliest moving pictures, such as the silent two-reeler *A Fool There Was* (1915), in which vamp Theda Bara debuted as a monstrous femme fatale called "The Vampire." Destroying the men she seduces, the deadly character is clearly meant as a cautionary metaphor for the false attractions of woman. Celluloid misogyny reappears in early German classics like *The Blue Angel* (1930) and *The Devil Is a Woman* (1935), in which pretty women are again portrayed as evil temptresses who endanger not only the individual men they victimize but also the very moral fabric of society (Dijkstra 1996).

Such a cynical view of the female sex shows no sign of receding in either Western writing or art. As Marianna Torgovnick shows in *Gone Primitive* (1990:17) women are still being linked in the masculine aesthetic and moral imagination to the concept of the Primitive, and in twentieth-century art are still being portrayed as lower, less evolved, and more susceptible than men to sensual temptation and depravity. Like the medievalist Howard Bloch, literary critic Ruth Abbey (1996:250) sees misogyny as the single touchstone uniting the entire European intellectual tradition, its unifying topos. Critic Katherine Ackley (1992:xi) sees misogyny as one of the most deeply entrenched traditions in Western culture, from Ovid's *Art of Love* to Norman Mailer's *An American Dream* and *Tough Guys Don't Dance*.

Even Shakespeare, whose female personae defy any single moral characterization and many of whom are noble and wise, sometimes reflected contemporary misogynist sentiment. In Hamlet's "Frailty, thy name is woman!" harangue, the flaws of women are enumerated in lengthy detail. Antiwoman animosity attains a fever pitch in King Lear's diatribe against his two treacherous daughters, in which Lear calls all women "centaurs down below" and rages about the "sulphurous pit" that the "fiends do inhabit." The obvious mixed moral and physiological connotations are of the kind found above in primitive antivagina tropes (Hattaway 1993). But Shakespeare's antifemale lapses are nothing compared with the venom spewed to denounce women by his contemporaries John Webster, George Chapman, and Ben Jonson.

Not surprisingly, two surveys of world cultures (Hays 1964; Lederer 1968) conclude by arguing that misogyny is a near-universal phenomenon. Anthropologist Robert Murphy (1977:22) has gone so far as to call it "the masculine project," regarding woman-hating as a psychological trait uniting males everywhere. Is misogyny universal? What is wrong with men?

Definitions and Scope of the Study

This book is an inquiry into misogyny as it occurs and has occurred in cultures around the world. By examining why so many men fear and hate women, why both learned and not so learned men — as Christine de Pizan put it — believe and repeat these terrible lies about women, this book is a belated attempt to answer de Pizan's despairing questions. But before we can begin this journey, we should decide what misogyny means, and how we will be using the word in this study.

Webster's Unabridged Dictionary (1978 ed.) defines "misogyny" (from the Greek root *misogynia*) simply as "hatred of women." Aside from implicitly revealing the venerable provenance of woman-hating, Webster's provides no other meanings and gives no sample usage. It is clear, however, from the multifarious beliefs and practices described above, that misogyny is more complicated than this simple tag would indicate, with many nuances, cognates, and variations.

For purposes of this book, by "misogyny" I will mean an unreasonable fear or hatred of women that takes on some palpable form in any given society. Misogyny is a feeling of enmity toward the female sex, a "disgust or abhorrence" toward women as an undifferentiated social category (Gelber 1986:95). I want to emphasize that this feeling finds social expression in the concrete behavior: in cultural institutions, in writings, in rituals, or in other observable activity. Misogyny, then, is a sexual prejudice that is symbolically exchanged (shared) among men, attaining praxis. It is something that is manifest in the ways people relate to each other. It is, of course, specifically acted out in society by males, often in ritualistic ways.

How Widespread Is *Horror Mulieris*?

As the cursory review above shows, antiwoman feelings appear to be almost universal. This *horror mulieris,* as Gelber calls it, occurs in some degree among men wherever the sexes live together (which is everywhere). As will become clear as we proceed, the position taken in this book is that misogyny is indeed close to being universal, as our data will amply demonstrate, and therefore requires an explanation that goes beyond any ad hoc functionalist or structural interpretation and demands a psychological dimension in interpretation. I further argue that misogyny is the result not of a single-sided hatred of women or a desire to dominate, but rather of affective ambivalence among men. The data will show that most men love and hate women simultaneously and in equal measure, that most men need women desperately, and that most men reject this driving need as both unworthy and dangerous. The misogynistic denigration of women is not always an attempt to politically dominate or control women, but often a psychic attempt to diminish the importance of the object of man's inner struggle and to reduce the bifurcated object to worthlessness. In so doing, misogynists attempt to relieve their inner turmoil by demolishing its source.

The near universality of misogyny has been noted by a number of scholars (Hays 1964; Lederer 1968; Coole 1988; Bloch and Ferguson 1989a, 1991), as well as by clinicians currently treating abusive male patients (Jukes 1994). Yet few observers have tried to gather empirical evidence from a diverse spectrum of cultures and time periods to corroborate this inference. This is why a comparative and historical approach, sorely lacking until now, will be useful here in establishing the global scope of the phenomenon, its strength, its timelessness, and its connection to male psychic development. By bringing together data from every time and place, including the contemporary West, and by including virtually all political systems, economies, and religions in our purview, a boundless comparison will show that no factor in the external environment can account for the ubiquity of the phenomenon and that the answer must lie in the shared psychic course of the male of the species.

The second part of my argument is that, although psychogenic in origin, misogyny is often exacerbated by certain social and cultural conditions, and under special conditions can reach the proportion of a full-blown epidemic. These special conditions include certain forms of patrilineal, patrilocal organization, a certain kinship ideology that favors fraternal solidarity at the expense of the husband-wife bond, the persistence of chronic warfare, feuding, or other forms of intergroup violence, religious puritanism or other forms of asceticism such as sexual prudery, unrealistic moral idealism, and certain kinds of domestic arrangements that occur in exogamous preindustrial societies.

Previous Work

Most previous studies of misogyny have been written by historians and literary critics and have taken a specific cultural tradition or a specific epoch as their subject (e.g., Rogers 1966; Coole 1988; Bloch 1991; Ackley 1992; Solomon 1997). Some very good studies have been confined entirely to Western society, usually even more narrowly to artists and to members of the intelligentsia. Most of these studies center on the classic eighteenth- and nineteenth-century woman-haters like Swift, Schopenhauer, Nietzsche, Strindberg, Monterlant, and Rémy de Gourmont (Coole 1986; Noddings 1989; Abbey 1996; Dijkstra 1986, 1996) or on Western fiction writers and poets from the Greeks to D. H. Lawrence (Rogers 1966; Nixon 1986; Gallagher 1987; Wilson and Makowski 1990). Some studies focus on representational Western art, especially Victorian homiletic painting (Dijkstra 1986; Kestner 1989). So the tendency in misogyny studies has been to mark off specific temporal or cultural areas, or specific aesthetic genres, and to seek causes for the phenomenon within that specific context; comparative and synoptic studies of continuities within cultural variation are rare. The general tendency to isolate eras and genres leaves us with an impression of uniqueness for each case, as though misogyny were either confined to, or unusually pronounced in, a particular place or age or tradition. As we shall see, this creates a spurious singularity that leads to a certain ahistorical shortsightedness and consequently to some distortions in theorizing and in formulating correlations.

There are, of course, a few exceptions to this restriction of scope: comparative studies by psychologists, like the Jungian Wolfgang Lederer (1968) and the more orthodox Freudian H. R. Hays (1964), take a global perspective. These two fine studies use a wealth of comparative data about misogyny, sometimes in insightful ways. But, because the authors are not anthropologists and draw on ethnographic sources that are often dated, they use ethnography in a cavalier way, sometimes repeating data that are sensational or distorted. Also, both Hays and Lederer emphasize the Oedipal complex, especially castration anxiety, as the principal causal factor in misogyny, placing most of their emphasis on the boy's sexual conflict. Both writers also tend to see the problem in light of the principle of psychic *ambivalence* (love-hate) as the main affective ingredient. Their orthodox psychoanalytic perspective is of course very useful in this focus, but it leaves out other points of view, other interpretations, and other aspects of male-female relationships.

In this book I do not try to provide a single or definitive answer to the problem of misogyny, but rather attempt to formulate a series of pertinent questions about it. The first question is the inescapable echo of Christine de Pizan's plaintive query: why do so many men, in so many places and times, fear and rail against women, who are, after all, at least physically, the weaker sex? What danger do women pose to men? Second, why are masculine delusions about women's "evil power" so intense that men must surround themselves with countless prophylactics and austere taboos and often inflict painful rituals of purgation, expiation, and decontamination upon themselves and their sons? That is, why must men hurt themselves as much as women in their efforts to avoid woman's imaginary evil powers? Third, from a slightly more complex perspective, why do misogynist rituals so often appear in cultures where men also perform paradoxical rites of woman-idealization? Why does the worst misogyny seem to go hand in hand with rituals of female impersonation, with bizarre glorifications of femininity, with florid ceremonies of cross-sex identification, with bloody simulations of menstruation, with the institution of the couvade (male imitation of labor and parturition)? What causes all this passionate sex confusion, this ambivalent, dualistic, *paradoxical* obsession with women? What is the nature of this male ambivalence, and what forms, aside from the obvious sexual one, does this ambivalence take?

Reciprocal Analogues?

Before going any further, let me put the problem into social-psychological and gender perspective. The first question we must ask in addressing these others must be: "Is there a clear-cut female equivalent to misogyny?" Do women return the favor by hating men and inventing magical dangers? The answer seems to be a resounding no. Male-hating among women has no popular name because it has never (at least not until recently) achieved apotheosis as a social *fact,* that is, it has never been reified into public, culturally recognized and approved *institutions* complete with their own theatrical repertory and constituent mythology and magic.

We do have some words in English that come close to man-hating: "misanthropy," for example, or "misandry" (Bloch and Ferguson 1989a, b). But misanthropy means the dislike of all humans rather than of males, and misandry, which literally does imply hatred of males (Greek, *andros*), has little currency. So, in the absence of any generally accepted label for man-hating, I concocted the word "viriphobia" in another context (Gilmore 1997) to describe the kind of hatred and fear of heterosexual masculinity that one finds today, for example, in the work of radical feminists like Andrea Dworkin who despise the human male as constitutionally evil, and many social-constructionist gender scholars, such as R. W. Connell (1995) and Miguel Vale de Almeida (1996). These last two writers disparage "hegemonic maleness" for what they imagine is its irredeemable crudeness and brutality. (For more on this very recent outpouring of vituperation against traditional male values and masculine norms see the useful summary by Matthew Gutmann [1997].)

But such neologisms as viriphobia and misandry refer, not to the hatred of men as men, but to the hatred of men's traditional male role, the obnoxious manly *pose,* a culture of machismo; that is, to an adopted sexual ideology or an affectation. They are therefore different from the intensely *ad feminam* aspect of misogyny that targets women no matter what they believe or do, whatever their sexual orientation, or however they comport themselves. Moreover, such antimale terms have little application in cultural anthropology for one other important reason: there are virtually no existing examples of culturally constituted antimale complexes in traditional cultures that can be designated by such terms. (This excludes the modern-day feminists like the redoubtable Dworkin who believe that all men are rapists and ipso facto evil.) What certainly exists among many more sensible women is the fear of and resentment against individual men who are often obnoxious or abusive. What also certainly exists is the dislike or disparagement of specifically "masculine" *quali-*

ties that some men have, like machismo, bravado, or the puerile braggadocio that sometimes appears in the locker room. But a generalized pan-sex complex of hatred against males that is acted out in public behavior and ritual seems rare for women, at least until very recently. There seems to be no good example of antimasculinism as a traditional "institutionalized phobia" or organized dogma among women in any traditional cultures (Stephens 1962:93). As a cultural institution, misogyny therefore seems to stand alone as a gender-based phobia, unreciprocated. In what might stand as a general observation about the sexes, Marilyn Gelber (1986:13) summarizes her research by saying that women as a group do not appear to have a dogmatist ideology regarding men as a group.

These differences in etiology and symptomatology in themselves testify to the fact that sexual prejudice, as a matter of public culture, seems almost exclusively male, a point that Bloch (1991:79–80) also makes in his study of medieval misogyny. This one-sidedness is no less salient in "primitive" cultures, as we shall soon see, and this in itself poses many questions about the psychology of men. It also raises questions about male sexuality and masculine gender-identity, and about the fantasies, sexual or not, that men make up out of their longings and feelings about the other sex. There seems to be something about being a human male that produces a painful conundrum in relating to and living with women. Misogyny has to be studied, then, as an aspect of male psychology and of subsequent cultural representations and their vicissitudes, an example of a "gendered psychosis," as Adam Jukes describes it in his book on woman-hating in Britain (1994:xxvi).

Semantics: Misogyny and Male Chauvinism

As I perceive it, misogyny is not the same as simple male political dominance, which we might distinguish semantically as "male chauvinism." For heuristic purposes, I would like to make a distinction between what political scientist Glenn Tinder (1997) calls "patriarchal traditionalism" and *cultural* misogyny. The former is a matter of defining women's proper place and social status within a broader constellation of political beliefs; the latter is a specifically emotive sensibility that feeds off phobias, terrors, and fantasies, regardless of women's position in the social structure. The ideology of male chauvinism is a political dogma regarding decisions about the proportionality of civil rights and power between the sexes; misogyny, although having political ramifications, is essentially an affective or psychological phenomenon based on passion, not thought. Visceral and irrational, it has no formal political program or position other than to denounce and harm women. Misogynists are "essentialists," positing a stereotypical "essence" in women, a basic, immutable, and evil nature allowing for no individual variation.

Additionally, I want to omit noninstitutionalized kinds of *disapproved* antiwoman behavior from this study. So I will not treat things like criminal rape, sexual abuse, and domestic violence. This certainly is not because I do not think these things are important. They are and have their own significant studies, such as Jukes's book (1994) on batterers in England. Rather, what I am interested in is group behavior taking on the form of generally accepted institutions in public culture — women-hating as examples of culturally constituted projective mechanisms, institutions that are part of a public value system, imbedded within the normative structure, shared by all or most men: what Durkheim (1933) called collective representations.

The Plan of This Book

My thesis in this book is that misogyny stems from unresolved inner conflicts in men. The argument that a powerful ambivalence lies at the core of misogyny requires an exploration not only of its negative side, but also of its positive side: the love, need, and identification that men experience in relation to women; and such a view also requires that we look at how these two opposing tendencies interrelate and interact in mind and in culture. My contention, further, is that this powerful masculine ambivalence stems not only from overtly sexual conflicts, that it is not reducible to the Oedipus complex and its derivatives (which most previous explanations have overemphasized). It also has deep roots in other, permanent, but less obvious, needs that men have for women: for mothering in infancy; food, support, and shelter from life's woes in childhood; care, comfort, and approval in adolescence; and later in adulthood, for heirs, especially sons, to continue the god-given task of continuing the family line. Perhaps most prominent among these extrasexual factors are the regressive and alimentary conflicts that men experience, however one conceives of them: unconscious wishes to return to infancy, longings to suckle at the breast, to return to the womb, the powerful temptation to surrender one's masculine autonomy to the omnipotent mother of childhood fantasy. All these secret desires spark unconscious opposition, internal conflict, and consequently psychic turmoil in men. My thesis is that man's multitiered ambivalence toward woman creates an uncomfortable and endless tension at every psychic level, which leads to effort to diminish the source of the turmoil by attacking its source: women.

The last two chapters of this book take up the issue of man's counter-balancing feelings for women. These positive feelings, too, are ambiguous, labile, and emotionally unsettling, and lead to ritualizations and to other cultur-ally constituted sublimations such as folklore and myth, exposing an emotive dialectic. The reader will have to wait (patiently) for a full exposition of my concluding theory of misogyny. In the final chapter I propose an eclectic inter-pretation that includes some original components but integrates these with a number of the theories already proposed. The reason for the delay in presenting a model of causality is that such a comprehensive model cannot take form before we discuss, analyze, and — especially — juxtapose the voluminous data on both sides of the love-hate complex. We must also familiarize ourselves with the many interpretations offered by psychoanalysts, anthropologists, sociolo-gists, political scientists, historians, literary critics, Marxists, and, of course, feminists.

Thus the plan of this book is as follows. I start with an exploration of body-oriented misogyny in Melanesia and tribal Amazonia, followed by a look at parallels in other parts of the world, including the West. I move on to a discussion of misogynistic beliefs centering on woman's moral and spiritual failings, including how negative feelings about women are corroborated and exacerbated by the world's great religions and holy texts. In the next phase of my argument, I consider social-structural factors that worsen misogyny, espe-cially in patrilineal, patrilocal tribal societies. Then I address aesthetic and intellectual misogyny in Western art and literature, as well as in the social sciences. This is followed by a summary of the common denominators, after which I introduce and critique the many theories that have been proposed. Fi-nally, I turn to a description of counterbalancing rituals and beliefs of woman-adoration and woman-emulation, and a consideration of the scope and measure of male gender ambivalence. In the final chapter, I construct my eclectic theo-retical model and end with a prognosis for the future.

Before presenting the data, I should point out that they derive from varied ethnographic publications and also fiction and the visual arts. Some readers may find this mixture promiscuous, since it is hard to tell if sentiments ex-pressed by characters in fiction express the author's own feelings or are simply plot devices. Questions may also be raised about the comparability of the anthropological material, since some is old, some recent, and once again, it is hard to tell if the anthropologist who is being cited has accurately described the prevailing culture or the attitudes of a few misogynistic informants. Not wishing to delve too deeply into the epistemological implications raised by such questions, let me say the following. First, in many cases of the fictional literature, it is obvious that the author is expressing his own views. This holds true for example in the work of writers like Semonides and Hesiod, Webster, Swift, Tolstoy, Strindberg, Pound, D. H. Lawrence, Mailer, and many others. In other cases, for example Shakespeare, Ben Jonson, William Wycherly, and others who also express mixed attitudes toward women, the misogynist sentiments expressed by their characters seem to reflect common attitudes of the time rather than those of the authors. But this, too, indicates a prevailing attitude to which the author is appealing. My feeling is that the invocation of data from such varied sources is not an exercise in butterfly collecting, but rather serves to reinforce the main point of this book, which is that rather than being culture-specific, misogyny transcends time and place.

I acknowledge the validity of holistic or systemic analysis of distinct and individual cultures, but I want to stress that the core of the anthropological method is the comparative testing of propositions stating necessary interconnections between certain features of distinct sociocultural systems. Further, I reject a ceteris paribus clause; that is, I argue that for the observer to achieve valid inferences about the meaning of statistical covariation in the data, the miscellaneous features of the societies and texts in question should specifically *not* be equivalent or identical. Otherwise, the correlations we arrive at as covariant may simply reflect some other, unrevealed factor in these surrounding features, obscuring the comparisons. Thus we may tentatively describe the method followed here as attempting to identify the empirical extent and distribution of a cultural trait and its underlying forces through comparisons of variations in distinct contexts. Rather than comparing repetitive and isomorphic "objects" lined up in a neat row, we are comparing and contrasting the constituent variables or criteria that constitute the subject as a congeries of empirical categories, in this case, the beliefs and practices that make up misogyny.

All that said, let us start with a consideration of misogyny of the body, man's fear of woman as flesh and blood. We the begin the tale in the mountains and valleys of Papua New Guinea, a place where, as we have seen, men and women live strictly apart for health reasons, where a woman's body is seen as the source of pollution, disease, and death.

The fly that sips treacle is lost in the sweets,

So he who tastes woman, woman, woman,

He that tastes woman, ruin meets.

   —John Gay, *The Beggar's Opera*, 8, air 26

1. Melanesian Misogynists

IT IS NO EXAGGERATION to say that the greatest obsession in history is that of man with woman's body. Since time immemorial, men have rhapsodized about feminine flesh; the earliest known works of representational art, the European "Venuses," tiny stone statuettes of voluptuous females with huge, pendulous breasts and grotesquely enlarged vulvas, attest to the antiquity and primacy of this obsession.

But more than a mere sexual object or a model of beauty and fertility, the female body is also man's first home. The womb is the mystical place of origin and procreation, and the female body harbors the fetus, nurtures the infant, shelters the toddler, nourishes the young adult, comforts the man in his age, consoles him at the end. The body of woman not only gives life and form to the man throughout life, but also issues his progeny, his sons who perpetuate his race, spread his genes, ensuring him a small measure of immortality. Woman's flesh is that of mother, lover, wife, daughter, friend, helpmate and caretaker, conferring on man his most intense physical pleasure, slaking his wildest lusts, satisfying his deepest instinctual needs.

Man's fascination is the product of a certain mixture or balance of emotional states that is as dynamically unstable as it is irresolvable. This jumble of emotions is polarized to an extreme and dramatic degree: both desire and repulsion, neither unalloyed, for just as man loves and desires the female body, he also fears and distrusts it because woman's flesh is too desirable, too gratifying. Man especially fears the peremptory power that woman's body exerts over him, its enormous capacity to provoke feelings so uncontrollable that their frustration promises as much pain as their gratification does pleasure. For the body is also the source of man's most grievous frustrations. Through no fault of her own, woman is the cause of his greatest disappointments, his worst shame and guilt. For many men, consequently, woman's body inspires not only desire, but anxiety, self-doubt, anger, and terror. In some cases of preindustrial peoples, as we shall soon see, these negative feelings about the female body attain expression in magical delusions, phobias, and bizarre ritualizations.

Melanesia: Black Islands

The island of New Guinea consists of the present-day nations of Papua New Guinea in the east (granted independence from Australia in 1975) and Irian Jaya in the west (annexed by Indonesia in 1963). The two countries occupy approximately equal territory.

Situated north of the Australian continent in the South Pacific, New Guinea is the largest island in the Melanesian chain and the second largest in the world (after Greenland). The term Melanesia, or "black islands," comes from the fact that the people are dark skinned and Negroid in appearance, which surprised early explorers familiar with the light-skinned Polynesians. The highland region of New Guinea occupies the central cordillera of the island and boasts peaks as high as 16,000 feet, which are the source of the rushing rivers and streams.

Thousands of verdant valleys and ravines splinter the misty highlands. Shrouded in fogs, enclosed by towering peaks and dense rainforests, these highland valleys opened up to Western exploration only after the 1930s and 1940s (Brown and Buchbinder 1976:2), some not until the 1960s; the area was one of the last aboriginal stone-age holdouts to be penetrated by Western explorers after the Second World War. In fact, some areas were unknown to whites until well into the 1970s. Writing as late as 1978, the ethnologist Paula Brown notes in her survey of the highlands that "the western part of New Guinea [Irian Jaya] is still relatively unknown" (1978:4). Even today, in a new century, some areas are barely explored.

This place, with its dense populations of sweet potato horticulturists and pig herders, was one of the last truly pristine Neolithic regions of the world, and consequently the practices of the people there, which were observed and recorded immediately upon contact by teams of intrepid anthropologists, remained largely unchanged and uncorrupted in the more remote areas by Western contact, at least until about 1960. New Guinea is a place where ethnographers have observed cultural forms that are sui generis, pristine, virtually free from major outside influence. These aboriginal beliefs are most colorfully mirrored in native customs about sex and gender.

Many books and articles have been written about sexual relations in New Guinea, most recently Lewis Langness's *Men and "Woman" in New Guinea* (1999). This subject became a virtual industry in cultural anthropology between 1950 and 1990, and continues unabated to this day; literally all publications start off by noting a curious degree of sex antagonism as a salient feature, if not *the* standout feature, of most highland societies. There is probably no place on earth where men and women are so intensely antagonistic toward one another and where men have such a pervasive fear and loathing of women, a fear that centers on their reproductive functions and especially on their mysterious sexual organs and everything relating to the vagina. Aboriginal New Guinea is a place where all women are simultaneously "inferior, malevolent, weak, and polluted" (Meigs 1984:31).

One early observer, Ronald Berndt (1962:129), struck by the belligerent attitude of the men toward the women, wrote that sexual relations in the highlands resemble "a kind of armed combat." Brown and Buchbinder (1976:1), summarizing the voluminous mass of material on the subject, write in less histrionic terms that ambivalent and antagonistic relations between the sexes are a "prevailing theme" of highland life. Buchbinder and Rappaport (1976:13) add that this antagonism is certainly universal there. Gelber (1986:12) notes that there is probably no other place in the world where sexual hostility reaches such an apogee of both intensity and degree of elaboration into cultural practices, misogynistic beliefs and taboos, and prophylactic rituals.

Although basing her opinions on library research, Gelber summarizes this cultural theme more authoritatively than many observers, and writes that this sex antagonism is found in virtually all areas of daily life and pervades the most basic aspects of village organization — living arrangements for example. The men must live far apart from their wives in guarded all-male houses (the famous Melanesian men's houses) out of fear for their physical and moral safety. Sex antagonism is also found in religious rituals from which women are strenuously excluded on pain of severe punishment. The men worship secret phallic symbols (holy trumpets and sacred flutes) that the women are not allowed even to see. The men's cults and secret societies are in fact designed to combat female pollution and the danger women pose to men's equanimity and health. An extreme visceral misogyny is found also in such phenomena as routine physical violence, including gang rape meted out as punishment for any wayward woman (Lindenbaum 1976:56), ritual mock battles between the sexes (Meggitt 1964:204), the gender-specific murder of women by men for violation of any of the prevailing rules, as well as unprovoked attacks on women's genitals (Gelber 1986:12). According to Gelber, the list of misogynist behaviors and beliefs in New Guinea can only be called "flamboyant" (154).

It is perhaps useful to try to categorize this rich and colorful armory of misogynistic practices in comparative perspective. We start with highland male fears and apprehensions about the female body: flesh, bone, blood, and fluids. Nowhere else in the world does fear of the female body reach such a terrible, staggering pitch. Highland men tremble before the female contagion and effluvia, the "dangerous universe" of woman's flesh and blood (Lindenbaum 1979:129):

A boy is taught that his whole development may be jeopardized if he does not exercise extreme care in his relations with the opposite sex, and he is permitted only a minimum of contact with women of the community. He eats only foodstuffs which have been cooked by men, and he is not permitted to sleep in the women's houses. He is, moreover, warned of the danger to himself if he succumbs to the blandishments of women . . . his strength may be impaired by contact with them. (Read 1954:867)

Boys are repeatedly cautioned not to spend too much time with women; if they do, "their skins will be 'no good,' their work will 'go wrong' and they will die young" (Langness 1967:165).

What is it exactly that boys are taught to fear so much? Is it sexual seductiveness? Are the men afraid, like the New England Puritans, of their own proclivities, blaming their sexual impulses on women? Oddly, the men are not sexual prudes; they actually like sex and, like most men, pursue opportunities for intercourse. Nor is it sexual desire in the abstract that torments them. Here we see right off that it is not sex alone that produces the fear and the hatred in men, that other psychic conflicts are equally involved. Rather, it is woman's physical body itself as a source of pollution that inspires the terror: her skin and her menstrual blood, her mysterious genitals, her reproductive effluvia, her very physical being in all aspects and forms. Mother, wife, sister . . . no matter; woman's body is the harbinger of all human evil.

For woman's body is regarded as a polluted thing. Its excretions and products are almost indescribably debilitating and deadly to all male creatures.

The female body must be avoided whenever possible. In a curious paradox, even sex itself, though desired by most men, is terrifying, since it means entering into a frightful world of contagion and death.

The idea that women are dangerously polluting and that their bodies are the source of contamination is widespread on the entire island and its outlying archipelagoes. This belief relates especially to notions about menstrual blood, parturitional fluids, childbirth itself, and, of course, the sex act. For example, Mervyn Meggitt (1964:210) writes that the Mae Enga of the Mount Hagen range in the western highlands think that copulation is in itself detrimental to male well-being. Overindulgence will dull a man's mind and leave his body permanently exhausted and withered, and any contact with a menstruating woman will sicken a man and cause persistent vomiting, turn his blood black, and corrupt his vital juices "so that his skin eventually darkens as his flesh wastes, permanently dull his wits, and eventually lead to a slow decline and death." Similar ideas are entertained by the Hua (Meigs 1984), the Gururumba (Newman 1965:42), the Kamano, Fore, Melpa, Gahuka-Gama, and many others (Gelber 1986:94). All these highland peoples fear woman's body as the fount of disease and death for men.

An Anti-Vagina Complex

In the highlands men and women live apart, the men secluded in male-only huts built to protect them from the noxious female contamination that surrounds them. Women radiate evil, a withering power from within; their bodies contain pollutants and vicious scourges poisoning food eaten by men and their animals, desecrating the sacred objects men worship, wrecking men's lives, and, finally, wasting and killing men. Everywhere in the highlands, writes Paula Brown (1978:150), men believe that women may make them shrivel and dry, that they sap their "juice" and that female sexuality, menstruation, vaginal secretions, childbirth, discharges from parturition, and so on are potent, dangerous, malignant things.

The Ndumba of the Mount Piora region, in the eastern highlands, believe that prolonged contact with women can make men's bones dissolve, their breath grow short, and generally lead to debilitation and even death (Hays and Hays 1982:206). Elsewhere — for example, among the Ilahita Arapesh, who do not live in the highlands — the men are more focused on breast milk than sexual effluvia: they believe that woman's milk is polluting and fear its contaminating effects on adult males (Tuzin 1982:337–38). More than simply unhygienic, woman's biology is inimical to man, a hostile force of nature. The Gimi of the eastern highlands treat both menstruation and childbirth as hostile and contagious acts. A woman with her period, or one holding a newborn child, is considered dangerous and has to be confined and avoided by males (Gillison 1993:4). Note that these extreme beliefs are not reciprocated by the women of the region, for there is no elaboration of reciprocal sexual fears by women (Paula Brown 1978:150), no terror of men's biological functions, no supernatural fears about the polluting power of their sexual organs.

As one might expect, the terror of women's contamination focuses on the vagina. There is a virtual "anti-vagina complex" (Shapiro 1989) among highland men, featuring specific beliefs in the devastating malignancy of magical vaginal secretions (Lidz and Lidz 1989:54–64). Everything connected with the vagina is deadly to men. Vaginal discharges are so poisonous that they can be used by witches to kill a man overnight, simply by depositing them near his clothing. Everything from the vagina is considered to be polluted, even nonsexual things like babies. Having passed through the mother's birth canal, the neonate of either sex is tainted. In traditional Hua society, for instance, until the baby was ritually purified, the father never touched it but only poked it playfully with a small stick, keeping a safe distance (Meigs 1984:64).

Even clothing worn over the female genital area is contaminated; a woman's skirt can sicken a man and cause early death (Meggitt 1964:209). For example, Buchbinder and Rappaport (1976) were told of an incident among the Maring people, a fringe highlands group. Their informant said that anything that has the slightest contact with the vagina can debilitate or even kill a man, including the seemingly innocent little apron strings with which women cover their genitals. When a young man visiting the Fugai-Korama (a neighboring people) found pieces of such an apron in his food, he concluded that someone was trying to kill him (21).

Any object that passes over or near the vagina can no longer be used safely by a man. This prohibition includes clothing, tools, food, and other domestic items. Even proximity of an object to the vagina requires ritual cleansing or disposal. If a woman's genitals are physically higher than a man's head, serious health risks ensue to him. For instance, if a woman steps over a sleeping man in such a way that her vagina passes above him, he will sicken and his body will rot unless immediately treated with an exorcism. Women, therefore, are not allowed to climb above men in trees or on ladders or to step across prone or sleeping men, an act that is both sexually exciting and frightening to the men. On the basis of fieldwork among the Mae Enga, Mervyn Meggitt provides a long list of prohibitions connected to this "height" phobia: a woman must not climb on the roof of a house lest a man be inside; she must never walk over a boy's hair clippings lest he become stunted and stupid; she may not step across the legs of a seated man or else his blood will die; she must not pass over his bow and arrow lest they lose their efficacy and he will catch no game (1964:208–10).

So deep is this fear of pestilence that whenever the Mae Enga people gather in mixed groups, as at weddings, they must segregate the sexes. The right-hand side is reserved exclusively for men, where they sit, kneel, or lie down in relative safety; the left side (associated with mystery and evil) is for the women, where they stand, step, or promenade as they like, avoiding contact with the vulnerable males. Women are barred from crossing this Melanesian Maginot Line. Among the Maring people, a man who suffers the terrible misfortune of being stepped over by a woman is afflicted with such hideous symptoms as slack and wrinkled skin, putrid pustules, and subcutaneous ulcers. It gets worse: eventually the unfortunate Maring man's flesh wastes away, his thoughts drift uncontrollably, and his belly painfully bloats (Buchbinder and Rappaport 1976:21); then he may wither away altogether. Gilbert Herdt (1986:71) reports similar ideas among the Sambia people of the southeastern highlands. Because of their polluting vaginas, the Sambia women are told not to walk above the male clubhouse, an act that would contaminate the initiates, ruin war weapons, and spoil the ritual paraphernalia. "Women belong down below, men on top," the men like to say, and they enforce this rule with a vigor borne of fear.

Raymond Kelly (1976), working among the Etoro of the central cordillera, reports that the men are so exercised by the dangers of the vagina that a man must throw away any food that a woman has stepped around or nearby, even if not directly over it. It an Etoro woman should chance to pass over such food, even unintentionally, the people say it has passed "between her thighs" (41) and has been poisoned by her polluting genital zone. The woman's vulva (and, therefore, the woman herself) must never be above a man's nose. The genitalia menace with lethal radiation and must remain below a man's organs of sense (what better metaphor for an inferior status?).

Women are at all times enjoined from stepping over a man's personal possessions, smoking pipes and tobacco, and especially food and the items employed in its cooking and consumption. Thus a woman must never step over split firewood or sit on the woodpile at the front of the longhouse. If a man consumes a morsel of food cooked by such firewood . . . he will suffer *hame hah hah* [wasting sickness] and a general lack of strength while pursuing his daily activities. Should a woman step over his ax, it will become dull. (Kelly 1976:41)

The Fore of the eastern highlands also believe in a topographical scheme of female pollution and sexuality. Among the Fore, female sexual organs that "surmount" male things in space (i.e., are above them), bring about illness and death to those who touch those things (Lindenbaum 1979:134).

As Lewis Langness indicates for the highlands generally (1974:207), the vagina phobia applies to both menstruating *and* nonmenstruating women; women are always somewhat polluting because of their periods' residue; there is no escape for them. For example, Gillian Gillison says about the Gimi of the eastern highlands:

The source of a woman's danger was her menstrual blood, and during her periods she was banished to a tiny shelter on the outskirts of the settlement. But even when a woman was no longer menstruating and emerged from seclusion, vestiges of blood remained beneath her fingernails and in the crevices of her vagina so that she was always polluted to some degree, infecting whatever she handled or stepped over and so "passed between her thighs." (1993:4)

As a result, most New Guinea men always hang their food in net bags suspended from walls so that the women cannot pass above them. They keep their pipes, tobacco, and other paraphernalia either hidden away in the men's house or else hung safely from high walls or ceilings so that women may never contaminate them (Kelly 1976:43–44).

So deadly is the female organ that among the Maring the female genitals are synonymous with death. Simply put, in Maring culture the vagina *is* decay, rot, and death. Symbolically, the vagina is likened to the grave. Such a conflation of vagina and grave is not unique to the Maring, but is a common highland symbolism, say Buchbinder and Rappaport (1976:32). The symbolic connection, as the authors astutely point out, occurs not only throughout Melanesia but also in many other distant cultures in which men associate the vagina with earth, dirt, and rotting things.

All this anxiousness of course does intrude into Melanesians' active sex life. Although they like sex, so fearful are the men of female genitalia that they avoid touching the genitalia, even during the height of sexual passion. A Wogeo man, for example, will scrupulously wash and purge himself after intercourse if he thinks genital contact has occurred even inadvertently (Hogbin 1970:89–91). Igniting the most ardent desires among men everywhere, the vagina simultaneously provokes intense disgust and nausea among the men of Melanesia. Anthropologist Raymond Kelly, who worked among the Etoro people, tells the following story, which illustrates men's confusion about the female organ. The episode involves a wronged husband and the public response to his actions to humiliate his unfaithful wife.

The woman openly betrayed her husband with a younger lover, who, as it turned out, was his nephew. Outraged, the cuckold dragged his deceitful wife into the center of the village to castigate her publicly. After a long harangue in which he rebuked her and her lover in great detail, he dramatically yanked his wife's skirt above her waist, thereby exposing her pelvis to the entire village (the women do not wear underwear). However, the response, of the assembled youths and men to this exhibition was rather unexpected. Rather than showing arousal or curiosity, the male observers responded with revulsion, nausea, and vomiting: "Several young men (including my informant) retched forthwith and the adulterous youth himself became a queasy and visibly discomfited. Older men turned their faces aside with expressions of disgust" (1976:43).

Menstruation

As might be expected, this anti-vagina delusion centers on the major effluvium of the female organ, menstrual blood, which is regarded as the world's most deadly substance and a magical scourge. Of course, a menstrual-poison fetish is almost ubiquitous in cultures around the world, but it reaches its apogee in highland New Guinea, where it attains the status of an authentic persecution mania. Paula Brown (1978:62) summarizes this widespread attitude by saying that during menstruation women are believed to be especially likely to pollute food and water, which can cause illness to men who eat or touch or even glance at such things. Further, the Melanesians believe that an angry wife will deliberately harm her husband by giving him such contaminated food. Or she may trick him into having intercourse while she is menstruating, and if he succumbs, he may then become seriously ill, even die. It is interesting that so many of these phobias involve a polluted parody of food and food preparation — the main social function of women in these societies.

Hays and Hays (1982:206) report that the Ndumba men of the eastern highlands believe that women often commit premeditated murder of their husband by dropping menstrual blood in his food. Among the Fore people, the men believe that female menstrual blood is a potent item in sorcery, and that a woman may use it intentionally to sicken or even kill her husband or his male relatives. "A wife who wished to eliminate her spouse can use this polluting substance as a poison" (Lindenbaum 1979:59, 131).

Examples of this blood-food phobia have been culled from ethnographies written shortly after contact was made in the 1950s. These few cases cited below, which are just the tip of the iceberg, give the reader some notion of the deep sense of actual beleaguerment and terror caused by menstruation and the extent to which the men preoccupy themselves with avoidance techniques and magical prophylactics, many having to do with food intake.

The Gururumba people live in six large villages in the upper Asaro Valley, bounded by towering mountains, some rising to 15,000 feet. Anthropologist Philip Newman (1965) studied them in the late 1950s, only a decade after discovery. He found that Gururumba men shrank in terror from the mere thought of menstrual blood, and they responded to his queries with visible discomfort. Fearful and vulnerable, these men have elaborated an extensive series of taboos and prohibitions to protect themselves from the horrid female scourge. For example, a man should never let a menstruating woman touch his bow, his food of course, his drinking tube, or his skin; a woman should destroy all trace of menstrual discharge lest a man come into contact with it indirectly and inadvertently through the mouth or nose; a menstruating woman should be isolated from the men and placed in a special hut from which she may not exit until her period ends. The men are equally fearful of the afterbirth and any other vaginal discharge. All these things are treated with dread and surrounded by the same taboos. The slightest infringement of these rules will sicken a man and cause his skin to shrivel; in some cases, he will waste away and die. So powerful is the vaginal poison that a man who simply *glances* at a menstruating woman imbibes her poison and becomes ill (Newman 1965:77).

The Bena Bena people of the Asaro River area, studied by Langness since 1961, observe similar proscriptions, or did so until very recently. Traditionally, they maintained a fairly rigid sexual separation of adults, grown men sleeping together in the segregated men's houses, the women sleeping with their children (of both sexes) in their own huts. As elsewhere, the Bena Bena abhorred a menstruating woman, for menstrual blood was regarded as dangerous. Women were secluded in special huts of their own construction during their menses and at childbirth (Langness 1999:6). Bena Bena men also maintain rigid taboos against a menstruating woman's touching a man's head, coming into contact with his hair or any part of his clothing, preparing food for men, "casting a shadow" on any man, or, once again, being in any way physically above a man or boy.

The island-dwelling Wogeo, although not highlanders, share many of these misogynist myths and have equally strict rules. The blood from a woman's period is virulently polluting; she may not touch anyone or anything while in this dangerous condition, nor may she touch her husband's food, lest he die (Hogbin 1970:86). A woman in her menses must wear a special skirt proclaiming her polluted status; she must use specific instruments for eating and drinking. The blood shed in childbirth is even more toxic than menstrual blood since it represents nine months' accumulation of pollution. The new Wogeo mother is highly polluted and becomes untouchable for at least three months. Anyone who touches her is in principle as polluted as she and must then observe the same taboos and restrictions, which will continue until the day after the next full moon (La Fontaine 1985:128–29).

The Siane of the eastern highlands regard menstrual blood and parturitional fluids as the most dangerous and polluting of all substances (Meigs 1984:111). The same is true of the Gimi of the eastern highlands. The latter, dauntless warriors who cheerfully battled and killed each other in innumerable wars, seemed more afraid of the women in their midst than of their enemies' spears and arrows, believing their health and vigor to be threatened more by menstrual blood, which was hidden and pervasive, than by their enemies' deadly weapons (Gillison 1993:4).

Similarly, the Ndumba people of the eastern highlands say that a menstruating woman is the custodian of a "lethal weapon" between her legs (Hays and Hays 1982:228). Girls are taught to exert special care as to where they walk while having their period; otherwise they may face accusations of assault and battery, or even murder if a nearby man sickens or dies from magical pollution. So convinced are the Ndumba men that menstrual emanations can kill them, if a man got sick or died from unknown causes before pacification in the 1950s the men would try, convict, and severely punish — even execute — any woman found guilty of having stepped near his food while menstruating. Slightly less draconian punishments are still inflicted: Hays and Hays report that during their fieldwork, for example, one woman was severely ostracized by her husband and other men because she was believed to be responsible for her brother's death by having stepped over his bow. For weeks afterward no one would speak to her or even recognize her existence (1982:228).

A Special Case

All this terror reaches its height among the Baruya people of the Kratke Mountain Range in the eastern highlands. Anthropologist Maurice Godelier spent

much time with them, studying their gender relations, and was struck by the
degree of dread provoked by menstrual fluid:

The attitude of the men toward menstrual blood, whenever they talk or think about it,
verges on hysteria, mingling disgust, repulsion, and above all fear. For them, menstrual
blood is dirty, and they rank it with those other polluting, repugnant substances, urine
and feces. Above all, though, it is a substance that weakens women whenever it flows
from them, and it would destroy men's strength if ever it came into contact with their
bodies. (1986:58)

In the Baruya scheme of things, menstrual blood is even more dangerous than
the vilest sorcery; it signals invisible death (59). But beyond this a woman's
orifice is dangerous to men always, not only during her periods. In fact, the
Baruya view women as a permanent danger by virtue of the very shape of the
sexual organ, by the inevitable fact that it is a slit that can never altogether keep
back the liquids it inwardly secretes. These fluids are thought to seep into
cracks in the earth and to join forces with "evil, chthonic powers" that live
there and threaten men and their possessions (59). So through her sexual organs
a woman, even if unintentionally, is believed to act as a constant magnet to the
evil powers that populate the world's subterranean realm. Women attract these
evil powers without even being aware of it, and thus seriously endanger both
nature and society (59–60).

Such extreme, almost apocalyptic manias about menstrual blood abound
in the highlands. Mervyn Meggitt tells us that the men of the Mae Enga group
regard menstrual discharge as not merely harmful and dirty, but also "truly
dangerous," malignant, death-dealing. The Mae Enga, he continues

believe that contact with it or with a menstruating woman will, in the absence of countermagic, sicken a man and cause persistent vomiting, turn his blood black, corrupt his vital
juices so that his skin darkens and wrinkles as his flesh wastes. . . . Menstrual blood
introduced into a man's food, they say, quickly kills him, and young women crossed in
love sometimes seek their revenge in this way. Menstrual blood dropped on the bog-iris
plant (*Acorus calamus*) that men use in wealth-, pig-, and war-magic destroys them; and
a man would divorce, and perhaps kill, the wife concerned. (1964:207)

In fact, Meggitt cites the example of a Mae Enga man who did just that: he
murdered his wife for the crime of menstruating. In the late 1950s, a male
informant told Meggitt that he had divorced his wife because she slept on his
blanket while menstruating; but afterward, still feeling threatened by her inju-
rious influence, he confessed to having killed her with an ax (206). He believed

he was justified by the rules of his culture. Acting entirely within tribal concepts of self-defense, he suffered no punishment whatsoever.

Prudent, But Not Prudes

It is important to emphasize that New Guinea men, as we have seen, are not sexual prudes. Actually, they enjoy sex and want it as much as men anywhere. Virtually every anthropologist agrees that what is involved is not moral priggishness but only fear of the supernatural and the need for hygienic prudence. For example, Buchbinder and Rappaport (1976:21) write that among the Maring the older men, who are notably less fearful than younger men about female pollution, are often openly lecherous and outspokenly ribald, and younger men too, despite their fears, "show a keen interest in sex." Maring men use tricks and love magic to proposition girls; they spend hours preening and generally are preoccupied with erotic conquests. Other New Guinea males, especially older ones, are likewise keen about sex — at least under the right, nonthreatening circumstances — to the point of "lechery" (Gelber 1986:18–19). These men are definitely not prudes. In fact, Gelber describes the sexual aggressiveness and eroticism of the older men throughout New Guinea as being excessive and even "florid" (1986:19). So here we have lechers who are terrified of the vagina.

Obviously intercourse presents an existential problem of the kind we have argued is the source of misogynist rage: contact with woman and her vagina is ardently desired but also dreaded because of the possibility of lethal consequences. Thus the New Guinea men are confronted with a classic double bind when it comes to the matter of sexual satisfaction: they can achieve sexual pleasure only at their peril. This makes the sex act all the more alluring, but also all the more terrifying. It is almost a truism to say that anything one cannot live without but which is also dangerous is experienced as both exciting and painful, causing acute moral tension and psychological stress. Among the Kuma, for example, the marriage relationship is fraught with apprehension because of the inevitability of intercourse, if only for procreation or the wife's insistence; and Fore men, on account of the current idea that women are potentially dangerous to men (Langness 1976:98), both crave and fear sex at all times, not just during menstruation, and are always anxious and tense with their wives.

Let us take the Etoro as an example of how this distressing marital conundrum is reflected in upland New Guinea. Interestingly, the Etoro are somewhat less afraid of menstrual blood than are most other highland males (Kelly 1976:42). Nevertheless, they regard heterosexual intercourse as highly detrimental to their physical well-being, seriously contaminating. Etoro men are thought to possess a life force, *hame,* which is centered in their semen. This *hame* is irreplaceably depleted by coitus, to the extent that men who overindulge in sex are thought to be in danger of withering to death. The male attitude toward sex is therefore charged with ambivalence, ambiguity, and anxiety (Kelly 1976:43). The men are literally afraid of their own desire and, although desirous of sex, afraid of their wives and of intercourse.

To resist the enticements of sex and thereby protect themselves from their own dangerous erotic impulses, not to mention from the pollution of their wives' bodies, the Etoro males have elaborated a virtually endless list of taboos. The result, according to Kelly, is that the Etoro have ritually eliminated heterosexual contact of any sort for between 205 and 260 days of the year (unfortunately there is no way of knowing whether these prohibitions are followed to the letter). So dangerous and debilitating is sex with a woman that the Etoro prohibit intercourse within their village boundaries, which forces couples to steal away into the forest for lovemaking, so as not to contaminate the village or its inhabitants. Despite the low incidence of intercourse, the population remains stable.

It is perhaps not surprising that the Etoro, like many highland peoples, associate sex with witchcraft and blame both evils entirely on women. A woman who entices her husband into excessive sexual relations (more than a few times a year) is said to be purposefully driving him to an early death, and is actually thought to be a witch (Kelly 1976:51) because of her erotic depredations. Throughout the island, in fact, any woman who uses feminine wiles to inveigle a man into sex may be deemed a witch and killed (Lidz and Lidz 1989:5). Not so far away, the Gimi men fear that sexual intercourse both depletes the man and infects him with deadly poisons. Female secretions invade the head of the penis and make a man sick. One Gimi man said: "We men continually give up to women something that is ours, and we grow weak and old before our time. . . . But the blood of women enters men. . . . The moment a man ejaculates and is empty, a woman's fluid enters him and makes him sick. It's poison to men. The fluid women have ruins us. It bends our backs and makes us old" (Gillison 1993:205–6).

Given such attitudes, it is not surprising that many highland men regard coitus with a great deal of unease and anxiety, and avoid it if they can. Copulation is by its very nature — since it involves physical contact with woman —

detrimental to male well-being. Sexual contact is poisonous not only to the male but also to everything he touches, including his crops, animals, and food. He must use potent countermagic to cleanse himself after every act of copulation. Even then, the possibility of defilement lingers: "Even after using magic he should not enter his gardens on the day he copulates, lest the female secretions adhering to him blight his crops, or try to cook meat lest it spoil. As a result the ordinary husband copulates with his wife only as often as he thinks necessary to beget children, and, naturally enough, regards with abhorrence any erotic preliminaries to the sexual act" (Meggitt 1964:210).

Disease

Because vaginal penetration is a part of sex and is usually required for impregnation, the men of the Sambia group are terrified that coitus will cause pollution in their penises, and from there, systemic disease. Menstrual blood is contaminating in itself, they say, but when in vaginal penetration the penis comes in contact with female genitalia, internal pollution is possible. The blood and other vaginal substances can enter the man's urethra and then travel through the bloodstream and lodge precariously in his stomach, causing putrefaction. Stalwart warriors, proud of their courage in combat, the Sambia acknowledge that the possibility of this affliction evokes their greatest fear: "We aren't afraid of anything else; we are afraid of the blood of women, which can enter the stomach. . . . Coitus is contaminating; it can cause the stomach to distend and a man's skin to blacken and lose its taut, masculine quality" (Herdt 1981:244–45). Indeed menstrual blood is used in witchcraft as a deadly poison. For the Sambia, making love and making war are not so different.

So fearful are men of women in general and coitus in particular, not to mention their own sexual impulses, that many bachelors in New Guinea postpone marriage indefinitely, until they are forced to tie the knot by their own kinsmen, who understand the youths' apprehensions but desperately want children to expand the patrilineage. Since some contact with women is unavoidable in the small villages and hamlets where these people live, cautious bachelors as a group seek constant ritualistic protection from female pollution. The Mae Enga youths, for instance, find this defense in an intermittent series of magical prophylactic rites, called *sanggai*. The *sanggai* ceremonies are designed to cleanse and strengthen the performers, but also to shield them from the omnipresent pollution of women (Meggitt 1964:211–12).

Meanwhile, many of the married men of New Guinea practice sexual abstinence for much of the year. For example, in an unpublished report, Robert Glassie, one of Meggitt's students, reports that among the Huli people of the Tari basin southwest of Mount Hagen the men also keep to a minimum their contact with women — for exactly the same reasons as the Mae Enga (Meggitt 1964:206). Indeed, some of the more timid Huli men actually refuse to marry at all, not because of prudishness or some ideal of abstemiousness, but because they fear pollution. Although there may be some exaggeration here in reality, Gelber (1986:95) notes that such an ideal of abstention may indirectly decrease or cap the population of many highland peoples. Some New Guinea couples also claim to observe a four- or five-year postpartum period of sexual abstinence, which, if true, would limit births to a maximum of one every five years. Shirley Lindenbaum (1972) also argues that misogynist pollution fears are a roundabout method of population control. Reviewing the literature up until 1971, she suggests that belief in female contamination, along with fear of sexual intercourse, appears to have resulted in an effective cultural barrier to human reproduction in the New Guinea highlands (1972:248).

Many highland men follow an elaborate sequence of precautions during sex in order to reduce the chance of corruption. For example, Herdt (1981) describes the rather extensive set of guidelines and techniques Sambia men use to defend their health against heterosexual coitus. These include restricting the frequency of intercourse to a bare minimum (once a month or so), using certain medicines and prophylactics to prepare for the rigors of intercourse (for example, ingesting special botanical products such as redwood bark before coitus and placing spearmint leaves inside the nostrils to prevent inhalation of woman's vile vaginal exhalations), and holding a large seed in the mouth during sex to remind them not to swallow their own saliva, which is contaminated by close contact with a woman.

Coitus itself among the Sambia follows certain rules. The man must always be on top of the woman to prevent the infiltration of bad fluids into his penis. He must get up at once after ejaculation to limit contact with female skin. Afterward, he performs numerous ablutions to ward off pollution, such as rubbing his hands and skin with stinging nettles to remove microscopic traces of the woman's effluvia. He replaces lost semen by guzzling various magical botanicals. He must clean his fingernails with a cassowary quill until he draws blood to rid himself of any female substance, accidentally acquired during the sex act, that might otherwise drop into his food (Herdt 1981:248–49).

Male Bias?

Could these morbidly misogynistic data be skewed because of a male bias in the reportage? After all, most of the field information presented here was collected, recorded, and interpreted by male anthropologists who worked mainly with male informants. Would a woman ethnographer find something different in the New Guinea highlands? The answer is a resounding no. Many women fieldworkers have found exactly the same things. Not so far away from the Mae Enga and the others, for example, live the Hua people, studied by Anna Meigs (1984:41). Sounding exactly like her male counterparts, she reports that the Hua regard sex with a woman as a negative act and extremely dangerous. Sex depletes a Hua man's vitality, sickens him, and robs him of his vital spirit, all the while strengthening the women in equal proportion. Shirley Lindenbaum found the same fear of woman's sexuality as a "wild" and "dangerous" thing among the Fore people (1976:56), and Paula Brown discovered that sex was dangerous and debilitating in the estimation of the Chimbu people (1978:150).

Similar findings were reported by female ethnographers such as Georgeda Buchbinder (Buchbinder and Rappaport 1976), Patricia Hays (Hays and Hays 1982), and Gillian Gillison (1993). Striking a dissonant note, ethnographer Elizabeth Faithorn (1975, 1976) claimed to have found that women among the Kafe of the eastern highlands *also* worry about pollution from men (semen), but this has rarely been corroborated by other observers, male or female, working in nearby areas (Langness 1976:101), and there is no evidence that men are thought to pose a danger to women by their "very nature," as women are said to do to men (Hays and Hays 1982:205).

The curious question remains of the obverse effect of the sex act on males and females. This invidious perception reveals something else about highland males' views of women and their misogynist premises. For the New Guinea men, as overtly stated above in the Hua case by Meigs, believe that while sex pollutes a man, it conversely strengthens a woman, makes her healthier, more powerful. This may be the reason that the men claim the women are sexually voracious witches in the battle of the sexes, in which even love is a form of war. Among the Hua, for example, intercourse is viewed as purifying for the female while polluting for the male (Meigs 1984:65). This happens because the man's vital essence, his healthy "juices," are stolen from him by the woman while copulating. The essential male spirit is believed to reside in the semen, passing from male to female during ejaculation. Throughout the entire highland region, men conclude that women pursue sex precisely in order to capture semen, to enhance well-being, to deplete the male victim, and to strengthen themselves in the process (Lidz and Lidz 1989:54–55). All this, of course, adds an entirely new and equally poignant element to the men's already fiercely defense-oriented misogyny: psychopathic fears of depletion at the hands of wicked women.

Depletion

For the Melanesians, sex is seen as doubly dangerous for men. The woman not only poisons his food, but also pollutes the man with her vaginal juices, which, by entering his penis, magically render him degenerate and wreck his possessions; additionally, he involuntarily depletes his own store of vital essences that keep him strong and healthy. He fears not only what woman intrudes into his helpless body, but also what she steals: his semen, the vital spark of maleness which women inevitably extract, "sapping a man's substance" (Herdt 1982a:54). Thus repetitive sex for a man is not only debilitating as a hygienic matter, but also literally lethal; it sucks him dry and leads to complete physical breakdown: decline, disintegration, and even death (Buchbinder and Rappaport 1976:21). All the while it augments the woman's health and power.

The belief in the danger of ejaculation is common in highland New Guinea, where every orgasm depletes a man's vitality (Meggitt 1964:210). Many suspicious New Guinea men also believe that women engage in sexual intercourse only in order to capture semen for nefarious purposes. Loss of semen in heterosexual intercourse is also considered weakening, and young men are stringently warned against overindulgence, as they are not yet strong enough to withstand the powers of women and the loss of semen. "A man runs the additional danger that his wife might give his semen to a sorcerer — a certain way of procuring his death" (Lidz and Lidz 1989:54).

The symbolic connection among sex, food, depletion, and death for many reasons is found throughout South Pacific native cultures, but we will also encounter it in almost every society we observe, "primitive" or not. I cite the convergence of sex and a foreboding of danger and decay, of nurturing gone bad, because sexual contact with women elicits some of the deepest and most intractable terrors in the male psyche — a terror of loss and diminishment in the face of his own impulses that goes beyond gender and beyond sex itself to the defense of ego boundaries, and that lies at the very heart of the misogynist malady. Curiously, these beliefs again present a kind of bizarre parody of the normal male-female situation in which the female "feeds" the male like a good mother and thereby sustains him and gives him life: here the woman robs the man of vital essences which she then uses to both corrupt him and batten her own terrible powers.

What is perhaps most striking about all the Melanesian material is its familiarity. The same impulses, fears, disavowals, ambiguities, and ambivalences exist among other men in other places. Although men in what we like to call modern civilizations do not often resort to magic and rituals, there are haunting formal parallels between contemporary American males and the Melanesians we have been describing in the moral and technical mechanics of misogynist blaming, feelings of disgust and endangerment, of an inversion of the good-mother image into its terrifying opposite, modes of denigration and their corporeal and spiritual underpinnings. In the next chapter, we look far afield from New Guinea and find similar misogynist folklore and antiwoman practices in many other places, including the modern West. It is perhaps fitting, then, to close this chapter with an observation by Gelber, with whose work we began this overview of Melanesian misogyny. She notes (1986:2–3) that fear and disgust toward women, an intense interest in the body and its products, sometimes disguised by phobias and a feeling that men and women are so different as to be almost two different species — these are attitudes that exist in a milder and more repressed way in American society, but pervade highland society "in an explicit, almost flamboyant form." Subtract some of the flamboyance and the explicitness, perhaps, and, as Gelber indicates, we are left with some haunting reminiscences elsewhere.

The female

Is an element, the female

Is chaos

An octopus

A biological process.

—Ezra Pound, *Canto* XXIX

2. Flesh and Blood

MANY MELANESIANS ARE COMMITTED misogynists, living apart from
their wives out of fear, denigrating woman's bodies and whatever comes
from them, elaborating magical spells and rites to repel female dangers.
In espousing this kind of genderized Manichaeism, so firmly rooted in
images of insidious flesh and mephitic blood, these highlanders seem
bizarre. After all, in our enlightened Western world the voluptuous female
body inspires our greatest art. But the Melanesian style of body-hating
misogyny is by no means a rarity in the world; nor is the form it takes —
visceral disgust, enchantment by biological forces — all that unusual. It
is a matter of degree rather than kind; the fierce denigration of woman's physicality, the allegation of mortal danger to the pure but corrup-
tible body of man, the fear of poisoning, and the rigorous avoidance of
the contagion of femininity are more common than one might expect. In
fact, what the New Guinea highlanders fear is so widespread that it appears almost routine in the liberated modern West. As the feminist critic
Nel Noddings (1989:36) says in her survey of misogyny in the modern
world, the fear of female flesh did not begin with Thomas Aquinas and
the patristic condemnation of sex, concupiscence, and carnality. Rather,
the fear of women as physical bodies is older than the Judeo-Christian
tradition.

In her book *Women and Evil,* Noddings traces the male association of woman's body with decay, poison, uncleanliness, and evil since the time of the ancient Greeks. She argues that this fear and degradation of the female body and its functions persists today among the most exalted thinkers, poets, and artists (1989:39). In the medieval period, the depravity of the flesh became "gendered as specifically feminine" (Bloch 1991:46), setting the course for centuries of antiwoman discourse to come.

Thus the female body became identified as the *locus classicus* of Western misogyny through the Middle Ages and into the modern period (Bloch 1991:47). Instances are legion, as Bloch's grim compendium of medieval fulminations against female flesh makes clear. For example, Bernard of Cluny describes women in grotesque language that reminds us of Melanesian attitudes: "locusts of the soul . . . a guilty thing, a hopelessly fleshy thing . . . rottenness . . . a vessel of filth . . . a trench of lust, the arms of chaos" (Wilson and Makowsky 1990:122). Walter Map, another medieval churchman, compares woman with a particularly loathsome Chimera with mixed animal imagery: "blemished with the belly of a rooking [rutting] kid and . . . beweaponed with the virulent tail of a viper" (cited in Rogers 1966:ix). How like the Melanesians, with their venomous wives' poisonous, bloody entrails.

King Lear's denunciation of womanhood takes on a similar virulence in its nauseous imagery (*King Lear* 4.6):

Down from the waist they are centaurs
Though women all above:
But to the girdle do the gods inherit,
Beneath is all the fiends; there's hell,
    there's darkness,
There is the sulphurous pit — burning, scalding,
Stench, consumption, fie, fie, fie! pah, pah!

The line "beneath is all the fiends" is associated with the belief that woman's genital orifice was the portal of the fiend himself, the devil.

The fabrication of a single embodiment of evil, a personification of ugliness, sin, and physical, not to mention moral, corruption had serious consequences for the imagery surrounding woman and her fleshy, corrupted self in Europe. According to Claudette Hoover (1989:354), belief in a moral connection between woman (whose body provides entrance for evil into the world) and the devil himself, in all his moral and physical loathsomeness, was widespread during the European Middle Ages and Renaissance. As in the jungles of New Guinea, this personification centered on the female orifice as the gateway to hell. Hoover cites a popular writer of the time, named Harsnett — a possible inspiration for Lear's misogynist rants in Shakespeare's play — who denounced women as having evil centered "in a particular part of the body . . . the inferior parts," which, he assured his readers, was the human lodgement of the devil.

Later in the eighteenth century, Jonathan Swift expressed much the same qualms about women's crevices in various diatribes against the awful immediacy of her flesh. In his poem *Strephon and Chloe,* he pilloried woman in typically repellent terms: "Exhal'd from sour, unsavory streams . . . all her stinks." In *Gulliver's Travels* he railed at length against the repulsiveness of the female sexual organs as seen from the perspective of tiny Gulliver, cast among the naked, repulsive Brobdingnagian giantesses. Only half joking, Swift defines a beautiful woman, a "belle," as an "ugly, ill-smelling animal." So potent are his descriptions of female bodily corruption — malodorousness, physical repulsiveness — that the term "Swiftian" has been used to mark the extreme misogyny of writers with a similarly neurotic vision of a monstrous femininity (Francus 1984). The Anglo-Irish poet W. B. Yeats, for example, wrote that "Love has pitched his mansion in the place of excrement." A leading contemporary Spanish writer, Ignacio Martínez de Pizón, uses the same sort of excremental language and imagery to convey a similar hatred and horror of femininity, showing the nauseous usage to be no means an exclusively Anglo-Saxon or a Melanesian neurosis (Glenn 1992).

The French belletrist Montherlant in *Les Léprouses* (1939) similarly stigmatized women as carriers of a "spiritual leprosy" dangerous to the health and virility of men and a peril to society itself (Nixon 1986:5). Recently, feminists such as Margery Collins and Christine Pierce (cited in Noddings 1989) have accused more contemporary writers and seemingly rational philosophers — Jean-Paul Sartre, for example — of contributing to this same misogynistic fantasy: identifying the female body with "obscenity" and "slime." Pierce also notes that Sartre blames the female body for being one of the strongest sources of nausea (Noddings 1989:39). This conviction that woman's body is "poisonous," containing some kind of mortal substance or element inimical to man's spiritual and physical well-being is, of course, part of a wider masculine rhetoric renouncing carnality and providing a convenient metaphor in genderized terms for man's failed quest for spiritual perfection. Once again, it is woman, the object of displaced rage, who is stigmatized for man's own existential disillusionment.

Another Anti-Vagina Complex

In the West, these masculine fears often find their locus in female genitalia, the defining anatomical fact of womanhood. Psychologists have long noted Western man's aversion to the vagina as threatening and "sinister" (Hays 1964:53), and his deep-seated anxiety about the female organ as eerie, unsettling, or, as Freud (1940) called it, "uncanny." The vagina's unknown morphology fascinates and terrifies Western man as much as the stone age men of New Guinea. The female organ is of course hidden; it is a passageway to the original home and to all the mysteries. At the same time, it is the center of modern man's erotic fantasies and for some remains a visual enigma until adulthood, or even later, as among the Melanesians who are afraid to look or touch. The female genitals, therefore, assume a fetishistic life of their own in numerous cultures; given the sameness of human anatomy, the vagina becomes frightening everywhere to men because of this disturbing unknowability (Lederer 1968:3). Freud wrote a paper specifically on this subject, "The Medusa's Head" published posthumously in 1940. In the Greek myth Freud took as a metaphor for universal male anxieties, the mere sight of Medusa's snaky locks turns beholders to stone. Interpreting the icon of a serpent-coiffed goddess as an objectification for psychic conflict, Freud argues that Medusa's head represents the vagina in general and the mother's vagina in particular, the archetypal "hairy maternal vulva" (Lederer 1968:3). Here is the Oedipal terror displaced to the head: Medusa embodies both mother and woman, and the hairy vulva typifies incestuous temptation. It is not only the ancient Greeks, Melanesians, and Western poets and philosophers who regard the vagina as eerie and the mother as a dualistic figure.

The strange and powerful Melanesian beliefs reverberate, for example, among the inhabitants of aboriginal Amazonia. Far from New Guinea — in fact, halfway around the globe — the men of the neolithic Mehinaku tribe in central Brazil are equally squeamish about women and their bodies. They say that the female genitals are "revolting" and not of this world, that they are in league with the devil and other dark chthonic forces. Many Mehinaku men speak of the vagina as a "spirit," as something ghoulish, mysterious, otherworldly (Gregor 1985:71).

Melford Spiro (1997:22,41) reports that in modern Myanmar (known as Burma until 1989), the vagina is considered both ignoble as an organ and "dangerous and dirty" to men and their possessions. Women's genitals are places of extreme menace as well as sexual attraction. If a woman wants to terrify and degrade a man in rural Myanmar, her worst threat is to expose herself. When a village woman becomes extremely angry with a man, she may, as an ultimate gesture of her ire, raise her skirt to her knees, "hinting that she might expose her genitals is intended to arouse his fear" (Spiro 1997:34). But, extrapolating from his data, Spiro emphasizes the global prevalence of the notion that the vagina is inimical to men, pointing out that the concept is found among the Mehinaku of Brazil, the Zuni of the southwestern United States, the Jains of India, and modern Western societies, as well as Iran and other parts of the Middle East. Jain monks, for example, view the vagina as a spittoon, which is good enough only for spitting and vomiting into (Spiro 1997:34–35).

In some parts of the Middle East, for example, the aversion to this ominous orifice is so magnified that it leads to a preference for anal intercourse, homosexuality, or total celibacy (Baraheni 1977:47). In some parts of India, the antivagina imagery becomes more grisly, and the menace implied in the female genitalia may become concrete, magnified in horrific imagery in folklore: a chamber pot full of poison, causing death in the sexual act, or jaws lined up with sharp teeth. The motif of the death-dealing vagina is pandemic in Hindu mythology, according to Indian psychoanalyst and ethnographer Sudir Kakar (1981:92). He also says that the feminine principle is regarded as not only dreadful, but contaminating. This is likewise true in Melanesia and Amazonia.

Curiously, the association of the vagina with danger along with pollution and dirt is also encountered in numerous cultures where no formalized pattern of menstrual taboos or pronounced ideology of misogynistic behavior exists. For example, such representations appear among the gentle Zunis, whose "Corn Woman" threatens crops and men (Delaney et al. 1988:13). The same connection occurs among the Semai of Malaysia, an aboriginal people who are among the least male-chauvinistic in the world (Dentan 1979). Despite their gentleness and virtually androgynous culture, the Semai believe that a menstruating woman can metamorphose into a man-eating tiger. Today in Myanmar, among the peaceable rural peasants, the vagina is also regarded as dangerous to males (Spiro 1997:33); its essences, as in New Guinea, are considered "polluting," and are warded off with a panoply of ritual and magic prophylactics. Again, as in New Guinea, many Burmese men believe that any object touching the female organ becomes dangerous and must be deflected, isolated, or magically propitiated. A man can be seriously damaged even by the most indirect contact with a polluting vagina, so powerful is its contagion. For example, it is perilous for a Burmese man to go near a toilet, a bidet, or a bathroom that has been previously used by a woman; he may sicken and die. It is also dangerous for him to so much as touch her sarong, which, of course, has brushed against her genitals; it is equally treacherous to walk near, or especially under, a clothesline from which her genital-touching sarong hangs drying. Similarly, a man is endangered if his own clothes are laundered or ironed together with a woman's or placed on a shelf or in a closet with a woman's (Spiro 1997:26).

Spiro (42) observes that the fear of touching a woman's skirt because it has brushed against her genitals is found not only in Myanmar, New Guinea, and Amazonia, but also in some degree among the Egyptian Bedouins, in several areas of Southeast Asia, especially Thailand, and among Gypsies in many different parts of the world. In most of these places it is highly inadvisable for a man to let himself be passed over by a woman's genitals; therefore, in order to avoid this danger, men avoid lying down while women are standing nearby. Burmese men, for example, are said to tremble at the idea that a woman's genitals might be higher up than a man's head (33). Meanwhile, of course, the act of a woman stepping over a prone man and displaying her genitals to him is sexually exciting to men everywhere.

Vagina Dentata

The horror of the putatively dangerous female genitals finds symbolic expression in the far-flung image of *vagina dentata,* the saw-toothed orifice that waits to mutilate the male. Norman O. Brown (1966:63) describes the legend in Western lore: "the vagina as a devouring mouth, or vagina dentata, the jaws of the giant cannibalistic mother, a menstruating woman with the penis bitten off, a bleeding trophy." The mangling, devouring vagina, the terrible cannibalistic mother, occurs as a motif in male folklore in many locales in the preliterate world (Thompson 1956, vol. 3), as well as in Freud's musings about castration anxiety and in his study of the Medusa figure.

Using reliable data, Hays (1964:55–56) reports, for example, at least twenty-two variants of this biting vagina myth in aboriginal North America alone, citing at length a variant found among the Wichita Indians of Kansas, who believe that the *vagina dentata* pursues a man and enters into his dreams to castrate him in sleep. Wolfgang Lederer (1968:44) also stresses that the subject is "incredibly prevalent" in both North and South America. Robert Murphy (1960:108) reports a *vagina dentata* theme among the Mundurucú Indians of Brazil, who refer to the female organ as the "crocodile's mouth." Even without the specific tooth evocation, there are innumerable New World myths and folktales in which the female cleft is felt to be a castrating scissors (Hays 1964:60). In anthropologist William Stephens's survey (1967:143) of folklore in seventy-one tribal societies, he found that in all but fourteen, the female genitalia are associated with injury and danger as biting, snapping mouths, sharp scissors, or jagged-clamp traps. The Mehinaku of the Brazilian Amazon are no strangers to the fanged vulva either, as their story "The Toothed Vagina" shows:

In ancient times, there was an angry man who constantly berated others. One evening, a woman took many tiny shells — they looked just like teeth — and put them in her inner labia [labia minora]. Later, when it got dark, the man wanted to have sex. "Oh, she is beautiful," he thought. The woman was pretending to sleep. "Let's have sex," he said. Oh, but his penis was big. In it went. He ate [penetrated] her, he ate her, it went all the way in. . . . *Tsyuu!* The vagina cut his penis right off, and he died right there in the hammock. (Gregor 1985:71)

Ferocious female castrators abound in the Old World as well. In Hindu India, for example, the mother of all she-demons, Kali, the fearsome warrior goddess, exults in her castrating vagina as well as in the swords she wields in her armada of arms to behead boys and men. In Orissa, India, according to Verrier Elwin (1968:102), the *vagina dentata* is known as a ferocious orifice of the wind that not only mutilates men but also gobbles the rice crop, ruins the harvests, and consumes the seeds for next year's regeneration, causing famine. The Muria of Madhya Pradesh, in central India, have various toothed-vagina legends (Elwin 1968:102–5), in which the vagina devours babies, animals, and men.

Sudir Kakar (81), who has studied these myths, states that many Hindus believe that the vagina is a chamber full of poison, causing death in the sexual act, or a snapping jaws lined with fangs (1978:92). Spiro finds a similar belief in the rural areas of Burma (1997:163) and quotes a verse from the Buddhist holy script *The Book of the Discipline* in which the Buddha warns men:

It is better for you, foolish man, that your male organ should enter the mouth of a terrible and poisonous snake than it should enter a woman. It were better for you, foolish man, that your organ should enter the mouth of a black snake, than it should enter a woman. It were better . . . that your male organ should enter a charcoal pit, burning, ablaze, afire, than it should enter a woman. (26–27)

Similar to the toothed *vagina dentata* is the poisonous vagina, once again showing the strength of the male fantasy-fear of a perversion of the alimentary role of woman. Poisoned orifice imagery is commonly found in early modern Western lore, especially in medical and theological texts. According to Michael Solomon (1997:83), in fifteenth-century European writings on hygiene and medicine there were not enough words to express the types of poisons that women offer men. All this rhetoric portrays women as mortally dangerous to men, as equivalent to some natural calamity like flood, fire, or earthquake, their bodies equally out of man's control. Rather than being nurturing and gentle, women are disastrous, unfathomable, and, like the implacable spirits above, they wreak unimaginable devastation on man and his works. The equation of woman with the worst natural dangers is common in many cultures. For example, the modern island Greeks have a saying, "Fear only three things — fire, water, and woman" (Hirschon 1978:69). In northern Greece the saying goes that the three evils in the world are fire, women, and the sea (Danforth 1989:127). This warning or similar ones are found in all the other Mediterranean countries today. George Lakoff in *Women, Fire, and Dangerous Things,* shows how a common theme in most cultures is a metaphorical and semantic linkage between the concept-phonemes "woman" and "danger." An Australian aboriginal language, Dyirbal, has a category, *balan,* that actually includes woman, fire, and all other dangerous things (1987:5). Woman is depravity itself: if she fails to drown you in vice, pollute you with poison, or sicken you through her insatiable sex drive, she will burn you like fire. Woman, who should protect and nurture the man, instead rends his flesh, starves him, poisons him, burns him alive.

Menstruation Again

These universal male fears, again, center on flesh, blood, bone, and specifically on menstrual blood. Virtually every society in the world practices some form of menstrual taboo or recognizes some system of demonization involving female effluvia. The menstrual taboo itself is virtually universal, as Paula Weideger (1976:85) has conclusively shown, perhaps the only universal proscription other than incest taboo. Among stone age peoples outside Melanesia, this female blood takes on the emotive salience of a magical phobia. In some ways, it is preliterate man's most powerful fear, greater than his fear of death, dishonor, or dismemberment (Delaney et al. 1988:1).

Among the preliterate cultures in Stephens's comprehensive survey (1967), the fear of menstrual blood is the single dominant belief out of thousands, and the one with the most "luxuriant variations" (88). The psycho-analyst Otto Fenichel (1945:11) calls menarche "the first pollution" in the history of mankind. And Freud, in *Civilization and Its Discontents* (1931a:48), comments that, although this blood phobia might serve aesthetic and hygienic purposes in modern civilizations, it was originally directed mainly against man's deep fears and his horror at the base animality of sexual functions associated with the vagina.

Again, there is the connection with food. In most preliterate societies, menstruating women are especially dangerous to hunters. Women in menses must not go near a hunter or his weapons, for their blood weakens the hunter, diminishes his skill, hurts his luck, and warns off the game. Menstrual fluids are also polluting to crops, prepared food, and other organic things. To the Maori of New Zealand, the menses are the personification of all human dirt and can inflict the greatest harm on a man (Delaney et al. 1988:8–9). Among the Gisu of Uganda, it is said that a menstruating woman must keep herself from contact with many activities lest she spoil them; she may not brew beer nor pass by the homestead of a potter lest his pots crack during firing; she may not cook for her husband nor sleep with him lest she endanger both his virility and his general health. A menstruating woman endangers the success of any ritual merely by her presence. During the time she is menstruating, she must not touch food with her hands; "she eats with two sticks" (La Fontaine 1972:164–65).

In Mali, along the Bandiagar escarpment, the men of the farming Dogon tribe believe that a menstruating woman is a threat to the sanctity of religious altars where the men pray and make sacrifices to protect their fields and the crops that sustain them. If a menstruating woman comes near the altars, which are situated both indoors and outdoors, the Dogon believe that her aura of pollution will ruin the shrines and bring disaster to the entire village, especially famine. Any menstruating woman knows she may be held personally responsible should a calamity occur (Small 1999:27).

Among the Oriyas of India, any contact with a menstruating woman can kill a man. The Oriyas say that if a menstruating wife touches her husband on the first day of her period, it is an offense equal to that of killing a holy man, a guru. If she touches him on the second day, it is an offense equal to killing a Brahmin, that is, a man of the highest caste. On the third day, to touch him is like cutting off his penis. If she touches him on the fourth day, it is like killing a child (Shweder 1991:251). Having studied sexual beliefs of the Nepalese Hindus, Lynn Bennett (1983:215) provides a long list of menstrual fears and taboos from the high valleys of the Himalayan range. Lederer (1968:26–29) gives equally detailed and reliable information from aboriginal North America, including postpartum superstitions and other vaginal-pollution beliefs; Hays (1964:42–47) gives us stories and myths from the Old World; and Delaney et al. (1988) describe menstrual terrors from various cultures, preliterate and postindustrial.

These beliefs, incidentally, are not confined to what are referred to as male-dominated cultures, nor to patrilineal societies where women's position to low. Reviewing the ethnographic literature on menstrual taboos, Buckley and Got-tlieb (1988b:8–9) point out that there is no correlation between the strength of these taboos and the status of women. For example, among the matrilineal Crow, where women controlled significant property and held relatively high status, a menstruating woman was nevertheless considered polluting and was subject to typical taboos. The menstruating Crow woman was not allowed to approach a wounded warrior or to go near men heading out to a war party, lest she infect them and bring them bad luck. Nor was a menstruating woman allowed to go near sacred tribal objects; she was considered a contamination, a substantial pestilence to all good or vulnerable things (Lowie 1956:44).

Even among the !Kung San Bushmen of Botswana, a gentle, egalitarian people almost devoid of openly misogynistic practices and lacking any gender hierarchy, there are fears about menstrual blood. A menstruating !Kung woman is not allowed to approach a hunter or to step over his bow. If she did, he would lose his hunting prowess or become impotent and his family would starve (Shostak 1983:239). Nor may she go near the cooking area or serve food to her husband or sons; in fact, she is forbidden to touch or even approach cooking utensils (Lee 1979:155). The !Kung San also regard childbirth as polluting to men, and a woman in labor must go off into the bush to deliver her baby so that her husband is not contaminated (Lee 1979:451). These same hunter-gatherers, incidentally, are often offered as a model of gender equality by feminist anthro-pologists (see Lee 1979 for a review of this issue).

The same prohibitions and anxieties prevailed among the Yurok Indians of northern California. The Yurok people held (and hold) women in relatively high esteem, at least as compared with other preliterate Pacific Coast fisher-men. Although they are nominally patrilineal, the Yuroks observed a parallel form of matrilineal, matrilocal marriage that led anthropologists studying their social structure to classify them as transitional between patriliny and matriliny (Waterman and Kroeber 1965:12–14). The Yurok women fished, worked out-side the hut, made important economic decisions, often ruled the clans as matriarchs, and freely and openly did everything that men did.

Even though the Yuroks today are highly acculturated to modern American ways, they still harbor the usual menstrual fears. For Yurok traditionalists, a menstruating woman is "highly polluting" and will "contaminate the family house and food supply if she comes into contact with either" (Buckley 1982:48). Avoided by even her closest kin, she is consigned to a special isolated hut and may not mingle with others.

Perhaps a prime example to disprove any one-to-one correspondence between male political domination and menstrual anxieties is found among the Semai Semang people of the Malay Peninsula. Aboriginal inhabitants of the Malay upland forests, the Semai are possibly the least violent, least sexist group of people on the face of the earth. They make almost no real distinctions between the sexes and get along perfectly well without a shred of machismo (Dentan 1979). Male bullies are not tolerated, men never hit their wives or even speak crossly to them, anger is unknown, and men as well as women avoid confrontation at virtually all cost. In this paradigm of sexual equality, an exceptionally — if not uniquely — androgynous people, there is not even a hint of a masculinity cult (Gilmore 1990). Yet even among these Semai the men fear menstruating women; they hedge menstrual blood with taboos and proscriptions, and they flee from contact with a menstruating woman. The Semai men imagine menstrual blood to be as lethal as the fish poison they use to kill river fish; if a menstruating woman steps into a river, they say, she will turn into a man-eating tiger. While menstruating, she is essentially put under house arrest except to urinate or defecate. She may not cook for men or for other women, nor handle kitchen utensils lest she pollute them. Bathing, of course, is prohibited lest she undergo transformation into a flesh-eating tiger (Dentan 1979:99).

Like other groups mentioned earlier, the Semai men, although not prudes, are terrified of sex with women. The first time they have sex they often suffer tremors and blackouts. With more experience, they eventually copulate with more pleasure. A young male Semai told the anthropologist Robert Dentan that he was beside himself on his wedding night. His wife's vagina, he agitatedly explained, "looked like a house, a *big* house." He feared being swallowed up (Dentan 1979:63). To enter the vagina, in the mind of this timorous but typical individual, was a daunting undertaking, requiring all his courage.

The Tahitians of the South Pacific are also frequently cited for their androgynous gender attitudes and the high status bestowed upon women. Like the Semai, the Tahitians have no beliefs about male dominance and are unconcerned with masculinity, the men being rather feminine and the women being somewhat masculine according to Levy's masterful study (1973:234–35). But even among these gentle Tahitians, menstrual blood is terrifying, considered dangerous to the male (meaning any male creature, man or beast) and contaminating to all living things (Levy 1973:336). The Tahitians also practice strict menstrual taboos and quarantines.

The British anthropologist Sir James George Frazer wrote in the late nineteenth century about menstrual mythology in European folklore: "The touch of a menstruous woman turned wine to vinegar, blighted crops, killed seedlings, blasted gardens, brought down the fruit from trees, dimmed mirrors, blunted razors, rusted iron and brass, killed bees . . . , caused mares to miscarry, and so forth" (Frazer 1890/1951:702). These are among the most ancient, pervasive, and tenacious beliefs in the recorded history of human thought. In the oldest extant encyclopedia, Pliny the Elder's *Historia naturalis,* the list of hazards created by menstruation is longer than any furnished by mere barbarians (Stephens 1962). This disgust continues as a time-honored obsession among Orthodox Jews, who regard menstruating women as unclean and requiring ritual purification in a *mikvah* bath (Harrowitz 1994:34–35). In the Old Testament (Leviticus) there is the warning, "Whosoever that toucheth her shall be unclean"; she is one of the abominations that, again, mainly involve food (cited in Delaney et al. 1988:19). In Orthodox Judaism, menstruating women must wear special contrivances to warn men to keep their distance.

The Qur'an (2:222) states that menstruating women are "unclean" and orders men to avoid them for safety's sake: "Keep aloof from women during their menstrual periods and do not approach them until they are clean again." The Qur'anic scholar Abelwahib Bouhdiba (1985:51–52) reminds us that in Islam there is none of the usual ambiguity in other matters about a woman's vaginal discharge; it is impure, and, he says, "arouses considerable revulsion."

Similarly steadfast taboos bind menstruating women throughout traditional Hindu societies in India, Bangladesh, and mountainous Nepal. A menstruating Hindu woman may not prepare food, handle religious offerings, go near a holy place, enter a kitchen, approach a granary, or draw water from a well. Indian men have a mortal horror of being near a woman during the time of menstruation. Like many other customs in India, the menstruation taboos have a hoary tradition. Manu, the law giver, is customarily blunt on the subject: "The wisdom, the energy, the strength, the might and the vitality of a man who approaches a woman covered with menstrual excretions utterly vanishes" (Kakar 1981:93).

Further east, in traditional China, too, woman was considered unclean during menstruation and postpartum. Her blood is *la-sam,* which means dirty or soiled (Ahern 1978:270). Moreover, all bodily effluvia "associated exclusively with women" are unclean, including afterbirth and vaginal discharge. These female substances are said to pose a powerful danger to the health of children and men and to be abhorrent to the gods. Thus, anyone — male or female — coming into contact with menstrual blood is barred from worshipping at altars or shrines in China and must be sequestered for the community's well-being.

In the Japanese Buddhist tradition, menstrual blood is also considered polluting. A well-known Japanese sutra, or discourse of the Buddha, tells the story of the esteemed monk Mokuren, who, in a conversation with Buddha, describes this ghastly image: "Once I went to such-and-such prefecture, and saw in the middle of a large field there a Hell composed of a pond of menstrual blood. . . . The blood the women had shed polluted the deity of the earth. Because of these acts of uncleanliness, the women were now forced to undergo sufferings" (Momoko 1983:230). According to a Japanese Buddhist text published in 1801, menstrual blood is the embodiment of women's iniquity: "Because they were born as women, their aspirations to Buddhahood are weak, and their jealousy and evil character are strong. These sins compounded become menstrual blood, which flows in two streams each month, polluting not only the earth god but all the other deities as well" (Momoko 1983:235).

The Japanese folk religion that predated Buddhism is Shintoism, a form of nature-spirit and ancestor worship that became the official state religion during the Tokugawa period (1615–1868). Like its successors, Shintoism also condemned menstrual blood, parturition, and postpartum fluids as polluting. Bleeding women could not go near a Shinto shrine without purification: they must wait seven days, clean their bodies for three days, and may go to a shrine on the eleventh day after their menstrual period has ended. Childbirth also made a woman unholy: women who give birth may not attend a shrine for ninety days after the flow of blood stops and may not use the same cooking fire as men for one hundred days. Historically, in all Japanese religious traditions, woman's biological functions were viewed in an extremely negative light, inappropriate to shrines and dangerous to holy things; her effluvia were contaminating and dirty (Smyers 1983:14–15).

As in Islam, Christianity, and other world religions, the ancient Middle Eastern faith predating Islam, Zoroastrianism, also had strict menstrual proscriptions, some of which are still observed in western Asia. The few remaining followers of Zarathustra (popularly known as Parsees or fire worshippers) regard vaginal discharge as *nasu*: dead, decaying, polluting materials (Fischer 1978:204). Having lived among the fire worshippers in Iran, anthropologist Michael Fischer describes the Zoroastrian menstruation guidelines and taboos from their sacred text, the *Vendidad*: the Zoroastrian code requires the severest separation of menstruating women. According to the *Vendidad* (verse 16) no one may approach her within three paces, food is handed to her in metal vessels, and she should not be given meat or other invigorating food that might strengthen "the fiend of pollution."

In many parts of the Mediterranean region, modern Christians harbor similar anxieties about menstruation and vaginal secretions. Richard and Eva Blum (1965:33–34; 1970:20,46) and John Campbell (1964:31–32) provide ample evidence of such fears among the rural Greek Orthodox in mainland Greece, as does Stanley Brandes (1980:85–86) for the Roman Catholic town of Monteros in southern Spain. Among the Orthodox Sarakatsani, mountain shepherds of Epirus in northern Greece, for example, a menstruating woman must avoid approaching a lactating sheep or else it will stop giving milk (Campbell 1964:31). Throughout rural Greece, menstrual or postpartum blood is so powerfully baleful that it "weakens even God." A menstruating woman in Greece may not, therefore, enter a church, make a meal, or visit the sick. Women's bodily functions are said to be polluted before God, and woman is the epitome of pollution, equal in sinfulness to a murderer (Blum and Blum 1965:50,138). Indeed, there is something truly malignant, even demonic, about women's bodies in this culture, where women are called "devils," and their "shame" (specifically, their genitals) must be concealed and periodically purified, as in ancient times, by ritual bathing, not in a *mikvah* bath, but in the sea (Blum and Blum 1965:50).

Brandes (1980) says that in Monteros, in Catholic Spain, men consider menstrual blood to be polluted for the specific reason that it carries away the filth that inevitably accumulates over the course of a woman's cycle. In neighboring Portugal, a woman having her period must keep away from vulnerable farm animals and cannot participate in sausage making or other food preparation for fear that the food will become poisonous and the people who eat it will become sick (D. L. Lawrence 1982:84).

Protestant northern Europeans and Ashkenazi Jews (those from northern and eastern Europe) also have menstrual fears, as do many well-educated residents of metropolises. The psychoanalyst Theodor Reik reports the following incident that occurred when, as a child, he visited his Viennese relatives. At dinner Reik's grandfather curtly ordered his wife, "Mach den Tisch rein!" (make the table clean) and then motioned for her to leave the room. When Reik asked what was happening, his parents told him that his grandmother was "in her time" (menstruating) and was not considered clean enough to be at the table with the menfolk (cited in Delaney et al. 1988:13).

Menstrual disgust can be found, although less obviously, in the contemporary United States. According to recent research among American college students, young men find menstruation unsanitary, repugnant, or otherwise distasteful (Paige 1977:147).

Female Contagion: An Early Modern Example

A sense of peril or contagion, and of masculine beleaguerment in a world full of female poison, is nowhere more starkly expressed than in medieval and early modern European literature on health and healing. Medical works dealing with prophylaxis and the curing of corporeal afflictions show a discomfiting continuity: the idea that women were a source of disease and physical disorder had a long and venerable tradition in Western thought (Solomon 1997:69).

A prime example of this enduring misogynistic tradition in the curative sciences is from medieval Spain, where scientific medicine reached its apogee during the European Middle Ages. The fourteenth-century Valencian physician Jaume Roig and the fifteenth-century Castilian clergyman and amateur doctor Alfonso Martínez de Toledo wrote extensively about the ills of the body and its cures. Echoing the antifemale alarmism of their society, both warned against the pathological potential of woman's flesh and blood.

The misogyny in their works, as cited by Solomon (1997:72), is truly awesome. For Roig, woman was a virtual epidemic. He complains that hidden beneath a woman's clothing lies a foul region of deadly humors and venomous vermin. Here, according to Roig, surrounded by foul vapors and the stench of decay, grotesque insects mingle with worms, frogs, rats, and serpents (80). Similarly, for Martínez de Toledo, woman was a transmitting agent for infectious diseases. He outlined four ways in which women pose health hazards to men: they wound and poison the male flesh with ruinous vapors; they drain and deplete men through the "excessive sexual contemplation that they provoke in the male"; they weaken men through "emasculation, seduction and enthrallment"; and last, through "congenital disfiguration," their baneful presence in and of itself causes the male body to sicken and wither (81). Simply put, for Father Martínez as for the stone age Melanesians, contact with a woman's body causes putrefaction in men (86).

A Parallel Case: Amazonia

One conclusion we can derive from this colorful material is that misogyny shows no correlation with any particular form of society. Rather than being culture-specific, it occurs everywhere and reappears without much variation among hunter-gatherers, fishermen, horticulturists, peasants, medieval clerics and physicians, and modern urban Europeans. Throughout the preliterate world, magical beliefs proliferate, rivaling those of New Guinea in luridness, abnegating proscriptions and fears of poisoning. But a special case of ritual and magical parallelism is found in aboriginal South America.

In the remote rainforest regions along the Amazon River in South America lie huge swaths of jungle and marsh collectively known as Amazonia — including portions of Brazil, Venezuela, Colombia, Ecuador, Peru, and Bolivia. Although these lands are as geographically distant and culturally remote from New Guinea as possible, stunning ritual convergence and curious ideological analogues to Melanesian practices permeate the cultures of many Indian tribes in these counties. More than any other data, this convergence points to a supracultural origin for misogyny.

The parallels between the Amazon and Papua New Guinea cultures are striking. They include, for example, the secret men's cults with their cult houses from which the women are rigidly excluded on pain of death or gang rape; the residence of the men in the cult house separate from their wives and children; the same men's anxieties about having heterosexual relations; the belief that female witches or bewitched women attract in order to drain a man of vital essences and thereby kill him (Lidz and Lidz 1989:166).

Many other anthropologists have noted the striking similarities among views of women in these disparate parts of the world. Joan Bamberger (1974) has argued that misogynistic rituals and their symbolism are so similar in New Guinea and Amazonia as to suggest common if not identical masculine psychology, since the possibility of diffusion must be ruled out. In her review of literature on anthropology and women, Naomi Quinn (1977:216) notes that ethnographic accounts of institutionalized misogyny from Amazonia include virtually all the specific elements found in Melanesia, especially gang rape for women who trespass into the male realm, or "mass rape" (as she calls it) in the case of the Kalapalo Indians of central Brazil. In the latter instance, all the men of the village attack the errant woman en masse (Basso 1973:60). Among the Mehinaku of central Brazil, a woman who has mistakenly entered the men's house, or so much as caught a glimpse of the men's sacred flutes, will likewise be gang raped, because, the men say, "a woman's eyes are revolting to the spirits" (Gregor 1985:100). All Mehinaku women live with the threat of rape for such minor transgressions, and many have violent nightmares about it (Gregor 1985:103).

Other shared traits between New Guinea and South America include an intense preoccupation with female pollution, fears about male sexual depletion caused by sexual contact with females, and a ritual similarity in elaborate male ceremonial activities, knowledge of which must be kept secret from women. Finally, it has been universally reported that men and women just do not get along in either place: relations between the sexes in both societies are also characterized as extremely hostile and antagonistic (Quinn 1977:216). A good example of the Amazonian misogynist complex is found among the Tukanoan people who live in the Vaupés region on the Colombian-Brazilian border. The Tukanoans have been described at length by ethnographers Jean Jackson (1992, 1996), Christine Hugh-Jones (1979), and Stephen Hugh-Jones (1979). I will digress briefly here to compare these paragons of misogyny with their New Guinea peers.

The Tukanoans are a riverine people, living along numerous small tributaries of the Amazon. They number aobut 20,000, speak the Eastern Tukanoan and Arawak languages of Amazonia, and live in long-house villages scattered throughout the rainforest. The men hunt, fish, and clear slash-and-burn fields in the jungle, where the women grow bitter manioc and other tropical crops. The Tukanoans are a classic patrilineal, patrilocal society, entertaining assumptions of male authority and superiority. In their male folklore, females are denigrated not only as lower than men, but as truly vile: dangerous, treacherous, and "barely human" (Jackson 1992:4).

A great deal of physical and emotional brutality is directed toward the Tukanoan women. For example, the men engage in simulated gang rape, threatening the women by lunging at them and pretending to rape them as a warning to get away from the men's sacred areas. The men also practice ritual bride capture in which women are again menaced, whipped, and roughed up to the point of serious bloodletting. In some areas of Tukanoan territory, the men practice *real* — as opposed to ritual — bride capture, accompanied by violence and sexual humiliation. Women are excluded from religious rituals and are prevented — on pain of death, or in some cases, gang rape — from even glimpsing the men's religious paraphernalia.

As in the New Guinea highlands, in Amazonia sex with women is considered dangerous to men's health. Women's bodies are viewed as corrupting and polluting; women's sexuality is depicted in a highly negative way and as debilitating to men. The men fear women as being too close to raw and inimical nature. Their bodies are said to harbor mysterious chthonic forces that are far too noxious to be resisted without powerful countermagic; unprotected men succumb to these forces as easily as small animals yield to ravenous jaguars on the prowl. Before sex, a groom must be blessed by a shaman and must drink special sacred water to resist the vagina's awful contagion. Menstruation, child-birth, and all other female biological processes are fraught with lethal danger to unprotected males.

There is also the usual terror of a woman's sexual allure, which is consid-ered a peril to man's mental composure, morality, and physical health. Attrac-tive women who draw men's attention away from serious matters like hunting are referred to not as witches, as in New Guinea, but as equally wicked "sick-ness women." Again, instead of giving life and health to men, women are seen as enacting a perverse inversion of their role. As in New Guinea, menstrual fluids are seen as poisonous and death-dealing. Among the Brazilian Mehi-naku, for example, a woman beginning her period must abstain from all contact with food that is to be served to a man. A woman who fails to do so will be blamed for any consequent sickness or death of a man. Her punishment will be excruciating. Like the Melanesians, the Mehinaku believe that a homicidal woman will use menstrual blood to poison men she dislikes.

The Mehinaku believe that menstrual fluid is akin to acid, a corrosive and foul poison, destroying a male body: once in a man's body, menstrual blood acts like a *kauki,* a term derived from the word for pain. The evil opposite of mother's milk, a *kauki* is an intrusive, disease-causing object that is believed to be responsible for all illness. "Usually a shaman, who then shows the object . . . to the victim, can remove it. Menstrual kauki is particularly intractable and difficult to reach" (Gregor 1985:143). The leitmotif of danger to men from women's physicality pervades the entire Amazon culture and reaches its apex in central Brazil in Yurupary, the male rites of renewal and purification used to combat infectious threats from females (S. Hugh-Jones 1979:130; Jackson 1996:108).

Interestingly, these Amazonian peoples associate woman's body with de-cay and death in much the same way as we have seen in New Guinea. Women's cycles are thought to be at one with the uncontrollable nature of many natural processes associated with women. Among these are menstruation, gestation, childbirth, natural decay, and death. The Tukanoan men believe that men have a soul and are, therefore, above the level of beasts; but the women, as evidenced by their reproductive rhythms, have only a body like the moon, and are no better than animals and other natural things that have no humanity, that decay and die without hope. If a man neglects the myriad prophylactic rituals to ward off female horrors, the price to pay is "exhaustion, illness, and death" (C. Hugh-Jones 1979:272).

So intense is this loathing of women for their physical contagion that these Amazonian men speak of a mythical golden age when only males, magically and unisexually reproducing sons, populated the earth. In this fantasy, the men entirely rid the world of female influence. Jackson says that the men of the Tatuyo tribe are "haunted" by a nostalgia for a lost world that is devoid of women and where men reproduce through parthenogenesis. They describe the many joys of a clean all-male society "in which one might live among one's own" (1992:14). Clearly birth-envy is part and parcel of male confusion here.

Among the Tukanoans, also, men magically usurp woman's procreative powers through the Yurupary rituals of rebirth, in which the boys are "really" born, or reborn, as men (Jackson 1992:110). Jackson (117) calls this unisexual rebirth an example of the Tukanoan ritualized effort to minimize women's social role: "By appropriating female symbolic imagery and transforming it, these second-birth rites are unmistakable evidence that males can hold sway, that they can procreate, and that the spiritual and cultural birth that is necessary for true membership in society is not based in the messiness of a reproductive physiology located in alien, 'other' females."

Fear of Sex Again

Like many New Guineans, the Amazonian males fear sex, although they, too, crave it in equal measure. They too surround sexuality with all manner of taboos and proscriptions which have the net effect of limiting both sexual pleasure and any possibly rewarding contact with women. Many men are paralyzed by the thought of sex and refuse to marry altogether. A man engaging in sex must always purify himself afterward to avoid damaging himself and polluting those around him. It is recommended that he limit sexual activity to a minimum — again, for health reasons. Sexual desire is especially dangerous because it is symbolic of "both dependence upon and physical union with women," as Gregor says about the Mehinaku of Brazil.

There are similar data for Europe, both past and present, demonstrating once again man's intense ambivalence toward his own impulses. In medieval Spain, coitus was thought to produce pathological conditions in the male; it dried up the brain and caused baldness, nearsightedness, and early dementia (Solomon 1997:72). Even in this century, men in Spain were cautioned about the dangers of sex. Many educated Spaniards, including sophisticated writers like Miguel de Unamuno and Pío Baroja, feared women and regarded sex as a "negative, will-sapping force" used by women to deplete men (Mitchell 1998:65). Some contemporary Andalusians still believe that excessive copulation makes a man sick and prematurely old. Brandes (1980:86) reports contemporary male folklore from Monteros that warns: "Si quieres llegar a viejo / Guarda la leche en el pellejo" ("If you want to grow old, / Keep your semen in your skin") and "Agua de pozo y mujer desnuda / Llevan al hombre a la sepultura" ("Well water and naked women / Lead men to an early grave"). Many Andalusian men believe that a wife uses sexual enticements to sap her husband's strength and drive him to an early grave (Brandes 1980:84). In many parts of rural Greece, sex is also considered an evil or dirty act that depletes and weakens the male, and for which, of course, the woman is always to blame (Campbell 1964). Sex is like fire and it is the man who gets burned.

Depletion Again

But more than sex, men fear loss of vital essences. As in New Guinea, the danger of women as sexual temptresses is often expressed in an idiom of depletion of life-enhancing juices rather than fire and burning. The Andalusians of Monteros told Brandes that each ejaculation weakens a man and that sex therefore is unhealthy, but that a woman benefits from stealing this vital semen. The early modern Spanish medical men Roig and Martínez de Toledo warned that sex "dehydrates" the male body, damaging the eyes, ears, and scalp, and causing the body to wither and eventually succumb to lethal diseases (Solomon 1997:94).

In India, many men believe that with every ejaculation they lose virtue and manly strength (Lederer 1968:52). The Upanishads regard the loss of the male seed "as a kind of death" (Doniger 1980:31). Moreover, the sacred Hindu books hold that the power carried by the semen is lost to the man through ejaculation, but is transmitted through the sexual act "to a rival, one's own wife, or another woman." Thus, like the Melanesians, Hindu women grow stronger by stealing vital fluids from men. In Burma, according to Spiro (1997: 27), semen loss also diminishes a man's power while empowering his guileful female partner. According to Warren Shapiro (1996:6), preliterate peoples almost universally believe in "body-weakening through semen loss."

Moreover, as sex is dangerous to the individual man because it diminishes him, it is equally dangerous to the intricate, flimsy social system that men have created with such effort, and for much the same reasons, only at a higher level of abstraction. Sex weakens the moral fiber of all men in unison, of the collectivity, leading to mass corruption and social degeneracy. It is for this reason that the medievals thought of woman as a contagion or a disease afflicting the body politic. Thus woman, as the incarnation of sexuality, defeats man and desecrates his works — all because of her power, knowingly or unintentionally, to undermine man with her irresistable body.

The power of woman to diminish man is not confined to this largely involuntary malignancy of the body. A woman, after all, has no choice about what her body does. But her danger to man also stems from an attribute of mind, of spirit, of volition, and here too lies iniquity and deviltry. As well as fearing her dangerous body and her sexuality, men everywhere fear women's intentions: her innate hostility to men, her indifference to lofty purpose, her materialism and greed, her love of disruption and disorder, her perverse delight in doing evil, her malice aforethought. Turning from the corporeal theme in misogyny, the obsession with the physical body and with reproductive functions, we look next at the willful aspect of woman's wickedness in the mind of man: her diabolical spirit.

Who trusts a woman, that man trusts a swindler.

—Hesiod

3. Malevolent Maidens

MISOGYNISTIC FEAR centers on the flesh that makes woman man's opposite and renders her unknowable to him. Misogynists tremble before the bodily labyrinth: veins, intestines, sexual organs. With her lunar cycles and genital effluvia, woman destroys the idealist's illusions of a pristine universe. But physical repugnance is only part of the picture. For many misogynists revulsion grows into a an indictment not of feminine flesh but of her spirit, her intellect, her character and will. For the committed woman-hater, woman is malignant not only in body, but in her intentions toward man. Here man's fears transcend sexuality to encompass all manner of cosmic fantasies and images of purposeful evil: woman as malevolent and purposefully destructive.

Misogyny makes for a polarizing worldview, envisioning a supposedly relentless campaign to undermine the male of the species and to corrupt all his ideals. The resulting vision of embattled manhood under siege, an adversarial sexual cosmos, a beleaguered innocence, a perverse inversion of maternal nurturing, produces an existential dualism in which woman are *intentionally* the devil's advocate, his accomplice or agent, the personification of all that is demonic. The anthropologist Melford Spiro calls this crypto-paranoid belief, which he notes is extremely widespread in male folklore, the "ideology of the dangerous female" (1997:31).

The Dangerous Female is an idea found not only in medieval Europe and in Melanesia but throughout the world. It is the idea that woman is driven by some defect of nature to entrap and debase men and boys. Virtually every preindustrial culture has a myth or legend describing and warning against some terrible supernatural maiden who willfully destroys males. Found in many guises, this devilish creature always drags the innocent down to some dark and unholy place, to the depths of the sea perhaps, or into a tenebrous grotto. Or perhaps she traps the unwary man in her lethal vagina and suffocates him, or, like the lamias of antiquity, drinks his blood. Or she may be a diabolical sorceress as in many preliterate societies, casting spells, or a ghostly femme fatale like the heartless beauty in John Keats's "La Belle Dame sans Merci" (1820), who deceives and bewitches. Or else she is a vixen, a nymph, or a sprite.

Bad Girls

The mythic malevolent maiden lurks within the recesses of the masculine imagination, her purpose to stalk and to capture men, and to destroy them. But beyond this, a curious commonality is that her effect on the male always involves some terrifying humiliation or degrading transformation, which, if not death itself, may involve stealing man's sanity, or perverting his reason, or turning men into swine or some other lowly or disgusting creature. Or else her victims become centaurs or other degraded beasts, or even worse, insensate blocks of ice or stone. Using these transformative powers, the female succubus deprives the man of all moral judgment, dominates him, and debases his nature.

The earliest Western avatars of this nightmare femininity are Circe, the sirens, and Scylla and Charybdis in Greek mythology. Circe turns men into squealing pigs; the others lure them into a watery grave. Especially horrifying, Charybdis is depicted as a voracious man-eating female sea monster, a watery virago who pulls down whole ships. The philosopher Dorothy Dinnerstein (1976) finds the image of the siren or mermaid, the female sea creature who rises from the dark sea depths to drag men down, to be virtually universal in folklore. In his book on monsters and demons, David Williams (1996:187) calls this siren figure the most widely represented monster throughout history, putting a female face on the horrific and the grotesque for all times.

Often portrayed with lurid overtones of engulfing and sucking as in the case of Charybdis, the subaqueous siren or female sea serpent represents an archetypal dream image: that of losing control, being powerless, falling prey to powers beyond rational control. In narrative terms, the male sailor or voyager, bravely plying the surface of life in search of knowledge or wisdom, or perhaps salvation, is suddenly and without warning sucked into oblivion by terrifying submarine creatures that rise up from the murky depths like the biblical Leviathan. The female sea serpent, or mermaid, however, is a typically ambiguous image: both sexually seductive and monstrously evil at the same time. This ambivalent nightmare, which many men share regardless of social situation, metaphorically links male fears of erotic abandon with punishment, lowering of the critical faculties, and death.

One may interpret such a fantasy as uniting unconscious fears of the unknown (the murky sea bottom) with the specific anxiety of being drawn down into an alien, hostile environment, a foreign place where one cannot survive. The visual image that connects the varied and vague fears is that of inscrutable femininity and an inimical and bestial nature, the monstrous female figures taking on shapes that are half human and half animal, their hybrid bodies containing mysterious spaces and liquids both desirable and terrifying. Dinnerstein says that the prototype is the treacherous mermaid, who, "representative of the dark and magic underworld from which our own life comes and in which we cannot live, lures voyagers to their doom" (1976:5). While the anxiety includes sexual images and voluptuous sensations, the real fear is of sinking, suffocation, and death.

Fears of being lowered, pulled down beneath the surface to a watery tomb, which have obvious return-to-the-womb connotations, disturb men most where they live near the sea, lakes, rivers, streams, marshes, or other watery places. The early twentieth-century anthropologist Bronislaw Malinowski (1961:244) cited a mermaid myth from the Trobriand Islands, in which shipwrecked sailors washed up on the shore are tortured to death by cruel female spirits on a mist-shrouded Isle of Women with striking similarities to Greek mythology. Other examples of such horrible isles or remote riverbanks haunted by foul, demonic women abound in the mythologies of China, India, Central Asia, and medieval Europe (White 1991:188). These female water sprites seduce and defile men, copulate with animals, entertain devils, and wreak havoc on sailors and fishermen. Analogous tales occur all over the Americas as well. Some Brazilian peoples living along the banks of the Amazon River, for instance, believe today in a supernatural pink dolphin, the *bota,* which has the soul of an evil animal-woman and drags men down into the swirling murky waters. This belief, according to Brazilian anthropologist Mark Cravalho (1999:55), reflects both a fear of the unknown and the gratification of a heterosexual fantasy. Terror and desire go hand in hand in such gynaco-aquatic visions.

Indeed, almost every maritime culture has such a sailor-beware myth, full of female demons and attesting to a feminization of a species-wide fear of the unknown and of deep waters: the universal cultural tendency "to associate death by water with women" (Warner 1998:95). In Celtic folklore, the kelpie, a half-woman, half-seal spirit, lures men to death in icy seas (Dijkstra 1986:230). The ancient Celtic goddess Danu, also a water dweller, was said to call to men and to drive them mad purely out of spite. Other European fantasy figures unite

human and animal motifs to create theriomorphic monstrosities that are specifically both female and water-related. Originally a kind of Celtic water sprite, for
example, the melusine was found not in the open sea, but around fountains and
ponds. Always female in the upper part of her body, the melusine is a scaly sea-
serpent in the lower half. Gilbert Durand considers this Celtic demon to be
the European version of a universal symbolism of "ophidian malevolence,"
that is, the serpentine evil associated with slimy, wet, reptilian things (Durand
1969:325). Yet another north European woman sea monster was the *echidna,* a
savage beast who emerged from her ocean cavern to devour sailors. She is
credited with giving birth to such celebrated horrors as Cerberus (the watchdog
of Hades), the multiheaded hydra, the chimera, and the fire-breathing dragon of
medieval lore (D. Williams 1996:183).

In landlocked places, the malevolent maidens pounce from forbidding
terrestrial lairs. In ancient mainland Greece, nymphs were in the forests, sprites
in deep woods, and mythical huntresses prowled in overgrown meadows seeking male prey. The fierce lamias, man-devouring monsters, represented with a
woman's head and breasts and a serpent's body, hid in nooks and crannies,
waiting to bewitch men and boys and to sap up their life's juices. Tree sprites,
hamadryads, waited to entrap unsuspecting men and boys in enchanted forests.
Elsewhere in the wilderness, evil female figures inhabit quicksand or wastes (a
witch in the sand dunes in Japan), windswept deserts (the Middle Eastern
female jinn, or genie), mountain tops and malarial marshes (in highland New
Guinea, for example). In dark and sinister places, wherever man fears to tread,
there are women who use their beauty as a lure to attack and destroy a male
victim. Fear of the unknown in nature and peripheral places blends with fear
of the unknown sex, to create hybrid images of doom and monsters of the
imagination.

As well as the repetitive aqueous imagery, there is this parallel male fear
that I mentioned above of being *changed* in some degrading way, rather like
being dissolved in acid or returning to a demonic womb. The theme of female-
induced metamorphosis involves a dramatic alteration in physical shape and
moral conviction, a defilement of body and spirit. The objective correlative of
the metamorphosis imagery includes a variety of ontological objects depending
upon local conditions. At the dawn of civilization, for example, the Egyptian
sphinxes, similar in appearance to the Greek lamias, turned men into blocks of
sandstone (Lederer 1968:123). Wicked women do more than drag a man down
to a slimy, aqueous debauchery: they reduce him into some base thing: a pig,
sandstone, salt, stone. Moral and physiological devolution ensues, and the

man regresses to a primitive state, to the formlessness of primal chaos, mindless matter.

This objectified image of a mystical, feral female danger, allied with the horrors of an unknowable nature, is nearly universal in the world's religions, as well as in secular folklore, and most faiths issue dire warnings to boys and to grown men to beware of the transforming powers of this menacing female. Images abound of beckoning devils and sharp-clawed demons, of potent otherworldly forces. The richer the theological imagery, the richer the iconography of female wickedness, but the danger posed by such mythical she-demons actually pales before that presented by a much more insidious and prevalent foe: flesh-and-blood, everyday, garden-variety woman.

Demonic Yet Mundane

In classical Hindu lore, for example, it is not so much the imaginary sorceress of folklore and myth as the normal, everyday woman who is said to be the cause of sin in the world. Mundane women also lead men astray, disrupt order, and cause fights. More than committing trivial sins, ordinary women exemplify evil itself and are minions of the Devil Woman. In Hinduism, says Wendy Doniger (1976:27), human women are used as the specific instrument of the gods to corrupt individual sages and wise men and to turn men (and male gods) into demons. Thus deceived by the here-and-now woman, men lose their minds and are preyed upon by the evil forces of the supernatural world. Woman is perceived as either demonic herself or actively allied with the demonic forces. As in ancient Greece and medieval Europe, as among the Trobrianders and the Amazonians, in India, too, woman is the "genius of darkness, foul as falsehood itself" (Spiro 1997:31).

Not far from Hindu India, in predominantly Buddhist Burma (Myanmar), men harbor a similarly exaggerated view of the human female's tendency to ally herself with inimical forces. These attitudes color the Buddhist texts and the holy scriptures to an unusual degree. The basic tenor of the misogynistic Buddhist texts as summarized by a native scholar is cited by anthropologist Spiro (1997:31): "Women deceive the men, therefore they are a delusion. They cannot be relied upon, then they are like a mirage. They are the cause of all ills, and embrace men for their own gains. . . . They are always looked upon as full of wiles, which are said to be 64 in number. . . . They are whirlpools in the ocean of life, a taproot of the creeper of craving, a door open to purgatory."

In detailing the myth of the deadly women in Burmese culture, Spiro (1997) shows that the Buddhist texts identify women's principal sins as treachery and deceit. Aside from the typical aquatic imagery connoting danger and death, as in the quote above, and the common association of women with destruction and ill will, the Burmese say that there are four things on earth that can never be trusted: women, thieves, rulers, and the boughs of trees (because they always break). According to the *Lokaniti,* a sacred Burmese Buddhist book, women are said to be as bad as fire, water, serpents, and other dangerous things that must be approached "with great circumspection; for they may take [your] life in an instant!" (Spiro 1997:23).

Bad enough because of their unpredictability, women are said to be doubly evil in the Burmese culture. First, they are evil because of their treachery, because they use all methods, fair and foul, to usurp man's rightful place. Second, they are evil because of their sexual allure, which, by disguising all this teeming malevolence with a pretty exterior, puts men in physical and moral danger of immorality. This physical attractiveness is, in fact, the strategy for their treachery and duplicity, for it is their appeal to men's senses that cheats, betrays, deceives. And so women are among the most dangerous things on earth.

Like many other misogynists, the Burmese Buddhists entertain a constellation of beliefs surrounding attractive women's power to debilitate and to enslave men. In one proverbial warning, Burmese men say: If a woman cannot overpower her husband through trickery, she will probably insert a betel nut into her vagina, grind it up after it has absorbed her vaginal secretions, and then infect his penis with the concoction during sex or, if all else fails, feed the deadly mixture to her unsuspecting husband, thereby causing his mental collapse and spiritual paralysis. This power-hungry female can be a flesh-and-blood wife or one of the mythical creatures discussed above — they tend to blend into one another. Spiro also cites a class of half-human pretty succubi, who spend their time entrapping and destroying unsuspecting males through magical enchantments:

The epitomization of the sexually-enticing, male-subjugating female is represented by a class of female spirits known as *ouktazaun.* Because of sins committed in a previous existence, these spirits must guard the buried treasure of the future Buddha. To escape this lonely fate, some of them assume the guise of an alluring woman and entice a man to fall in love with them. Should the unfortunate male, unable to resist the spirit's attraction, have sexual intercourse with her, he will die and then must share her task. (1997:24)

Spiro cites numerous texts to demonstrate this thesis of female culpability, her alliance with the devil. For example, he gives us the following lines from the *Paduma,* a play taken from the sacred texts: "It is the habit of women to fall in love with any man they see. . . . they will even kill their rightful husbands the moment they want a new lover. Their lust blinds them. . . . They receive all, just as a roaring fire receives all rubbish." A similar view is expressed in *The Lokaniti* :

All rivers turn out to be winding
All forests are full of kindling
All women, given a secluded place,
End by sinning. (25)

Demonic Damsels: Parallels

Such beliefs about woman's natural affinity with evil spirits, coupled with belief about her malign secular intentions are widespread in the Old World. In a Muslim Arab village in Jordan studied by anthropologist Richard Antoun (1968:692), the men told Antoun that women's sexual appetite was twenty times more powerful than men's and just as many times more threatening to social stability. This belief is found in the Middle East, North Africa, and western Asia, in both Muslim and other Arab traditions. It is prevalent in North Africa, where women are said to be especially impulsive and assertive sexually (Geertz 1979:332). Driven by their "animalistic sexual appetite" (Mason 1975:650), North African women are "the devil's nets" for the credulous man (Bourdieu 1966:227). In Turkey, female sexuality is said to be "like gunpowder," damaging both individual men and society (Fallers and Fallers 1976:258). The theme of explosive female concupiscence versus noble male resistance reaches its apogee in the Maghreb, especially in Morocco, where any attractive woman is a "lascivious temptress" (Maher 1978:119), corrupting and destroying men through her insatiable lust (Dwyer 1978:151).

Myths of Matriarchy

Fears about woman's formidable power to do evil frequently assume origin-of-the-world mythic forms, expressing underlying male terror in colorful metaphorical language. What would happen if these devilish women actually ruled the world and implemented their wicked plans? In several preliterate societies, men in fact entertain origin myths that portray a long-ago time when women ruled the earth and tyrannized men. Such narratives are found scattered around the world, but especially in New Guinea and Amazonia (as one might expect). Anthropologists lump them together as "myths of matriarchy" (Bamberger 1974). Interestingly, the narratives in the Old and New worlds are strikingly similar, and they always have a "happy" ending: the browbeaten men overthrow the evil female despots, establish a salutary male hegemony, and thereby reverse the vicious matriarchal order. These male rebellions are always blessed by divine approval and lead to progress and order. The psychologist Adam Jukes (1994:312) calls this turn of events "phallus in wonderland."

The Mundurucú of Brazil, described by Robert Murphy (1960), are typical in many respects of other groups in the Amazon rainforest area. Their myths center on a metaphor of musical instruments. They believe that the gods provided sacred trumpets for the use of humankind. The mellifluous melodies of the hallowed instruments enabled humans to conquer nature and to thrive. But long ago, the guileful women of the tribe seized the sacred trumpets and gained dominance over men. The women abused this awesome power to enchant the men, making them do all the menial work (that women should do), and keeping them ignorant of the gods' plans for masculine sovereignty. Finally, at the dawn of "real" history, the men rose up and recaptured the holy instruments in a manly coup (Murphy 1960:108). Today, of course, the Mundurucú jealously guard their sacred trumpets in a special men's hut, which is forbidden to women on pain of the usual gang rape or execution. The men "feed" their magical trumpets in secret, all-male ceremonies. Women must not even glimpse the trumpets or the feeding ceremony lest they regain their loathsome dominance and the social order collapse.

Most New Guinea peoples have such myths of matriarchy with the same story line and moral injunctions (Herdt 1982b). The sacred instruments of the Fore people of the highlands have bamboo flutes instead of trumpets. Like the Mundurucú instruments, these flutes were once in the grasp of fiendish women, who, as usual, used their power to enslave and exploit the poor deluded men (Lindenbaum 1976:57–58). In *Guardians of the Flutes* (1981), Herdt describes various rites through which the Sambia of the central eastern cordillera ensure their tenuous control over the flutes. The Sambia men, too, believe that the precious instruments were once in the hands of females, and that women still plot secretly to usurp a godly male suzerainty.

Another anthropologist, Joan Bamberger (1974), recognizes the curious convergence of myths about musical instruments, which are always wind instruments of some sort — flutes, trumpets, pipes, and the like — in the Old and New worlds. She proposes a plausible feminist theory: these myths establish a religious justification for male dominance and female oppression by suggesting that it was once the other way around, but that things are much better with men in control.

Ideas about female conspiracies against the "good" male social order are not confined to South America or Melanesia. The Greeks and Romans also saw wooden flutes and brass trumpets as sacred instruments, given to men by gods. More than phallic symbols, these timeless musical fetishes represent a psychic male defense against the bossy, disorderly woman of misogynistic imagination. In the first century A.D., Juvenal in his *Satires* ascribes the holiness of masculinity to Pan's flutes and warns flawed women to stay away: "Remain far off, ye unholy! / Women, remain far off: no females play on our trumpets!" (Hays 1964:98). The fear of castrating, malevolent femininity is identical to that found among the Fore or Mundurucú and is expressed in the identical musical metaphor and phallic symbolism. The flutes or trumpets may, psychologically, represent the tumescent penis; politically they may represent male dominance and their music male sexual power. The myths of usurpation can therefore symbolize castration anxiety, at least at one level. But the entire panoply of beliefs seems however to indicate an even deeper fear about female intentions against the social order. These fears, as Rogers suggests (1966:271–72), probably derive not from Oedipal or sexual conflicts, but from residues of infantile fears of abandonment and maternal rejection. The omnipotent women of the matriarchy myths may symbolize the infant's omnipotent mother.

Goats and Devils: A Modern Greek Example

We move on to a modern case of this kind of moralistic misogyny in contemporary northern Greece. Hellenist John Campbell (1964) describes the Sarakatsani shepherds who live in the Epirus area near the Albanian border. A Greek Orthodox minority, possibly distantly related to the Vlachs (transient ethnic Albanians in Greece), the Sarakatsani herd sheep and goats and sell their milk in urban markets for cheese making. These shepherds follow a typical Mediterranean pattern of transhumance, moving to the high plateaus in the summer and descending to the valleys during the winter months. Clinging to tradition, they stubbornly retain ideas about the differences between the sexes, especially about the evilness of women.

According to Campbell, the Sarakatsani entertain a dualistic view of sexual morality, linked to wider dualisms. Their cosmos comprises balanced oppositions between complementary categories. Everything regarded as good has an evil mirror-image; the polar contrasts represent constituent dyads in the dichotomous cosmic structure, much like the Melanesians "good" male order and contrasting "evil" female chaos. The dyads in this overarching scheme include the moral contrasts such as good-evil, God-devil, and left-right, but also social and ontological divisions — rural-urban, sheep-goat, kinsman-stranger, and so on. The primary binary opposition, perhaps not surprisingly, is man-woman.

In accordance with this black-and-white worldview, many Sarakatsani see man as noble, honest, and fair, while woman is treacherous and ignoble. The relegation of woman to the nether side relates to Sarakatsani concepts of honor, a noble virtue attainable only by males. *Dropi,* or female shame, is enmeshed with the taint of woman's sexuality:

If man is nearly all nobility, a natural predisposition to evil . . . is the most striking feature of the female character. She is above all cunning, especially in the sense that her cunning involves the corruption of another, that is the man. She is a constant threat to his honour. "Cunning" is typically the adjective which also describes the Devil, and the Sarakatsani believe that the Devil has a hold over women, who are his particular emissaries, dispatched to provoke men's hearts with sexual passions. (Campbell 1964:277)

These Greek shepherds use knowledge of their herd animals to explain gender polarities, comparing sheep to Christ, consistent with Orthodox iconography of Jesus as sacrificial lamb. Sheep are indeed passive, gentle, and stoic, like the long-suffering Christ, and, of course, sheep shed their blood so that man can live (by eating lamb). But the Sarakatsani regard the goat, which they do not eat, as lustful, dirty, cunning, and predisposed to trickery. This contrast leads to a corresponding association of the dyad sheep-goat to that of Christ-Satan. In the dualistic universe inspired by such contrasts, women are goats (the devil), while men retain a purity and innocence through association with both sheep and the martyred Christ. In the Sarakatsani view, women are not devils themselves, but their morally flawed nature makes them willingly, or unwillingly, agents of the devil's will (31). As in the malevolent maiden myths or in Burmese and Indian lore, common everyday woman, luring man with physical beauty, lies in wait to defile manly honor and goodness. "The female is a constant threat to the honour and integrity of the male, and must be disciplined and dominated" (Campbell 1964:57). The woman's very sex carries the emblem of sexual shame, the mark of the devil. Every woman is a mermaid.

Goats and Vipers

The Sarakatsani's cynical image of woman finds expression elsewhere and in various cultural guises. Most striking are the animal tropes found in many systems of witchcraft beliefs, in which women are depicted as the devil's agents, disguised primarily as the awful goat, once again, but also as other lowly or supposedly lascivious animals. For example, Noddings (1989:44) in her study of women as witches shows how medieval artists depicted woman accompanied by the iconographic symbol of fleshly depravity, the goat. Much primitive folklore and oral tradition portrays women as wild animals — if not goats, then whatever native animal symbolizes unbridled lust, evil, or disorder: snakes, scorpions, apes, asses, or pigs. Thus, in a curious reversal of the male-metamorphosis theme we examined earlier, in which women turn men into swine, for example, woman is again linked to coarse nature through identification with disgusting or feared animals. Again widespread in Old World religions, the woman-turning-into-a-snake image is, of course, the central metaphorical device of the Fall in the Old Testament, as well as in later art and literature. Bram Dijkstra (1986) shows that the woman-as-viper image was a common theme in Victorian fantasy painting, in which serpentine coils were used to exemplify women's treacherous and poisonous nature.

The same vicious-animal imagery is found in modern popular culture. For example, a study of American boys' comic books by the sociologist Kenneth Adams shows that a large proportion of stories featured boys being lured to their death by sexually enticing lamias. The "woman-as-monster" image — with women depicted as snakes, spiders, reptilian extraterrestrials, and scorpions — is very common in boys' literature, not only in the United States but also in Europe and Japan (cited in Gregor 1985:202). It is all very similar to the *vagina dentata* image we have already examined.

Such a melodramatic view of women's dangerous powers is especially pervasive in the literature of the Middle Ages, where woman is represented as in league with satanic forces arrayed against a noble and besieged manhood. Bloch notes that a Manichaean tendency runs throughout early patristic and medieval thought, not only in its reliance upon binary oppositions polarizing the sexes, but also in the condemnation of womanhood as stigmatized by reptilian evil and thus as morally poisonous to the male (Bloch 1989:43). This tendency to link woman with primary evil and to perceive her as a moral threat to mankind finds expression in early Christian theology in the admonitions of Tertullian (c. A.D. 160–220), the theologian who first denounced woman as the

Devil's gateway. Accusing women of original sin, as well as all manner of lesser evils, Tertullian addresses them directly:

> Do you not know that each of you is Eve? The sentence of God on this sex of yours lives in this age: the guilt must of necessity live too. *You* are the Devil's Gateway. *You* are the unsealer of that forbidden tree. *You* are the first deserter of the divine Law. *You* are she who persuaded him whom the Devil was not valiant enough to attack. *You* destroyed so easily God's image, man. On account of your desert[ion], that is death, even the Son of God had to die. (Noddings 1989:52)

Other Men, Other Misogynies

In the West the misogynistic tradition is perhaps less melodramatic than in some preliterate societies, but it is equally entrenched. In a book on Western misogyny, Nancy Harrowitz (1994) finds a typical nineteenth-century attitude toward women expressed in sociology texts on deviance and criminology. Foremost among these for vitriol is the work of the Italian criminologist Cesare Lombroso (1835–1909), who, with Guglielmo Ferrero, wrote the book *The Female Offender* (1890), a relentless attack on female "nature." The authors aver that woman is "atavistic" and argue that there is a "latent base of evil" in every woman (cited in Harrowitz 1994:31,33).

Classicist Robert Meagher (1995) points out that at the dawn of Greek civilization, men were blaming women for evil and for animality. This theme crops up as early as the seventh century B.C. in the work of the poet Semonides, in the first known piece of literature specifically written about the fair sex. In his lengthy poem *Woman,* Semonides identifies the female sex with *kakon,* or base evil, and says that Zeus created woman from animals: lazy donkeys, gross apes, stinging bees, and dirty pigs reposing on dung heaps. In much early writing, woman is depicted not as only one of many evils but as the worst *kakon* invented by the gods to torment mortal men. Woman's primary iniquity is bound up with her inherent deceitfulness, synonymous with her superficial attractiveness, which baits the trap for man.

Thus, in early Greek poetry, after Semonides' foray into misogyny, woman is characterized not just as a necessary evil but as *dolon,* a trick or baited trap (Meagher 1995:53). An early Greek legend describes her in ambivalent terms: "Woman, the recipient of all that is bright, is the giver of all that is dark!" (Meagher 1995:55). In his lengthy poem *Theogeny,* Hesiod (eighth century B.C.), continuing the indictment, says, "Thunderous Zeus made woman to be a *kakon* [evil] for mortal men" (Meagher 1995:52). Although some of Homer's noblest characters are women (e.g., Penelope and Andromache), nevertheless throughout the Homeric tales women are constantly excoriated for their moral failings, which men see as the source of most, if not all, of the vexations and disillusionments of the world.

Legends, myths, and folktales describing women's infamy may begin with the ancients but grow and proliferate in the Christian era. In a study of the *Grimms' Fairy Tales,* a mid-nineteenth-century compilation reflecting ageless central European folk themes, Ruth Bottigheimer (1987) finds a similar misogynistic condemnation of female guile. While wayward boys in the German folktales are treated leniently and forgiven their indulgences (usually brought on by female treachery), the girls are condemned for eternity and seen as hopelessly evil. Bottigheimer regards the dualistic moral code as a reflection of German culture and gender mythology of the period (94). Hence the title of her book: *Grimms' Bad Girls and Bold Boys.*

We have already seen ample examples of inadvertent female destructiveness in the writings of medieval Spanish physicians. Ethnographer Stanley Brandes shows how many men in modern Monteros regard women as intentionally evil, malicious, and disposed to spread their bodily poison. Women's machinations start early in life, when their mothers teach them to paint their faces and make themselves desirable in order to ensnare men. Once these heartless huntresses have trapped a hapless man in the chains of marriage, their true ambition is revealed: to exploit him and to drive him to an early grave. "Once the man is bound by an official, indissoluble wedding ceremony [there was no legal divorce in Spain at the time], the woman begins to demonstrate her true ambition, which is nothing less than to dominate completely, to rule her husband and children, and above all to sap her husband's strength by forcing him to engage in heavy sexual activity and physical labor until he gradually expires" (Brandes 1980:84).

Witches

Woman's iniquity also achieves incarnation in the universal image of the witch. Beautiful or ugly, witches consort with the devil, change shape, commit heinous acts of sexual depravity, and resolutely wreak havoc on males and their good works. In his fascinating study of witchcraft in colonial Salem, *Entertaining Satan* (1982), historian John Demos notes that the New England colonists perceived the devil himself to be male, but his minions as mainly female. Since deviltry was conceived as "entertaining" Satan, meaning erotic fraternization, it seemed logical that women were more susceptible to Satan's blandishments than men. This opinion reflected the view that women were weaker, less trustworthy than men, not only in their sexuality but in their judgment, if not inherently wicked. Throughout the early modern period of European (and colonial American) history, imagery of satanic women reflected standard gender cosmology for notions of good, evil, and the supernatural proclivities of women.

The Church made it official. The celebrated book of witchcraft lore, the *Malleus maleficarum* (The hammer of evil) — a virtual guide for witch hunters — continuously identifies woman as the source of evil magic and infernal machinations. Throughout the Latin text, written in 1486, she is called an "evil of nature," a "necessary evil," and a "calamity." When menstruating she is said to be especially vulnerable to Satan's lures (Kramer and Spengler 1971:43). The authors of the *Malleus,* in fact, state that "all witchcraft comes from carnal lust, which is in women insatiable. . . . Wherefore, for the sake of fulfilling their lusts they consort with devils."

The phenomenon of the consorting, consenting woman was frequently depicted in medieval art and architecture, especially on church facades. The art historian Henry Kraus shows that the sculpted presentation of the Vice of Unchastity, which appears on so many church facades of the high Middle Ages, is invariably a woman, suffering the torments of hell, and that she is usually shown in a revolting posture, her naked body entwined by serpents or gargoyles which feed from her breasts and sexual organs. Sometimes, too, she is accompanied by the devil himself, who often assumes an intimate erotic relationship with her (Hoover 1989:354).

Given the connection of woman, devil, snakes, and sin, it is perhaps not so surprising that the identification of woman as witch is nearly universal. In a worldwide study of such beliefs, anthropologist J. L. Brain (1996:78) finds evidence that in most societies witches are predominantly, if not exclusively female. In fact, the most striking and consistent social correlation in magic beliefs is that between witchcraft and women. In an anthropological text on supernatural beliefs worldwide, Arthur Lehman and James Myers (1993:196) note that although in certain areas and for brief periods of time, more men were accused of witchcraft than women, the opposite has almost always been true, and over the entire history of the European witch craze, women outnumbered men by at least three to one. In New England, for example, 80 percent of the accused were women. As Lederer puts it (1968:199), witchcraft is a "woman's thing," and not only in medieval times or in Salem, Massachusetts. In preliterate societies men are often depicted as sorcerers, sometimes malignant, sometimes not, but evil witches are almost always women.

The distinction between the male sorcerer and the female witch may seem pedantic, but it is also quite important in understanding misogyny. Since the 1965 publication of Evans-Pritchard's magisterial work on African tribal magic, anthropologists have made an almost canonical distinction between sorcery and witchcraft. Both involve human figures using supernatural power, but sorcery is a learned, acquired craft (e.g., as in Dukas's orchestral scherzo, *The Sorcerer's Apprentice,* itself based on a ballad by Goethe), while witchcraft implies innate or inherited powers, often represented as organic material transmitted through blood or by a biological process (Lehman and Myers 1993:187). Contrary to witchcraft, which is always evil and antisocial, sorcery may not always be nefariously or illegitimately used. In fact, sorcery may be beneficent in the hands of a shaman, or witch doctor, who cures illnesses.

Born with the power to destroy men's souls, therefore, the female witch is usually much more powerful and deadly than the male sorcerer. The sorcerer's spells can at best make people sick or cause minor mishaps — nonfatal accidents and broken limbs. In most preliterate belief systems, the witch can kill, but the sorcerer can only injure or vex. Thus, in a famous Melanesian case described many years ago by Reo Fortune in *Sorcerers of Dobu* (1932), all the men were sorcerers, practicing either malevolent or beneficial magic, while the women were far more dangerous witches, flying around at night, changing shape, and exerting their inherited skills to destroy the souls of men and kill them. Their victims (no surprise) are most often their inept husbands.

Wicked Wives and Stepmothers

Given the depth and ubiquity of such attitudes, it is not surprising that literary scholars such as Katherine Rogers (1966), Howard Bloch (1991), and Katherine Ackerly (1992), as well as political scientist Linda Coole (1988) have described this kind of characterological misogyny as a unifying, ramifying theme running through the range of both Western and non-Western cultural history, a topos to which men always return. These beliefs in innate wickedness are broadcast in hosts of virulently negative gender stereotypes, through stock characters that find their way into works of literature, folklore, mythology, and ritual. Such perennial favorites as the shrewish wife and battle-ax mother-in-law have few male equivalents; the father-in-law gets off scot-free.

By the time of Homer's *Iliad,* women were already being shoe-horned into the "bad-wife" stereotype, even among the gods. The blind poet's portrayal of the bossy Hera who persecutes her husband Zeus is typical. Nagging wives populate supernumerary Greek myths and stories; they drive their husbands to distraction, culminating in calamity (Coole 1988:7). This bad-wife stereotype among the immortals is a prime motif in the Nordic myths from which Richard Wagner drew his tetralogy, *Der Ring des Nibelungen.* In act 1 of *Die Walküre,* the termagant Fricka persecutes her husband Wotan, father of the gods, forcing him to withdraw support from Siegfried, thereby indirectly causing the hero's death, as well as fomenting other disasters that occur on- and off-stage for the next twelve long hours. Whether right or wrong, Fricka exemplifies the stereo-typical vexatious, domineering shrew.

Of equally ancient provenance are the meddlesome mother-in-law stereo-types, all too familiar to American audiences from overexposure to situation comedies. Another misogynistic standard, the wicked stepmother, has been part and parcel of folklore and mythology in the West since classical antiquity. (And where is the wicked stepfather?) In contemporary humor, fathers-in-law get kid-glove treatment. In *Ancient Stepmothers: Myth, Misogyny, and Reality* (1995), the classicist Patricia Watson affirms the depth and ubiquity of this stock female villain in the male pantheon of demons and devils.

We find wicked stepmothers (and stepsisters) in popular children's tales such as *Snow White and the Seven Dwarfs* and *Cinderella,* and in other Euro-pean folk stories. In these tales, the stepmother is always the main villain: she tries to seduce her stepson or persuades her husband to disinherit his children. The Grimm brothers offer stories in which the stepmother perpetrates even more heinous crimes. For example, in *Darling Roland* the stepmother attacks her sleeping stepchild with an ax, but inadvertently decapitates her own daugh-ter. In *The Juniper Tree* the mercenary stepmother kills her stepson so that her own daughter will inherit her husband's fortune.

Animal transformations are prevalent in sinister stepmother tales, once again reflecting woman's ability to manipulate those near and dear and to turn people into beasts. The stepmother often turns her stepchildren into wolves or lambs marked for slaughter and the family's dinner table. Watson cites nu-merous modern variations of this theme from Iceland, England, Germany, and almost every other western European tradition. In comparing the structure of these European tales, she shows that the archetypal stepmother's evil takes one or more of three predictable directions. The stepmother may be an outright murderess (usually using poison); she may disinherit her stepchildren in order to steal their patrimony, forcing them into destitution; or she may be a mendacious sexual predator, incestuously seducing her stepson and cuckolding her husband. In some cases, the stepmother is guilty of two or even all three miscreant behaviors.

Watson traces this threefold evil paradigm to the earliest written sources. As early as the fourth century B.C., the wicked stepmother was a stock dramatic device in legends and myths, appearing in works by Herodotus, Euripides, Sophocles and many others. In Attic tragedy, the stepmother rarely deviates from the monstrous model; she is nearly always painted as evil and described as invariably malignant, cunning, and treacherous — in Watson's words, "intrinsically evil" (222). She is often shown plotting to disinherit her stepchildren, betraying her spouse, seducing her stepson, murdering her stepdaughter, and generally being lustful and immoral, spreading devastation wherever she goes.

A marked feature of Greek mythic literature is the stepmother's tergiversation, her skullduggery and "sneakiness" (29). Watson argues convincingly that this repellent motif in the Greek texts and legends attests to a deeper core of pure misogyny in Athenian society. The prejudice against the stepmother in the Greek texts may be explained in terms of gender, she says; in other words, it is part of a more general misogynist tradition, the recurrence of certain character traits in the depiction of individual stepmothers in the ancient myths. On the whole, these correspond to the qualities regarded by writers, such as Aristotle, as quintessentially feminine, notably jealousy, treacherousness, shamelessness, lack of self-control, and sexual avarice (84).

Later, in Roman literature and drama, the same virulent theme reappears even more powerfully. On the Roman stage and in Latin verse, this character is *saeva noverca,* the wicked-witch stepmother, a model of unmitigated evil. Watson cites examples from Seneca and Ovid, especially from Seneca's *Phaedra,* in which the murderous stepmother not only is unconscionably evil, but also acts from simple, unmotivated spite. Since such wickedness is unfathomable from the Roman poets' point of view, it must stem from the very wellspring of her nature rather than from the social conditions and pressures that push men into villainy (Watson 1995:110).

Watson also notes the black-and-white imagery of the stepmother and her victims. She is always totally evil while her prey are pure as the driven snow, like Snow White. This paradigm obviously distorts the reality of stepparents, because empirical studies have shown that in all cultures and at all times, stepfathers are much more dangerous to their wards than are stepmothers, since the men are much more prone to domestic violence and sexual abuse (39–40, 216–17). Thus this wicked-stepmother topos is just another misogynistic fantasy.

In the stepmother's homicidal schemes there is an emphasis on poison as the weapon of choice. Watson notes that Attic tragedy is replete with images of female poisoners — often visibly stigmatized with reptilian features — especially those who pour deadly potions into the food and drink of their charges. In Aristophanes' *The Thesmophoriazusae,* for instance, the First Woman proposes to kill Euripides for exposing female vices, either by poison or by some other oral "artifice" (217).

Numerous other women in Greek and Roman mythology, Medea and Deianira for instance, employ poisons and potions as murder weapons (Watson 1995:87). This identification of women as poisoners — polluters of the body — forms a homology with the Melanesian ideas about the innate danger of female substances and women as congenitally venomous; artificial potions and concoctions are simply another method of polluting and infiltrating unsuspecting males, in this case with malevolent conscious intent. It is probable that this imagery and the underlying poison phobia lead to the snake and reptile imagery so often bound up with misogynist rhetoric.

Watson is left with only one adequate explanation for the pervasiveness of this motif:

> Since the character traits associated with the stepmother correspond in large measure to those regarded by the ancients as quintessentially feminine (for instance, jealousy, lack of self-control, treacherousness), the stepmother was an especially powerful paradigm of the negative side of women. . . . The wicked stepmother of Greek and Roman tradition is an outstanding example of the translation of misogynistic attitudes into a stereotype, the best possible illustration of the dictum from Seneca's *Phaedra,* "dux malorum femina" ("woman is the chief source of ills"). (222)

Mulier Loquax

The belief in woman's evil is pervasive; her evil deeds are matched by her equally evil words. Dripping honey and acid, her tongue is venomous (the poison motif yet again). Her soft and sinuous speech, always disingenuous, is full of falsehoods, malice, and duplicity (Solomon 1997:83). The Spanish medieval physicians actually believed that woman's speech could physically harm a man by lulling him into noxious states of confusion. In reviewing German folklore of the early modern period, Bottigheimer (1987) shows how in the tales collected by the Grimm brothers, the honeyed female voice often heralds female viciousness. The Grimm collection also spins off another female stereotype, *mulier loquax,* the noisome, garrulous woman.

The vexatious chatterbox of myth and legend is also the mellifluous-mouthed serpent, equally fork-tongued. Woman talks too much, and uses bad words to deceive and injure; she "must be silenced" (Bottigheimer 1987:170). In German folklore one finds constant complaints about women's hypocritical, frivolous, and gossipy speech, which debases human discourse, poisons language, and lowers the intellectual level of mankind (169). In fact, in most cultures woman is associated with ill-intended use of words, malicious gossip, and character assassination. Literature critic Patricia Spacks (1985:38) notes that the ferocity of male attacks on gossip throughout Western history can be largely explained by the traditional connection of gossip with women. Although Spacks cites mainly contemporary American popular culture and modern Western literature to prove her point, this connection is especially powerful in traditional oral cultures and in peasant villages, where it is said that women do untold damage with their vicious tongues and their backbiting.

In the villages of contemporary Spain, for example, women are called *malas lenguas* (evil tongues); women use their speech like knives or swords, or, as one sophisticated man said, "interpersonal ballistic missiles" aimed at the unwary, ruining lives, and destroying reputations (Gilmore 1978:60). Many Spanish villagers claim that men never gossip; malicious speech is by nature a "woman's thing." Voicing a general attitude, one man told me that women's tongues "should be cut out." Women's idle speech is always likened to rumor-mongering, innuendo, and calumny. Nothing good, the men say, can come from women's words.

Writing about the Aragonese village of Oroel, for example, Susan Harding also found that villagers there regarded "bad words" and women as inextricably linked, and gossip and character assassination are exclusively female diversions. The male villagers told her that "The tongues of women — and their thoughts about others as well — are dangerous, wicked, and sinful." The men used umpteen terms to describe women's talk, all with the connotation of malice, wickedness, sin, and pollution. Gossip is dirty work and polluted, not because it is so intrinsically, but because women do it (Harding 1974:303). Thus it is not only women's bodies that pollute the fastidious world of men; their words defile, their speech poisons the art of oratory.

Nor is this stereotype of the *mulier loquax* confined to Spain. In a French village, Jeanne Favret-Saada (1980) found that in the male villagers' minds women's intimate conversation took on the status of verbal warfare. Female verbosity was in fact compared to black magic and even witchcraft. Another anthropologist, F. G. Bailey, studying a community in the Italian Alps, noted the differences ascribed to male and female speech: "For men to sit around in public and gossip is quite acceptable since, it is generally assumed this exchange is . . . a friendly, sociable, light-hearted, good-natured, altruistic exchange of news, information and opinion. But if women are seen talking together, then something quite different is happening: very likely they are indulging in . . . gossip, malice, 'character assassination' " (Bailey 1971:1). Bailey notes that people in such villages connect women's words with poison; hence the title of his book, *Gifts and Poison.*

The link between women and poisonous language goes far back in the West. In early Christian thought, woman's evil speech started with Eve, who first "speaks" to (i.e., consorts with) the devil, while Adam remains silent, if not resistant, and remote. Thus Eve's voice — woman's voice — is the "primary cause of sin in the world" (Bottigheimer 1987:170). This mixed scriptural image combines various elements of misogynistic discourse — woman as snake, woman as poisoner, woman as agent of the devil, woman as malicious gossiper — into a devastating assault on her character.

In medieval French literature, woman's words are again identified with lies, dissimulation, and verbal trickery that poisons the soul. Women's innate tendency toward casuistry is entwined with sensual seductiveness and its cohort, physical corruption (Bloch 1991:21). Furthermore, woman is blamed for being the author of deceitful language; she turns speech into liars' weapons: woman is the equivalent of the deception of which language is capable, a "prejudice so deeply rooted in the medieval discourse on gender that it often even passes unnoticed."

This image of poisonous tongues continues into later ages in the western European tradition at all levels of society, all degrees of education and sophistication. Bloch points out that in the nineteenth century, respected criminologists such as Cesare Lombroso associated women with abundant orality — loquacity, gossip — with speech to the exclusion of writing, and thus, without the restraint of script, to capriciousness, falseness, deception, and fraud (1991:60). The German philosopher Arthur Schopenhauer accused women of lying constitutionally, blaming natural sexual selection: "They are driven to rely not on force but on cunning; hence their instinctive subtlety and their tendency to tell lies" (1970:83). Not to be outdone, Schopenhauer's intellectual heir Friedrich Nietzsche denounced womanhood in even more fustian terms: "What is truth to a woman? From the beginning, nothing has been more alien, repugnant and hostile to women than truth — her great art is her lie" (1967:163). Women, lies, and witchcraft remain bound together throughout the ages among peasants, philosophers, and poets. As Bloch points out, there is also the sense of woman as transitory, temporary, contingent, sensual, rather than intellectual, using ephemeral speech rather than substantive, masculine writing. Men write in lofty words; women ply the foul art of gossip.

Dissolution and Depletion

Viewed in retrospect, most of these derogatory images have a degree of commonality. This underlying thread links the moral condemnation of women as having consciously malicious intent toward men with the bodily misogyny we looked at in earlier chapters, and which we have called Melanesian. Running along both avenues of antipathy is the same deep dread that focuses obsessively on woman's putative innate evil, manifested particularly as the power to corrupt, contaminate, pollute, and thereby undermine man's best efforts, and to wreck his body and spirit. This intrusive female scourge takes on two special concrete representations: first, the power to intrude evil substances and evil words directly into man; and second, the power to steal something valuable from him, to take away some priceless property or degrade some virtue.

The theme of noxious intrusion revolves around the use of poisons (liquid or verbal) or other substances, which have come to stand for moral rot, eating away the will and the soul from within. The obverse theme, that of extrusion, of theft, takes the opposite valence: the siphoning off of vital substances. The latter image, the fear of being sucked dry or depleted, invokes the sense of loss of some life-enhancing substance, usually semen, or the symbolic larceny of moral purity, the spiriting away of life-sustaining vital values, the corruption of innocence, the defilement or emptying of the soul. As Gelber notes, this sense of masculine helplessness before the forces of decay embodied by woman represents a formal reification of man's fear of uncontrollable nature, universal fears that do not die when technology advances and civilization flourishes.

Such beliefs about female pollution, contagion, and destructiveness seem to be inextricably linked to other anxiety-provoking subjects, such as death and rotting, Gelber adds (1986:59). Again, these are morbid anxieties that know no cultural barriers. The pervasive masculine fears specifically about semen loss are also worthy of note. It is clear that the anxiety about woman's trying to remove something valuable, sapping inner strength, or sullying probity is linked to both the fear of death and to castration anxiety: something valuable is being stolen or diminished.

In a fascinating study of such terrors and their objectifications in fantasy worldwide, Sander Gilman (1988:1) shows that these apprehensions are often projected onto real objects, or scapegoats, in order to psychologically "localize and domesticate" them, and thus to resolve inner conflicts so that the sufferer can launch a restorative attack. In many such cases the victim is some ethnic group or race, as in the persecution of Jews in Nazi Germany. In the case of misogyny, the scapegoats are women.

Many of the beliefs we have looked at in this chapter go deeper than the fulminations of individual men about the evils of women. Because these notions are tied up with deepest moral values, they also have religious dimensions. Often men appeal to sacred texts or traditions to justify their personal animus toward women, and all the great faiths have their misogynistic side, as we have seen in brief references to Buddhism, Christianity, Hinduism, Zoroastrianism, and Islam. We now turn to the scriptural dimension of misogyny, and look at some of the more egregious examples of woman-hating in the world's most sacred texts. We examine how these rich growths within the fields of religion serve to legitimize man's inhumanity to woman.

The woman was first deceived, and it was she who deceived the man. Hence the apostle Paul told that women were subject to the stronger vessel, obeying their husbands as their masters. And Paul says: "Adam was not deceived, but the woman was deceived and was in sin."

—St. Ambrose, De Paradiso

4. Scriptures

WE HAVE ALREADY SEEN religious teachings that condemn women. Virtually every faith, monotheistic, polytheistic, apostolic, or animist, has something hostile to say about menstrual blood and female reproductive functions. In addition, most religions blame woman, not man, for concupiscence, because it is supposedly her irresistible attractiveness that provokes male lust. Most religions contain an ascetic tradition and therefore a potentially misogynistic component.

In most of the world's messianic religions — in which God's revelations are set down in writing by prophets — sin is brought into the world by women. It is always First Woman, never First Man, who, because of innate character flaws, capitulates to the devil's blandishments. As St. Ambrose (c. A.D. 339–397) writes, the First Woman, weak and sensual, is easily deceived and in turn deceives the man, thereby condemning all mankind. Eve is the guilty party in Christianity as well as in its sister faiths, Judaism and Islam, but Eve's role as the devil's gateway is played by female surrogates in practically all other origin myths, such as the Greeks' Pandora. So in a sense, one can say that the malevolent-maiden motif finds expression in the guise of First Woman, the primum mobile of evil.

Burmese Buddhism

When we discussed Buddhism as practiced in Burma (Myanmar), we cited some examples of sacred writings, theological dramaturgy, and homiletic poetry that criticize woman for her grave flaws. More than other East Asian Buddhist traditions, the Burmese form of Buddhism takes umbrage at feminine treacherousness, and warns men repeatedly about letting down their guard against this ubiquitous menace. Spiro shows that Buddhism regards human biological drives, especially libido, as unhealthy and anarchic, interfering with the search for salvation. Buddhism emphasizes the moral defects of woman, the primary one being her supposedly exaggerated libido, unrestrained and surpassing the male's. If Buddhist monks are believed to be morally pure because of an ability to control their sexual appetites, females are morally defective since their sexual ardor is said to be insatiable (Spiro 1997:21).

The result of this moral defect is that women are excluded from attaining the spiritual levels reached by men. The highest goal in life is to achieve perfect wisdom, or nirvana. The main obstacle to this goal is libido, which enfeebles self-control and impedes the spiritual quest. Not only does women's insatiable sex drive make nirvana impossible for them, it also presents a danger to men who seek transcendence:

according to Buddhism . . . sex is a base drive and an insurmountable obstacle to ultimate salvation (nirvana) whose achievement requires, among other things, the extinction of sexual desire. The stronger one's libido, then, the lower one's position on the scale of spiritual progress — which is one reason that females, given their putatively powerful libido, are believed to be spiritually inferior to males. (Spiro 1997:154)

That women are sexual predators who lead men to perdition is enshrined in the traditional writings in the Burmese canon, in particular the *Culla-Paduma Jataka,* a traditional text that is the basis of a famous drama in Burmese classical theater (Spiro 1997:154). In this lengthy narrative, a virtuous and naive young man is seduced by a woman and dragged down to sexual debauchery. His fall is explained by a character in the play who says that a woman is to blame. According to Burmese Buddhist lore, the female libido is as wide as the ocean and as intense as a roaring fire. Note again the association of women with fire, sin, and other dangerous things. Enshrined in writ, this unity of women and fire takes on canonical authority.

Other Burmese religious authorities assure us that a woman's sexual impulse is eight times stronger than a man's. Her libido is also much less governable, less amenable to cultural constraint than a man's (Spiro 1997:22). In the many texts cited by Spiro, man comes across thus as morally superior to woman, who is invariably depicted as morally defective and spiritually inferior (22–24). His anarchic sexuality is governable, hers not; she is more animal-like.

Such misogynist notions are enshrined in other sacred texts, such as the homiletic poem the *Andabhuta Jataka,* which holds, for example, that "All women work iniquity" upon the world (23). They do this by seducing men from the righteous path and debasing them with lustful thoughts:

'Tis nature's law that rivers wind;
Trees grow of wood and kind;
And, given opportunity,
All women work iniquity.
A sex composed of wickedness and guile,
Unknowable, uncertain as the path
Of fishes in the water — womankind
Hold truth for falsehood, falsehood for the truth! (23)

As well as charging women with falsity and sexual guile, the texts call them faithless and dishonest. Much the same accusation is made in Burmese secular folklore and ideology. Again, woman's iniquity is a thickly layered, insidious danger requiring unflagging vigilance in both secular and spiritual realms. In the authoritative traditional play *Paduma,* the eponymous hero proclaims women's infidelity in a celebrated diatribe known to every Burmese schoolboy: "They will even kill their rightful husbands the moment they want a new lover. Their lust blinds them. . . . They receive all, just as a roaring fire receives all rubbish. . . . One is more certain of one's ability to drink up all the waters of the ocean, than of the faithfulness of one's wife" (Htin Aung 1937:231). Another passage in the *Andabhuta Jataka* says: "You couldn't be certain of woman, even if you had her inside you and always walked about with her. No woman is ever faithful to one man alone" (Spiro 1997:25). It is clear that woman is being blamed as a scapegoat for man's sense of disillusionment at the faithlessness of life. Aside from all this emphasis on woman as sinner and corrupter of man through her carnality, Burmese Buddhism denounces her for intentional cruelty and perversity. Such categorical indictments can be found in a host of companion works of literature.

Rather than being unique to Burma, according to Spiro, these prejudices are found in the Thai and other versions of Buddhism. He summarizes all these Southeast Asian Buddhist misogynistic beliefs as follows: woman is intrinsically dangerous to man because she leads him astray through sexual enticement; she distracts man from his spiritual quest through her false promises of love and tenderness; rather than nurture him, she betrays him. In all versions of Southeast Asian Buddhism the cause of this wickedness is the same; woman is cursed with three defects: an immodest and powerful libido, a polluting vagina, and a powerful sexual allure. The dangerous female who burns men to ashes is an inherent aspect of the Burmese and Southeast Asian ascetic complex and cannot be separated from coexistent and everyday supernatural beliefs and practices.

Other Buddhisms

Burma reflects a set of holy teachings stressing what might be summarized as an ascetic misogyny, placing the blame for temptation of all sorts on women. Such devotions are therefore necessarily aggressively hostile to women and to sex itself, with which of course women are linked (Sponberg 1992:18). Some of this sexual hostility may derive from prevailing East Asian social views regarding sexuality and gender predating Buddha, but it is consecrated by incorporation into the early texts of Buddha's teachings, as Alan Sponberg (1992) argues in his syncretic study of Asian gender attitudes. But the antagonism goes beyond woman's sexual allure, and woman is blamed for virtually all human flaws, and specifically for a perverse failure to nurture man as he wants and expects. An example of what he calls this particularly "virulent" brand of all-encompassing antifeminism in early Buddhism comes from a dramatic text, the *Anguttara Nikaya,* which tells the story of the wandering hero Ananda.

At one point in his adventures, Ananda comes across Buddha and asks, "Pray, Lord, what is the reason, what is the cause why womenfolk neither sit in a court [of justice], nor embark on business, nor reach the essence of [any] deed" (that is, why are women to be excluded from rational discourse?). The Buddha replies, "Womenfolk are uncontrolled, Ananda. Womenfolk are envious, Ananda. Womenfolk are greedy, Ananda. Womenfolk are weak in wisdom, Ananda. That is the reason, that is the cause why womenfolk do not sit in a court of justice, do not embark on business, do not reach the essence of the deed" (Sponberg 1992:18–19).

Sponberg also cites excerpts from an even more virulent antiwoman text, "The Tale of King Udayana of Vatsa," which is a component sutra from the *Maharatnakuta,* an important sacred collection:

All desires are suffering, the vilest of evils
The impurity of pus, extremely despicable . . .
Like the overflow from a toilet or the corpse of a dog or a fox.

In the Sitavana cemetery pollution flows everywhere.
The evils of desire are contemptible like these.
Fools lust for women, like dogs in heat.
They do not know abstinence.
They are also like flies who see vomited food.
Like a herd of hogs, they greedily seek manure.
Women can ruin the precepts of purity.
They can also ignore honor and virtue . . .
As the filth and decay of a dead dog or dead snake are burned away,
So men should burn filth and detest evil.
The dead snake and dog are detestable,
But women are even more detestable than they are . . .
Women are like fishermen; their flattery is a net.
Men are like fish caught by the net. (Sponberg 1992:21)

Burma's northern neighbor China also partakes of the Great Tradition of classical Buddhism, but with some differences. Unlike Burma, Tibet, or Thailand, which are largely monolithically Buddhist, China, a much larger and more diverse country, hosts numerous religious traditions, none of which can be said to be central. These overlapping traditions include various forms of Buddhism, Confucianism, Taoism, and remnants of ancestor worship, as well as the mystic teachings of sages such as Mencius. We have already seen that in traditional Chinese Buddhism and Taoism, women were not considered clean mainly because of menstrual blood and other bodily effluvia (Ahern 1978). Likewise, in Chinese traditional ancestor worship, which often coincides with Buddhist observance, the ancestral spirits are highly offended by the presence of menstruating or lactating women.

In a recent study of modern Chinese literature, the Chinese-American literary critic Tonglin Lu (1993) mines another rich vein of misogynistic thinking. She ascribes this attitude to ancient concepts stemming from sacred and philosophical texts in the Chinese literary tradition. For example, she places what she calls the "misogynist discourse" of popular writing within a venerable context: in China, she argues, the search for a marginalized and demeaned Other has essentially taken the form "of misogyny" (1995:4). With few ethnic divisions to inspire prejudice, the majority Han Chinese focus on the female sex as the denigrated other, the opposite, the negative mirror-image. Woman's beguiling sexuality is part of the blanket condemnation, but not all of it.

Tonglin Lu supports this idea by noting that in the Confucian tradition women are seen as "inferior men" (*xiaoren*) who have none of the qualities of superior men. A famous Confucian saying reflects this notion: "Women and inferior men are difficult to deal with," stressing woman's perverse and wayward nature (Lu 1993:13). Other Confucian proverbs stress woman's animal-like impulses and passionate nature, her lack of emotional self-control, her evil tongue, and her susceptibility to disorder and sin. Lu shows that women are often portrayed as beastly or atavistic in contemporary fiction, just as they are in ancient texts in which femininity is often related to animality (1994:145). She notes that in Confucius's writings, the sage usually refers to women as *xiao,* "little, mean, inferior" (1995:9).

Early Christianity and the Bible

Western feminists have often denounced official Christianity, especially Catholicism, because of the blame it places on Eve as well as for its all-male hierarchies and proscriptions against female "rights" such as sexual freedom and abortion. But the Christian Bible contains very little that could be called overtly misogynistic. However, a number of villainesses do appear in the Bible, women who tempt good men into sin or worse, and themselves scalp, behead, and castrate heroes with abandon. But these femmes fatales are no more prevalent and no more evil than the myriad male villains of Christian myth; a man, Judas Iscariot, for example, is the prime villain in the New Testament. The chief scourge of the Old Testament, Satan, is without any real sexual identity in the texts, but is nevertheless normally presented as male.

Yet the scribes of the Bible are not free of antiwoman pronouncements. In Proverbs we find the rhetorically misogynistic question: "Who can find a virtuous woman? For her price is far above rubies." That evaluation certainly attests to a stereotypically negative attitude toward woman's moral nature in the Judeo-Christian tradition in general terms, rather than toward individual female sinners for specific acts of sexual transgression. In her study of literary woman-hating, Katherine Rogers also points out that the story of Genesis, by inverting a normal birth and portraying Eve as emerging from Adam's body rather than the other way around, provides evidence of antiwomen feelings, since it steals from woman the power of procreation and thus makes woman secondary, an afterthought (Rogers 1966:3). Feminist political scientist Linda Coole agrees, musing that the biblical reversal of birth implies that women are inferior (1988:44).

More tellingly, there are several lines from biblical apocrypha that might arouse feminist indignation. One warns against "the ruinous power, which women can exercise over men." Another addresses the iniquity of womankind: "All wickedness is but little [compared] to the wickedness of a woman" (cited in Rogers 1966:13). But these sporadic critiques, after all, come from the apocrypha, the suppressed writings, which means that they were bowdlerized by a male interpreter, whereas the Bible, the official, edited testament of the Christian faith, cannot be labeled as misogynistic as the Buddhist texts we have examined above.

Still, if one takes a closer look at the uses made of Christ's teachings especially among the theologians of the early Middle Ages — a time of great obsession with sin and the devil — one can see the validity of feminist assertions against the European Church and its pronouncements. Flesh-and-blood men twist lore and shape sacred revelations to suit their irrational antiwoman beliefs and feelings, reinventing holy writ for their own purposes.

Eve, the Devil, and the Fall

Biblical scholar Elaine Pagels in *Adam, Eve, and the Serpent* (1988), as well as other students of early Christianity, have shown that ecclesiastical misogyny is a product of the formal association made by the founding clerics between sin and woman's nature, their belief that carnality originates in the woman's genitals, which are viewed as a trick or trap in which the devil ensnares the innocent male. This, of course, is only a crude form of what I have called Melanesian misogyny, in which sex is denounced as a trap or a pollution. "The guilt is hers, not theirs [the men's]" (Blamires 1992:4). In medieval Christianity especially, as in Burmese Buddhism, woman was not seen simply as a passive object of man's carnal appetites, but as "the incarnation of sin, the temptation of the flesh" (Bakhtin 1984:240).

As Bloch argues (1991:78), much of this emphasis on the sinfulness of female sexuality and woman's shamefulness as sexual predator stems from St. Augustine's defining struggles with his own lusts and his angry renunciation of the pleasures of the flesh. The patristic writers concluded that the idea of woman was virtually identical with the supervenient and the contingent, with the realm of the senses, that woman existed in the flesh in specific revealed contrast to the world of the spirit, which is both pure and male, "virtuous and godly" (65). The Manichaean division between man (spirit) and woman (flesh) is thus God's intention: unquestionable and immutable.

So again we see male sexual guilt as the emotive inspiration for antiwoman feelings as a system of self-serving morality: an effort to exonerate the self by isolating and blaming the other. By claiming that the *object* of desire is the *source* of desire, one neatly sidesteps complicity. As Bloch astutely notes (1991:59), the Manichaean worldview of the early Christian puritans was one of ceaseless temptation in which flesh-and-blood women were not autonomous human beings with a soul, free will, and a chance of salvation, but were "snares" and "lures" — that is, the bait of the devil, the embodiment of sinfulness, objectified things rather than complex and feeling human beings. And of course the aspiring male saints and holy men were surrounded by such subhuman temptations living in the real world, so that the *mundus mulieris* (world of woman) was not a neutral place or environment, but a living assault on their senses, an insidious temptation to be renounced and denounced if salvation were to be achieved.

In a typical diatribe, Bishop Marbod of Rennes (c. 1035–1123) writes about the wickedness of women in his popular book *La Femme fatale*: "Countless are the traps which the scheming enemy [the devil] has set throughout the world's paths and plains: but among them the greatest — and the one scarcely anybody can evade — is woman. Woman, the unhappy source, evil root, and corrupt offshoot, who brings to birth every sort of outrage throughout the world. . . . Woman subverts the world; woman the sweet evil, compound of honeycomb and poison" (Blamires 1992:100–101).

The message about "sweet evil" and poison originates not with Marbod in the twelfth century, nor with St. Augustine in the fifth, but rather with the apostle Paul in the first. Paul (or the writer of some of the material attributed to him) can be legitimately cast in the role of the first official Christian misogynist, as is indeed suggested in Ambrose's attribution in the epigram that opens this chapter, credited with the epochal act of inextricably linking sensuality and woman with sin in the Western world. A recurrent theme in the great world religions, sexual sin in formative Christianity, takes on the additional feature of *original* sin, a "poison" (once again) in the human bloodstream; even in marriage it retains a certain detrimental connotation within the bounds of scripture.

First Corinthians expresses contempt for woman and stresses repeatedly that she must remain subservient to man, not just to preserve an orderly family life, but for moral reasons, as ordained by God. She represents not only raw sexuality but also childlike depravity, and only man can act responsibly: "Let wives be subject unto their husbands in everything," urges Ephesians, with the underlying message that male dominance is necessary because woman is morally weaker and more susceptible to sensuality than man. Besides, women have the awesome power to lead men from the straight and narrow and to defile them with lascivious thoughts. Women are more dangerous to men than anything else on earth because of the seductive power of their bodies (Rogers 1966:11). In her treatise on Western political misogyny, Coole (1988:44) sees this theme as simply a carryover from the ancients or, as she puts it, a mental recycling of classic Greek misogyny. But there is of course an additional impetus in Christianity: women are not to be trusted because of their association, through Eve, with original sin; they carry the burden of the Fall (Coole 1988:43–44). Woman constantly *betrays* man; she disappoints and disillusions him like a bad, indifferent mother.

This antiwoman dogma inherent in the Christian liturgy continues throughout the early period of Roman Christianity and the dark and early middle ages. Saturninus, in the second century, declared that "marriage and procreation are of Satan," and he called chastity the supreme Christian virtue, upon which every moral quality depended. Not long afterward, St. Athanasius proclaimed that virginity and chastity were the supreme revelations brought into the world through Christ's teachings and declared concupiscence to be the primary obstacle to a state of grace. "Every woman," said St. Clement of Alexandria, "ought to be filled with shame at the thought that she is a woman." And St. Ambrose equated even conjugal relations with sin and shame: "Married people ought to blush at the state in which they are living, since it is equivalent to prostituting the members of Christ" (Lederer 1968:162–63).

Theological misogyny, which achieved a kind of formal legitimacy in the earliest thinkers, gathered steam throughout the high middle ages, culminating in the works of such clerics as Walter Map, Andreas Capellanus, and Jean Le Fèvre (author of the *Lamentations of Maltheolus* that so incensed Christine de Pizan). Included also are Tertullian (of "Devil's Gateway" fame) and of course the martyrs and celibate mortifiers-of-the-flesh like St. Jerome the hermit and St. Anthony, who likewise took a detour from the way of all flesh by hiding out in the wilderness.

Saints Jerome and Anthony, perhaps, represent the archetype of virtuous men tempted by female softness, then depicted as soldiering against enticing but deadly sirens. Numerous Renaissance and early modern paintings of St. Jerome in the desert and St. Anthony in the wilderness portray the valiant struggle of these saints who turned their backs on lurid voluptuaries and retreated into Spartan sanctuaries. Prime examples are Hieronymus Bosch's surreal *St. Anthony Tempted by the Devil-Queen* (ca. 1500), in which the seminude siren is depicted coyly concealing her private parts with a diaphanous curtain, and Francisco de Zurbarán's *Temptation of St. Jerome* (1638–40), in which the maidens are depicted as pretty musicians, playing come-hither music as the virtuous saint fends them off. Thinking aloud in his work *Adversus Jovinianum* (393), Jerome reproaches woman as a human "atrocity," the scourge of mankind, the principal cause of sin in the world.

While focusing on specific females as examples, Jerome's condemnation is categorical and dogmatic. Like Juvenal in his *Satires,* Jerome maintains that women cause war, incite murder, and abet other atrocities (Coole 1988:53). Considering these categorical views, the celibacy of the Catholic priesthood is a foregone conclusion, as is the resultant strength of male resolve against the iniquitous enchantments of female flesh: as the Church struggled gradually to "shun the two-legged she-beast," it is not surprising that there was a hardening of the inclination among those same clerics to see woman merely as a sexual snare employed by the devil.

Gendercide?

Many of these ascetic fanatics were so suspicious of the "two-legged she-beast" and so consumed by sexual guilt and other frustrated longings for tender female ministrations that they either ran away from human society to become recluses, as in the case of desert-dwelling St. Jerome, or remained celibate and permanently avoided female contamination. Not even the sanctity of marriage was immune to the shame of sex; these anchorites fulminated not only against women in general but against marriage as an institution. This convergence of phobias, mixing misogyny with *misogamy* (fear and hatred of marriage), produced a curious sexual nihilism, almost exclusive to Christian Europe, that is purely male and that reverberates throughout Western history, to an extent rarely encountered elsewhere, except perhaps, as Spiro argues, in Burmese Buddhism.

Like misogyny, misogamy is firmly entrenched throughout Western literary history, as is shown in a book by Katherine Wilson and Elizabeth Makowski (1990). A classic example, in modern Western literature, is Leo Tolstoy's novella *The Kreutzer Sonata.* In this misanthropic diatribe written apparently during a period of marital troubles, Tolstoy has his puritanical hero, Pozdnyshev, denounce all sex as sinful, even conjugal sex. Not unlike St. Jerome, Pozdnyshev advocates universal celibacy. This view, although extreme, reflects Tolstoy's attitudes at the time and, in fact, Tolstoy himself spoke of this novella as reflecting precisely his emerging ascetic religious beliefs (Rancour-Laferriere 1998:65). As a specifically *Christian* thinker, concerned with questions of sin and redemption, Tolstoy is, it is sad to say, in good company. For example, both Ambrose and Tertullian declared that the extinction of the human race was preferable to its propagation by sexual intercourse (Lederer 1968:163). Deeply disturbed by visions of sensual, gratifying women, saints Jerome, Anthony, and

Hilarion would probably have also agreed. But obviously, the extinction of the human race is only a second-best solution to the extermination of the female sex, or as Jukes (1994:315) calls it, "gynicide."

The antiwoman, antisex hysteria reaches it apogee, perhaps, in the early Christian period with Quintus Septimus Florens Tertullian (c. 160–c. 225), a pagan from Carthage who converted to Christianity around 197, became a priest, and as we have seen, began a tradition that identified woman as the gateway to hell. Another example of misogynist rage appears in the works of Walter Map (c.1140–1209), a respected member of Henry II's court who later became the influential archdeacon of Oxford. In his misogynistic screed, *The Letter of Valerius to Ruffinus, Against Marriage* (c. 1180), he reproaches women in the most scurrilous terms for sin and depravity, holding them accountable for causing the men who love them "bitterness of fear, anxiety, and frequent misfortune," as well as for being demonically deceitful, lustful, and for harboring in their breasts the unending desire to do harm. Map envisions a world without women and is mightily pleased with the image.

Women, for Map as for so many other of these clearly disturbed male thinkers, are equivalent not only to carnality but to the failure of the human enterprise itself. Taken to its extreme, this prejudice comes close to advocating something akin to gendercide — the elimination of women — if not by actually murdering them (none of these writers went that far), then through the demographic device of attrition by celibacy and ultimate human extinction (for which male extinction would be an acceptable price to pay).

Biblical Bad Girls

We have seen that except for the story of the Fall (Genesis), some snippets in the Apocrypha, and a few allusions to menstrual pollution (Leviticus), the Bible does not dwell specifically on the malevolence of womankind (as, one might argue, do the Qur'an and some Buddhist texts). Yet the Old Testament does in fact conjure up a stereotype of the destructive femme fatale in several hyperbolic mythical incarnations. One could refer to these ancient villainesses as biblical bad girls, because in their maliciousness and disastrous impact on men under their influence, they resemble the bad-girl model of today.

These biblical temptresses cut a wide swath: Jael kills Sisera the Canaanite after lulling him to sleep with soothing milk and a surfeit of maternal concern (Lassner 1993:24); cruel Delilah does a hatchet job on Samson's glorious mane; the witch Jezebel manipulates men with her evil wiles; and demonic

Lilith is an enigmatic and powerful force of nature whose corruption is exposed in Hebraic scriptural caveats.

Biblical scholar Jacob Lassner, in a lengthy book about the "demonization" of females in Christian lore as well as in Hebrew and Islamic texts, argues that this constantly reappearing portrait reveals "a terrifying fear" that grips men throughout the history of the Middle East — where all three religions originated — and that still lingers there and in the mind of Christian Europe. The fear is that woman, circumventing man's domination through deceit and seduction, would make short shrift of civilization and reduce men to servitude, obliterating their chance at salvation; that is, left to their own devices, dangerous female creatures would change the nature of the world as we know it.

Destroying civilization is bad enough, but these inherently amoral females would also defile motherhood. By evading maternal responsibilities, they would unleash chaos in the nursery, and humanity would ultimately become extinct:

The implications of this course [rejecting motherhood] are self-evident. If the danger to the newly born and those [who] would be born is realized, humankind will not be able to sustain the species and in time will become extinct. Therefore, it is imperative that men, and the women of their household as well, do everything to maintain the separate roles that nature has designed for them at God's behest. In any event, that is what texts ancient and medieval say they ought to do. (Lassner 1993:35)

This fear of wanton, amoral women who reject the duties of motherhood has deep roots in many cultures, Lassner concludes, and is as insistent as the fear of woman's unleashed sexuality (33). It is in fact both curious and disturbing to see how woman as a human transgressor is magnified in male fantasies into a threatening and nonhuman *force*, super- and subhuman at the same time, allied with Satan and Chaos, endangering the universe. The contradictory messages reflect the extraordinary degree of male inner conflict and confusion: woman wants to overpopulate the world by enticing man into frenzied fornication, yet she also wants to extinguish the human race by abrogating her maternal role and renouncing sex.

This ambiguity along with the contradictory imagery of condemnation will become a major focus in later chapters, when we explore the psychological and cultural roots of many male distortions and inconsistencies. Nowhere is this gender ambivalence manifested so strikingly as in the cult of the Virgin Mary in southern Europe. Latin Christianity, unlike other world religions, places a woman, and a mother once again, at the heart of God's grace. The Madonna is both a beacon of goodness, a goddess in her own right, and the mother of God—the essence of purity. Marian worship therefore presents a significant counterweight to misogyny in Christianity. Consequently, all is not so clear in the Christian vision of woman; we will look more closely at this basic contradiction in Chapter 10.

Islam

The Islamic scholar Abdelwahab Bouhdiba, in a book that can be seen partly as a defense of Islam against its feminist critics, admits that misogyny constantly recurs as a theme in Arab culture (1985:119). He acknowledges that the Qur'an and other Arab-Muslim holy texts swarm with resolutely antifeminist declarations (117), a leitmotif in historical and contemporary Islam (the topos once again). Many staunchly feminist anthropologists concur with this assessment, even though there has been much recent emphasis on reconciling feminism with Mohammed's teachings (Ahmed 1992; Stowasser 1994; Varisco 1995). The revisionists contend that the Qur'an is less misogynistic and more sexually "egalitarian" (Ahmed 1992:66) than some feminists allow. According to these observers, the feminist anthropologists have distorted the holy texts for their own realpolitik (Stowasser 1994:134) and are guilty of "orientalism."

Bouhdiba even maintains at one point that Islamic civilization is essentially feminist (1985:116)—definitely a minority view, but one supported by Arabist scholar Daniel Varisco and a few other Arabist ethnographers. Furthermore, Middle Eastern and Mediterranean misogyny, they claim, certainly did not appear suddenly with Islam but rather predates both Mohammed and the Christian era by centuries. Lila Ahmed, for example, claims that whatever the cultural source or sources, a fierce misogyny was a distinct ingredient of Mediterranean and eventually Christian thought in the century immediately preceding the rise of Islam (the seventh century A.D.). One form it took, she notes, in the pre-Christian era was female infanticide: the practice of infanticide, predominantly of girls, predated both Christianity and Islam (1992:35).

However, even with the best intentions, this Islamic "antiorientalist" revisionism resembles the frequent effort of Marxists to revivify communism by pronouncing that all current socialist regimes are corruptions of the one true faith. Despite the ambiguity and even ambivalence in the Qur'anic view of women and her "nature," for the most part, Islamic cosmology and morality, as adumbrated by Mohammed and his followers, indict woman: for her body, her incendiary sexuality, and her spiritual defects.

The Qur'an (4:34) says quite unequivocally that God made men superior to women, that men "have a status above women," and that men have the right to command over "the inferior sex." It also stipulates that a male should inherit twice as much as a female (4:11); in addition, the scripture gives men, but not women, the right to initiate a divorce (the aggrieved husband only has to call two honest men to witness), and to take more than one spouse (65:1). "Women are your fields," says Mohammed in sura 2; "go, then into your fields whence you please," thus making women chattel for men to own, use, and abuse as they wish. Many other elements supporting women's inferiority have been identified in Muslim texts, including the following: men are permitted multiple wives, women may only have one husband; virginity is required for the bride but not the groom; in case of divorce, children belong to the husband, not the wife; women must observe a strict curfew from sunrise to sunset, while men may wander at will; husbands, not wives, are empowered to select the place of residence after marriage; women may not make eye contact or talk with a stranger, while men are at liberty to do so; women must be covered from head to toe, men not; women cannot work outside the home without the consent of their husbands; most marital property belongs to the man except for the woman's personal jewelry; women are generally excluded from mosques, courtrooms, and all other places of power and privilege; for management of property belonging to her own children, a male relative must usually give consent, and so on ad infinitum.

Legally, the secondary sacred Islamic texts — not the Qur'an but the law books such as the Hadith and the Shari'a, restrict women's freedom, providing males exclusive authority not only in divorce but in most contractual, domestic, and religious matters. In what is essentially a feminist defense of Islam, the social historian Shala Haeri asserts that Middle Eastern women do have some defined rights in these scriptural texts but she admits that women's rights are always inferior to those of men, and that woman is generally considered "half a man" (1989:27).

This diminishment holds true in both the orthodox Sunni and Shiite branches of Islam. Assumptions of female deficiency, presumably rooted in anatomy, saturate Shiite literature (Haeri 1989:68). In his typically understated way, Bouhdiba says, "Male supremacy is fundamental in Islam" (1985:19). He emphasizes the *moral* rather than political justification for masculine privilege; women are considered innately amoral, obdurate, frivolous, and therefore incapable of religious purity and moral gravity. And because of their passionate nature, women are not only lesser humans, innocent waifs needing masculine protection, but also dangerous and even demonic figures.

Picking up the common misogynistic thread uniting the world's great religions, Islam makes a direct association of woman with satanic powers. The Muslim *Book of Marriage* equates woman with the devil: "She resembles Satan in his irresistible power over the individual" (cited in Mernissi 1987:42). Upon his nocturnal ascension to heaven, Mohammed declared (in an infernal vision vouchsafed by Allah) that "hell was populated above all by women" (Bouhdiba 1985:117), who were the devil's agents in their power over men. The Prophet also warned that "No group prospers that appoints a woman to rule over them" (Lassner 1995:74). And in a verse attributed to Mohammed on his deathbed, the still-wary Prophet cautions against woman's terrible destructive power: "After my disappearance," he warned, "there will be no other greater source of chaos and disorder for my nation than women" (Varisco 1995:10).

Finding ammunition aplenty in such declarations, Mohammed's misogynistic followers often advanced his radical view of woman as evil. The Imam Ali, an influential early theologian and political leader, said that "woman is wholly evil; and the worst thing about her is that she is a necessary evil" (i.e., for lawful procreation). The pious fourteenth-century Muslim poet Zayn Ibn al-Wardi wrote that "women constitute the basis of all *fitna* (revolt against God), since they are the principal element in Satan's traps" (Bouhdiba 1985:118).

The allusion to *fitna,* or chaos, is the kernel of Islamic condemnation of woman. A polysemous word in Arabic, *fitna* means not only chaos, disorder, and social anarchy, but also, in a curious homology, a nubile, pretty woman (Stowasser 1994:55). Virtually all Islamic scholars agree that *fitna* signifies the importunate sexual attraction of women as well as moral collapse and general societal destruction (Varisco 1995). Indeed, according to the Moroccan feminist scholar Fatima Mernissi (1987:31), the *fitna* concept unites "chaos or disorder" and femme fatale, the beautiful woman who makes men lose self-control; thus the term suggests and encourages an unconscious identification of woman with illicit sex and sin. No matter what one's views about woman in Islam, one is drawn to conclusion that woman's "nature" is dangerous to the established moral order and that women are inherently defective in the eyes of Muslims. Barbara Stowasser (1994:13) points out further that the diatribes against female sexuality and women in general are immutable because Mohammed's words represent *literally* God's words and an unchangeable revelation to humankind.

The attack on woman as the source of sexual shame and sin is nowhere more antagonistic than in Muslim North Africa. Throughout this region women are unambiguously considered to be more impulsive, less self-controlled, and more sexually aggressive than men (Geertz 1979:332). The theme of *fitna* reaches a climax in the Maghreb, especially in Morocco, where woman is a "lascivious temptress" (Maher 1978:119), an evil seducer, corrupting and destroying men through her insatiable and peremptory lust (Dwyer 1978:151). In the eyes of many males in this part of the world, women are *the* major threat to male-created social institutions: women are a repository of powerfully destructive "id forces" (Rosen 1979). Even in non-Arab but Muslim Turkey, female sexuality is said to be explosive "like gunpowder" and equally destructive to social order (Fallers and Fallers 1976:258).

Mernissi supplies the reader with a multitude of Moroccan proverbs, verses, and holy writ that hammer home the misogynistic consensus and that harp on female defects both sexual and ethical. One of the best examples of the Muslim distrust of women is found in the still popular verses of the sixteenth-century poet Sidi Abderahman al-Majdoub. Throughout Morocco his sayings are household axioms:

Women are fleeting, wooden vessels
Whose passengers are doomed to destruction.

And:

Women's intrigues are mighty.
To protect myself I run endlessly.
Women are belted with serpents
And bejeweled with scorpions. (Mernissi 1987:43)

Poisons and serpents yet again.

Deeply appalled, Mernissi perhaps goes too far in her blanket statement: "The entire Muslim social structure can be seen as an attack on, and a defense against, the disruptive power of female sexuality" (45). In any case, one can easily see that the male fears constituting the essence of Islamic misogyny are yet again guilt-reducing projections of sexual desire onto women; the entire enterprise is a form of paranoid delusion in which women are scapegoats for all of man's own failings. Islamic misogyny, Bouhdiba states, is really "a flight before women as the source of uncontrollable desires in the male self" (1985:116).

Hinduism and the Goddess Kali

Varying little from Western monotheism in its basically negative view of the female sex, Hinduism also regards menstruation and other female bodily functions as defiling and unclean. Other similarities with the misogyny of the revealed religions abound. In Nepalese Hinduism, for example, there is the same striking emphasis on woman as chaos, social disruption, and moral disorder: woman represents all the unruly forces that work against purity, restraint, and reason in the world. The Nepalese Hindu man must constantly guard against the unruly and destructive forces of female degeneracy or face dissolution (Bennett 1983:218).

But Hindu misogyny also has a rare, peculiarly superheated quality stemming from the luxuriant imagery of deadly she-demons in its pantheon: diabolical figures that find few parallels in the Middle Eastern and Western canons. Throughout the Hindu texts, one encounters an upanishadic tendency toward misogyny and a "deep-seated" distrust of woman in all her guises (Doniger 1980:129, 133). This tendency, in accord with the rich iconography and pictorial mythology of classical Hinduism, assumes some highly idiosyncratic imagistic representations of the familiar malevolent maiden: mystical figures, deities, and exotic personifications. Doniger (133) refers to the Hindu women-blaming as yet another form of "ascetic misogyny," related to the underlying fear of sexuality as "extremely dangerous" to man's mental and spiritual health.

This view is endorsed by many other Hindu scholars. For example, Lynn Bennett, writing about Nepalese Hinduism, agrees with Doniger that the ascetic tradition, based as it is upon a profound misogyny, is quick to challenge the chastity of any woman, noble or not (1983:220), thus impugning the essential moral fiber of the entire sex. However, for Doniger, the question is not which comes first, asceticism or misogyny, but rather, how these themes interrelate and reinforce each another, especially in iconography and devotional practices.

Doniger seems to argue that the hatred for women is coterminous to, if not actually prior to, canonical anxiety over sex in Hinduism. She notes that the view that sex is evil is the natural consequence of the general misogyny of the Indian ascetic tradition and the upanishadic doctrine of the chain of rebirth: "reproduction traps men in the painful cycle of existence. Orthodox Hinduism, too, was prone to misogyny in its caste laws restricting the freedom of women" (Doniger 1976:27). In her opinion, the turning away from sex is only part of the problem, which is caused not only by liturgical injunctions against lust but also by a curious "gynecomorphic" preoccupation in the Hindu imagination that goes beyond sex, giving rise to a plethora of monstrous mothers and man-eating demons such as the famous death-goddess, Kali. Equipped with death-dealing weaponry and dripping blood, this ferocious she-creature turns desire into fright, intercourse into castration, motherhood into murder, love into death, dramatically embodying man's most profound terrors of the deadly female. The lurid figure of Kali is familiar to Westerners as the bloodthirsty, multiarmed, sword-wielding fiend of Hindu mythology. She is the goddess of death, the taker of life, oppressive and frightening, the impersonation of terror.

But Kali is not the only protean she-demon in Indian lore, which is richly populated with gruesome female figures — among them the bloodthirsty virgin warrior Durga and her emanations, Camunda, Mahisamardini, Yogi Nidra, and Ambika. The goddess Durga is one of the many forms of Devi (Bennett 1983:261). Carstairs (1958:157) describes the goddess Mataji in equally terrifying terms: "everyone worships the Mataji, the Goddess, who is a protective mother to those who prostrate themselves before her in abject supplication, but who is depicted also as a sort of demon, with gnashing teeth, who stands on top of her male adversary, cuts off his head and drinks his blood." This demon mother-goddess has the same appearance as a witch.

Deeply impressed by all this bloody imagery, part sexual part maternal, Lederer (1968:chap. 17) nevertheless regards Kali as simply one among a global multitude of fantasies about the diabolical female scourge dressed in religious garb along with witches and enchantresses: an iconography of feminized terror and a recurrent theme of *embodiment* or gyneco-anthropomorphism, the tendency to visualize and animate all manner of phobias in the shape of woman, often in the guise of monstrous mother. Lederer points out that Kali resembles the female figure of Chicomecoatl in pre-Aztec Mexico, the Terrible Mother who devours her husband and children. Kali also finds a parallel in the later Aztec Snake Woman, who appears in devotional imagery and drinks from a bowl of blood. Malekula, the man-devouring ogress of Polynesian lore, and various Celtic war-goddesses and Nordic woman-deities also mutilate, castrate, or kill their male adversaries. And of course, all these she-demons and murderous succubi bear uncanny resemblances to the sirens, lamias, naiads, sorceresses, evil stepmothers, and witches of Greek and Roman mythology: all female warriors and killers seducing men into moral amnesia if not murdering them and drinking their lifeblood with abandon. The sexual aspect is of course critical, but there is much more involved than sex; there is also the fear of the bad mother who gives death not life.

This kind of multitextured misogyny finds scriptural support everywhere. Whether or not religious antifeminism predates and stimulates its secular forms is a question often debated, especially by Islamic and Christian scholars, but essentially the question is a chicken-and-egg one. The causes of such complex feelings are deep and broad and resistant to any monocausal explanation, or one that relies only on sexual guilt and Oedipal elements. As we shall see in the next chapter, some other, purely secular causes of misogyny lie deeply embedded within the very structure and sinew of many societies.

What mighty ills have not been done by women!

Who was't betrayed the Capitol?—A woman!

Who lost Mark Antony the world?—A woman!

Who was the cause of a long ten years' war,

And laid at last old Troy in ashes?—Woman!

Destructive, damnable, deceitful woman!

—Thomas Otway, *The Orphan*

5. Social Structure

ONE ASPECT OF MISOGYNY has escaped most previous studies. It is linked to the way tribal peoples in preindustrial (or "primitive") societies reckon kinship and marriage, and involves the contemplation of woman as alien and dangerous, not because of her biology or her innate wickedness, but because of the tenuous position that she occupies within the social structure of such societies. The connection of misogynistic grievance to a distinctive form of social organization may explain the lack of interest among social scientists other than anthropologists, who are the specialists most concerned with kinship, for this is a specifically *ethnological* problem, derived from humanity's failure to solve an inherent contradiction in patrilineal social organization.

Structure and Sentiment

Patrilineal societies are those in which descent and inheritance are reckoned entirely, or largely, in the male line. *Patrilocal* means that postmarital residence patterns favor the male side; that is, women marry into, and reside after marriage, with their husband's local group (see glossary). Most patrilineal societies are also patrilocal; such societies are usually but not always *unilineal*; that is, the children are members *only* of the father's patriline, the mother's blood is not recognized, and her ancestors are excluded from the patrilineage. In such contexts, wives must always be "outsiders" to the host group because they must, as a result of stringent incest taboos, come from *outside* the male line, from a different patrilineage. Here, blood is all-important: the sense of unity and the self-identification of groups are centered on shared blood and genealogy. Thus, wives and mothers are outsiders not only in the sense that they were born and bred somewhere else, but also because they are not "of the blood." Indeed, in-marrying wives may come from a distant place and from a strange people who may be distrusted and even feared as potential enemies in times of war, economic competition, or other trouble (Jackson 1996:117).

In anthropology, the patrilineal, patrilocal kinship unit in such situations described above is often referred to as following the principle of agnatic solidarity, or having an ideology of agnation: that is, investing special importance on the unity of brothers (agnates: relatives whose descent can be traced to a common male ancestor). These terms are borrowed from ancient Roman law, in which a man's kin were divided into two categories: his *cognati* — kin through any link — and his *agnati* — kin through male links only. Relatives traced through females rather than males are called "uterine" (Fox 1983:51). As we have seen, uterine kin are excluded from the lineage in patrilineal societies. Relations traced through marriage are referred to in anthropology as *affines,* what we in the West call in-laws.

Patrilineal, patrilocal societies are legion historically and exist in great numbers in the tribal and preindustrial world. In fact, *most* societies that have ever existed — about 80 percent according to students of tribal social structure (cf. Murdock 1949) — have this specially patrilineal and patrilocal structural pattern. Recent studies in kinship have shown that this pattern is somewhat less rigid than originally thought and that flexibility is common (cf. D. Schneider 1984). Nevertheless, the general pattern is well documented and remains a classic in kinship studies.

Fraternal solidarity is a very important ideal in these patrilineal, patrilocal societies, because men wish to keep the agnates together in place and through time to augment sentimental solidarity and to maintain both genealogical continuity and material corporacy (joint ownership of property). This brotherly ideal of unity can usually be realized only through the retention of fraternal and filial propinquity — that is, by maintaining the physical closeness of agnates, as well as their moral, economic, and even military cooperation in forms of domestic organization centered on the joint or patrilaterally extended family (fathers and sons living together). The typical domestic unit and the ideal, therefore, is a three-generation affair, usually consisting of the father-patriarch and his wife living together in one household along with their married sons and their wives and children. Property is jointly owned, and the men share a merged (corporate) identity in the eyes of outsiders.

In such families, the ideal is for the sons of the clan to stay home and breed. Likewise, the grandsons in succeeding generations stay and propagate; the daughters and granddaughters are conversely mobile and must marry out and leave, to be absorbed by their husband's patrilines in the same way that mothers and wives are imported into and absorbed within the patrilineal kinship unit described above (Keesing 1975:26).

Often this ideal of fraternal unity has important military as well as economic and affective significance. Such unilineal societies are often based on the continuous replication of identical kin units that simply repeat the agnatic principle of cohesion in space by "budding" off from the apical, or original, lineage as the brothers grow up, separate, and go their own way. This splitting off or budding is called *segmentation* in kinship analysis. The clones make up the "segments" of the tribe, just as — to use a classic organic analogy — the segments of an annelid make up the whole worm, or the replicate cells of a beehive make up the swarm. The segments usually settle in nearby villages or tribal districts, and living close together, may cooperate, as is the ideal, but often, as time and competing interests push them further and further apart (e.g., third and fourth cousins), they often grow more competitive, as males tend to do. This segmentary-lineage model has also come in for scholarly reexamination, but the general outlines, as originally developed by Evans-Pritchard and others in the 1940s, seem true and resistant to major criticism.

The complementary balance of identical segments means that, despite the principle of agnatic loyalty, each extended family (segment) exists in potential opposition to all others. Since each is comprised of brothers and cousins, all the segments are theoretically politically equal and have equal claims upon resources. As time passes and fraternal loyalties diminish (replaced by commitments to one's own immediate family and descendants), the segments may compete with one another for land, wealth, flocks, or other resources. The essential nature of segmentary kinship is just this complementarity and structural balance of equivalent units, or, as Evans-Pritchard (1940) famously called it, "balanced opposition."

In the process of lineage segmentation, each extended family is surrounded by a concentric ring of agnatic kin, who are of course blood relations in decreasing degrees of closeness. Exogamous marriage in such situations presents a serious problem because the men must not marry women within this ring of settlement. These women are largely agnates, that is, blood relations through males. Owing to incest prohibitions, the men must instead look farther afield to the next ring of settlement or, failing to find a suitable wife there, to faraway nonagnates. Hence the women brought in as wives are often outsiders in two ways: first, they are members of distant and unrelated groups, and second, they may be from geographically remote places often not well known to local people. In other words, wives are doubly *aliens*: strangers who come from strange and suspect places, and aliens by blood.

Curiously, all this does not prevent men from marrying women from distant groups that they *actually* battle and compete against in deadly rivalries. The fact is that in many parts of the world where tribal kinship still prevails, the pattern of "affines-as-enemies" is the norm, not the exception. Wives often come from distrusted remote groups and are themselves distrusted until fully incorporated into the local lineage segment — a process that takes many births and much time, and that is sometimes never achieved.

Marital = Martial?

Frequently, then, wives come from distant outside groups which are seen as either actual or potential enemies. This situation of endemic distrust and warfare among in-laws is particularly pronounced in much of highland New Guinea, where exogamous clans are famous for making war on the very same people with whom they exchange women in marriage (Paula Brown 1964, 1978:166–67). Intermarriage may or may not lessen the extent of hostilities, but it has little ameliorative impact on killing, and the two combatant clans or villages simply continue to make war and love at the same time. New Guinea is famous for this paradoxical trait.

From a survey of literature on highland warfare before and just after European contact, Ronald Berndt (1964) reports that most fighting in the highlands took place among peoples who were also the main source of marital partners and that violence between these in-laws was especially "bitter" (193–94). Berndt stresses that there was a high correlation between rate of killing and rate of marriage throughout the area and notes that the highlanders were actually killing their own affines.

Even more specifically, Richard Salisbury (1962:25) quotes the Siane people of New Guinea about their in-laws: "They are our affinal relatives [in-laws]; with them we fight." Indeed, some of the New Guinea highland peoples say, as in a Mae Enga proverb, "We marry those whom we fight" (Meggitt 1958:278). Among both the Gahuka-Gama and the Gururumba, researchers estimate are that almost 70 percent of the wives come from enemy villages, so that a man's mother and wife may both be from enemy villages (Lidz and Lidz 1989).

In New Guinea, as in many tribal societies where war and raiding are common, "marital" therefore carries the connotation of "martial." In-marrying wives may be viewed not only as sinister emissaries from hostile lands but even, and for unfailingly logical reasons due to marriage and residence patterns, as a fifth column in times of war. As Paula Brown puts it: throughout upland New Guinea the loyalties of husband and wife may not only be divided, but are also frequently openly in opposition, placing the woman in the position of "suspected traitor" (1978:150). In these contexts, the wife never loses her alien status completely; her loyalties remain for a long time, at least psychologically, with her own distant group, a group that may constitute a looming menace to her husband's village. Brown notes that a man's loyalties are firmly set in his own place, while his wife's are established elsewhere: "A wife must acquire a new set of loyalties as a result of the marriage transactions." But this postmarital shift is not easily made in the pervasive atmosphere of distrust that surrounds the wife, for in the highlands, men must, as they say, "bring strangers into their houses," and strangers are always viewed as dangerous and treacherous regardless of where they come from.

Acknowledging the self-fulfilling-prophecy implications here, Brown goes on to point out that the new wife's alienation from her husband's clan may be both permanent and irreconcilable. Her husband and, especially, his agnates may never learn to trust her even after she settles in and has children, simply because she represents a blood connection to their mortal enemies (163). Meggitt (1976:70) reports that among the Mae Enga, the word for wife may also connote enemy.

Although there may be some degree of paranoia here, there are legitimate reasons for complaints about "enemy-alien wives." Many studies cited by Brown in her survey (1978) have shown that in-marrying women usually do retain feelings of loyalty with their distant fathers and brothers. Their divided loyalties will be especially strong if their husbands, to whose homes they must relocate after marriage, are negligent or abusive, as seems so often the case — thereby creating a vicious cycle of misogyny.

The structural alienation of women from patrilineal, patrilocal groups becomes a self-fulfilling prophecy of affective alienation. Even if the women are not acting as actual traitors sneaking military intelligence to their fathers and brothers, they are often suspected of some sort of magical betrayal — of using witchcraft against a spouse in favor of father or brother, or betraying a husband by giving intimate personal items, such as clothing or nail clippings, to his enemies, who will use these things in sorcery against him (Brown 1978:163). Many Fore men, for example, fear that their wives may even give enemy sorcerers the semen they retrieve from their underskirts to be used in black magic against them (Lindenbaum 1979:131). Among the Siane, the wife is literally the "enemy within the gates" who provides her husband's enemies (her brothers) with his fingernail pairings, hair, spittle, to be used in sorcery against him (Meigs 1984:106).

Even if the "alien" woman is not actively working for his military downfall, the husband fears that she is prejudicing their children against him and toward her own kin who have the power to "co-opt their young relatives' hearts" (Gewertz 1982:314). Whenever the wife takes her young children to visit her natal village, even briefly, the men worry and cavil about her betrayal of the agnatic principle. Thus, among the Chambiri of the Sepik River region, in-marrying wives are thought by their suspicious husbands to be "stealing away the essence of patrilineality" (Gewertz 1982:315) by turning the sons against the fathers. No matter what they do, the in-marrying wives are tarred with the brush of treason.

This "structural" embattlement by treacherous spouses adds a new wrinkle to the misogyny puzzle. It demonstrates an underlying current of suspicion and anxiety in very many tribal societies, not only between husband and wife, but also, as Brown notes, between in-marrying women and their husbands' kinsmen, who may feel threatened by the presence of an "enemy" woman, even if her husband comes to accept her. When warfare breaks out, these men have a concrete excuse to berate and blame the women, and since warfare is a constant threat, suspicions linger even during peaceful periods, probably leading to a degree of conjugal tension and irritability. The opportunities for scapegoating are therefore enormous, as the men release their subliminal and warlike aggressions on their wives. Clearly, in agnatically-oriented societies where warfare is common, all wives are in a delicate, precarious position.

This connection between a social structure and the intensity of misogyny has been pointed out in other parts of the world as well, primarily among patrilineal groups that resemble New Guinea highland peoples in their intensity of persecutory misogyny, such as the Tukanoan Indians of the Amazon Basin. Let us briefly reconsider them.

Amazonian Parallels

Writing about the misogyny of Tukanoan men, Jean Jackson (1992, 1996) reiterates the premise about the structural origins of their prejudices. In this case, the men's misogyny is centered not so much on warfare as on the fervent belief that in-marrying women are perversely impeding the men's desperate efforts to reproduce. Tukanoan men believe that their wives do everything possible to avoid getting pregnant and, if contraception fails, that they secretly abort their fetuses to prevent the men from expanding their clans. Their reasoning is that the women are "aliens" retaining loyalty to their own distant patrilines, which may be hostile to and competitive with their husbands': Jackson argues that one explanation for this misogynistic belief derives from the fact that women in patrilineal, patrilocal societies not only represent "not-us" in terms of gender, but also "not-us" in terms of blood. "Women, especially sexual women," she writes, "are depicted as not wanting to act for the collective interest. . . . Why *should* women want to have children who belong to another descent group, and thus make that group strong?" (1996:117). Fearful, frustrated, and angry at this imagined betrayal, the men say that woman is an uncontrollable and subversive element: the wild, distant, mysterious, and unknown principle in life that melts the glue of Tukanoan society (Jackson 1992:8, 12). Not only is she a probable traitor; she is also the greatest obstacle to the god-given male objective: to be fruitful and multiply.

Jackson goes on to argue that men in strongly agnatically-based societies tend also to view women as threats to fraternal unity; their very existence makes the men feel "vulnerable." But in all such societies, not only among the Tukanoan and in highland New Guinea, the foreign woman's presence produces "centrifugal tensions threatening male corporate relations" (that is, tensions that tear apart the society of brothers), and cause anxiety and rage among the always suspicious men (Jackson 1992:14). Given woman's tenuous position in this tricky social architecture, her subsequent role as prime scapegoat for every male dissatisfaction is virtually guaranteed. Women are simply scapegoated, she continues, because it is convenient to find an outlet to blame, "a patsy who diverts attention from the cracks in the united front of male agnatic solidarity" (Jackson 1992:13).

Sleeping with the Enemy

All this adds credibility to Louise Lamphere's (1974) useful observation about the inevitability of men's negative view of women in exogamous, patrilineal societies. Making a case for the structural underpinnings of misogyny, Lamphere argues that in these cultures, where the rules of strict clan exogamy dictate that wives marry in, women will always be strangers and foreigners, carrying with them the stigma of xenophobic danger.

Her argument finds much support also in classical anthropological literature on segmentary kinship organization in Africa. Although one may not extrapolate between African and Melanesian systems (which are different in many ways, as noted by J. A. Barnes (1962) and others), there are some important similarities. It is actually quite common in both places for men to intermarry with the enemy; therefore, again, affines are often foes, with women bearing the onus for this closed, paradoxical, and cybernetic system of relations. For example, Meyer Fortes notes that in Africa "marriages commonly take place between members of politically autonomous and mutually opposed, if not hostile, descent groups" (1959:209). As in New Guinea, this state of affairs takes on magical and occult dimensions, further inflaming sexual antagonism. In African literature, for example, the association of women with witchcraft and other imagined malignancies is more intense in tribes where the agnatic ideology predominates, especially where brothers live in proximity to one another, to their fathers, and to paternal uncles — that is, where the society is both rigidly patrilineal and patrilocal.

This same pattern is found in parts of China, where males also emphasize continuity of the patriline, or *tsu,* technically a clan organization. In traditional China, according to Emily Ahern (1978:275), a married woman's loyalties, at least initially, do not lie firmly with her new husband's family. As an outsider, she is expected to make her own way, if need be by undermining her husband's authority. "The people I could persuade to talk about sorcery," she writes, "mentioned one form of sorcery almost to the exclusion of any other: attempts by a new bride to dominate her husband."

A similar situation prevails in parts of India, where men also fear in-marrying wives. Anthropologist Scarlett Epstein (1967:150) writes about the village of Wangala in Mysore (now Karnataka) state:

Wangala peasants have never accused men of witchcraft. As far as I could establish, only women have been so accused. In a patrilineal community, such as that of Wangala peasants, women are outsiders. They marry virilocally into the lineage of their husbands but the absorption into it is only partial. They always maintain some links with their lineage and village of origin. In order to uphold the ideal of the unity and harmony of the patrilineal kin group in the face of conflicts arising in everyday relations between members of the group, witchcraft accusations have always been leveled against women, who are outsiders to the group. Similarly, women are always blamed for the break-up of a joint family.

James Brain corroborates the connection of in-marrying women and evil antimale magic. He concludes his global study of women and witchcraft by stating that the more rigidly patrilineal a society is, the more women will be portrayed in a negative light, especially as witches who attack men (1996:80). All this, incidentally, finds echoes in ancient European prototypes. For example, in classical origin myths the first woman is depicted as an outsider or afterthought who becomes a subversive intruder into the orderly world of brothers. We can perhaps now see these myths as providing a convenient nonsexual metaphor for the in-marrying bride's potentially ruinous effect on the ideal of an "orderly" fraternal world. Woman is the alien, the other, who once again poisons the idyllic world of cooperating brothers.

Classicist Robert Meagher puts it this way: in all these patriarchal traditions, but especially in the ancient Greek, the first woman is always portrayed as "an unwitting interloper into the original scheme of things, who disturbs the natural order, bringing sex, strife, suffering, and death" (1995:59). The underlying idea is that if the brothers could only get rid of women and reproduce asexually there would be no need to invite these dangerous, subversive, deceitful aliens into the harmonious fraternal society. Without women, strife and treachery would disappear and all would be well. As in the parable of the Fall, sin came into the world originally simply because Adam needed a wife to reproduce.

All this turmoil is compounded by the fact that in many parts of the world, men actually acquired (some still do) wives through the practice of "bride-capture," usually at the expense of hostile neighbors. Indeed, bride theft and raiding-for-wives are integral aspects of marriage in a large percent of reported societies in a tribal survey (Bates et al. 1974b:234). For example, a large proportion of wives among the polygynous Yanomamo Indians of the Venezuelan Amazon are abducted from enemy villages in violent raids in which many men are killed. As anthropologist Napoleon Chagnon (1997:126) notes, all Yanomamo women fear being abducted by raiders and always leave the village with this anxiety at the back of their minds when their men are at war.

It is perhaps no coincidence that the Yanomamo wife-kidnappers are among the most misogynistic men described in the ethnographic literature, and that the full fury of their abuse is directed against their wives. As portrayed by Chagnon, who has studied them for decades, these men are notorious wife-beaters, infamous for their brutality.

Most reprimands meted out by irate husbands are even more brutal [than beatings]. Some of them chop their wives with the sharp edge of a machete or ax, or shoot them with a barbed arrow in some non-vital area, such as the buttocks or leg. Many men are given over to punishing their wives by holding the hot end of a glowing stick against them, resulting in serious burns. . . . It is not uncommon for a man to injure his errant wife seriously; and some men have even killed wives for infidelity by shooting them with an arrow. (124–25)

The phenomenon of capturing a bride by raiding one's enemies is still widespread in both highland New Guinea and the Amazon area; in the latter case it was actually witnessed by reputable ethnographers as late as 1987 (Århem 1987). Even where bride capturing has been stamped out by the government, as recently among the Tukanoans, it remains a vivid memory: "Certainly bride capture as a theme and a fantasy was very much alive and well in Tukanoan society in the late 1960s" (Jackson 1992:5), as well as still being common in Amazonia. Wife kidnapping was practiced among some Mayan peasants in southern Mexico as late as the mid-1970s (Stross 1974).

But the practice of stealing wives is not confined to tribal, preliterate peoples. Bride abduction (*otmiča*) is an ancient and hallowed tradition among the South Slavs of the former Yugoslavia (Lockwood 1974:253). It also occurs in many parts of modern Turkey, for example, among the Yörük herdsmen of the southeast (Bates 1974:270). Bride abduction also still occurs in some parts of India; for example, among the Koya of the south, where it is casually referred to as "wife thieving" (Bruckman 1974:304). Wife and concubine capture was a common practice in classical antiquity as well. The Romans were notorious for this predatory practice.

To the widespread correlation between patriliny and misogyny, then, we may add the following proviso: negative attitudes toward women will increase when the in-marrying women come from groups that are geographically distant from the host group and with which the host group maintains relations of chronic enmity. The misogyny will escalate to overt persecution when such antagonistic relations culminate in physical violence; that is, when raiding or warfare are common. These criteria are met to a T in Amazonia and, especially, in the central highlands of New Guinea, the most virulently antifemale cultures known to anthropology.

However, even though most societies in the world have some patrilineal, agnatic elements, this explanation has limited applicability. After all, agnates exist in all societies; but an *ideology* of agnatic solidarity does not. The explanation fails, though, when applied to medieval or Victorian Europe, to much of the Far East, and to other areas where misogyny is pronounced but where in-marrying brides do not represent inimical social groups. It is irrelevant to those peasant societies where village endogamy is the rule, as in rural Europe and Latin America. This ambiguity of cause-and-effect points to the multicausal complexity of misogyny, its overdetermined nature.

Let us take a closer look at some ethnographic case studies outside New Guinea and Amazonia that illustrate this kind of structural kinship-based misogyny. In these examples, outright warfare is replaced by conditions of economic competition and rivalry. The misogyny is less ferocious than that of Amazonia or New Guinea, but it is still pronounced.

Hindu Structural Misogyny: A Nepalese Case

The Narikot villagers of central Nepal are a typically patrilocal, patrilineal people who practice clan exogamy and place the usual emphasis on the unity of brothers and cousins (agnates). Since the village is comprised mostly of a single clan, the Narikots practice village exogamy, too, seeking wives living in other villages. After marriage, the brides are brought from their natal villages to live in Narikot; the local women leave in the same way when they marry. This transaction is sometimes called sister-exchange marriage.

Lynn Bennett's monograph recounts the gender culture of these Nepalese, concentrating on the men's intense, but deeply ambivalent, antifemale attitudes and practices. The Narikot farmers are pious Hindus who uphold most of the misogynistic notions we have seen in the classical Indian canon. For example, they regard menstrual blood as polluting, and they are deeply involved in devotion to the fearful goddess Kali, especially her bloodthirsty incarnation, the warrior Durga. In addition, there is a strong emphasis on asceticism for males, who are expected to resist sexual temptation and to exercise restraint even in marriage. Nepalese Hindus regard sex not only as dirty and inimical to spirituality, but also as a trap set by evil powers to lead men to perdition. After marriage, a man should be virile, but only in the service of procreation (Bennett 1983:219).

Woman is impure. The Narikot villagers tend to stress her unruly nature as a sexual being and blame her for man's susceptibility to temptation and sin (218). As usual, all man's flaws are woman's fault. An unmarried nubile woman is regarded as an anomaly and as dangerous to the patriline, because until she is safely sent away in marriage to another lineage her sexuality is as yet untamed and can excite and perturb the men of the clan. In other words, a nascently sexual woman is like a moral landmine that endangers everyone in the patriline (240).

But even worse is the danger in-marrying women pose to male solidarity and the integrity of the patriline. The Nepalese follow the usual agnatic ideology described above: maintaining the unity of the patriline as a god-given duty. Unlike the New Guinea highlanders, however, these Nepalese villagers do not engage in warfare against in-law villages. On the contrary, they are peaceful, at least on the surface, and do not feel threatened in a military sense. Rather, the danger of the alien women is that they can cause wrack and ruin within the group, poisoning the body politic.

As elsewhere, the men's ideal is to maintain the unity of brothers at all costs and to expand the patriline, so they maintain at least a facade of unity. This is important because patrilines compete for scarce resources, just as villages compete for land and forage. Eventually, however, squabbles cause brothers to separate, to divide the formerly corporate patrimony, and to become competitors.

Why are women blamed for this inevitable separation of the brothers? The reasons will sound familiar. The men claim that it is woman's unruly nature that poisons fraternal harmony. It is women who argue and fight, usually over trivialities. Women gossip and haggle more than men do because women promote their children's interests at the expense of their nephews' and nieces'. Sharing blood and loyalties, the brothers, according to their self-image, are above such trifles. Since women are by nature more shortsighted and selfish than men and, most important, since they are unconcerned about the unity of the patriline (not sharing its blood), they are interested only in their own interests and those of their children. Therefore, ipso facto, whatever squabbles erupt within the family (or even among brothers) are by definition the fault of the small-minded women.

Despite what appears to be self-justifying male fantasy, one should point out a kernel of truth in the men's view, stemming not from women's nature but from the very real and very vulnerable "outsider" position of women. As Bennett says (219), the women do indeed fight over their children more than the men do, and they do tend to squabble with their sisters-in-law and mothers-in-law with whom they share living quarters (familiarity often does breed contempt here as elsewhere).

But the men blame women for *all* internal dissension in the patriline, for being the instigators of all strife. Even when the men fight among themselves, they say the women somehow caused it. Therefore women are always incriminated "ultimately for the inevitable segmentation of the joint family" (219). Women are, in short, typically held responsible for the breakdown of an *unattainable* ideal. It is their nature (read: their position within the social structure). Bennett sees such grievances as part of a radical indictment of the position of women in Nepalese society, which she calls the central structural conflict and the irresolvable contradiction of family life. Given the inevitability of human frailty and of the egoism of men, woman's position is inevitably "problematic" in such a society (214).

Bennett sees this irreconcilable contradiction in women's role as one of the central stress points in the system of Hindu culture, reflecting the deeply perturbing "Hindu ambivalence" about the female sex (316). Obviously men cannot have it both ways. The resulting frustration at the limitations posed by the structures of kinship and the strictures of sexual reproduction is foisted upon the shoulders of woman. Although this scapegoating has a specific structural provenance in Nepal, we will see more of it elsewhere.

A Bilateral Example

In the preceding chapter we introduced the Sarakatsani shepherds of northern Greece. Like other Europeans, the Sarakatsani practice bilateral rather than unilineal kinship. Their social organization, however, is based not on the nuclear family, but on the corporate kindred. Sarakatsani kindreds are basically large three-generation families stretched to include second cousins. Although these extended families are bilateral when it comes to descent, they are always extended patri-virilocally, that is, they consist of married brothers living together along with their in-marrying wives. In this way they resemble agnatic lineages in composition, at least in terms of local group residence. The Sarakatsani family pattern, incidentally, is not at all unusual in Greece but is in fact common in both rural and urban parts of the country, given the preference for patrilocal residence (Herzfeld 1985:52; Danforth 1989:98). Many Greeks other than Sarakatsani say that blood ties are "only through the father," and that blood is "transmitted by the father" (Danforth 1989:98). Michael Herzfeld remarks constantly upon the heavy emphasis on agnatic kinship and the territorial "patriline" throughout the islands (54).

The big kindreds are the backbone of the Sarakatsani society. Sarakatsani kinship also emphasizes a firm principle of patriarchal authority. They uphold fraternal solidarity above all other virtues, raising it to a religious ideal specifically sanctified by Christ; disunity among brothers is the worst thing in the world, a scourge of the devil, a sin that they say "goes against God" (Campbell 1964:350).

In this spiritually (if not genealogically) patrilineal context, the brothers therefore consider it not only a moral but also a religious duty, as well as a practical necessity, to stay together after the patriarch dies, thereby propagating the patriline in perpetuity, glorifying the ancestors, and honoring the father. The larger the family is, moreover, the safer, richer, and more honorable are its members. Sarakatsani kindreds are not a "descent group," being ego-based and transient, but from Campbell's description it seems that the Sarakatsani are following a nonexclusive patrilineal principle, combined with bilateral kinship reckoning for the purposes of defining an economic and a vengeance group.

Just as in tribal societies, the kindreds are exogamous: the men stay and the women marry in. Large families are called "companies" (*stani*), not only because they hold property in common, but because they function as the basic economic units. These companies are usually led by a respected autocrat, typically the elderly father or grandfather. Although the Sarakatsani are technically bilateral, nevertheless, as in patrilineal societies, they observe a rigid bias toward "agnatic affiliation" (Campbell 1964:41–43), favoring the father's side. Since the Sarakatsani are often involved in feuds with other kindreds, the agnatic principle comes to the fore especially during violent conflicts, when men rely mainly on their kinsmen for strategic support. Consequently, Campbell argues plausibly that the Sarakatsani, for all practical purposes, follow an agnatically based ideology, and that, with its "sentimental patriline," their society is indeed effectively patrilineal (43).

In addition to the constant blood feuding, the kindreds exist in complementary opposition to one another in other ways. As in segmentary tribal kinship, they are locked into a continuing relationship of rivalry for prestige and "honor" as well as for scarce resources (forage, markets, and cash). In short, the Sarakatsani people experience structural conditions breeding a spirit of intense and aggressive competitiveness and in this way strongly resemble the segmentary, exogamous model of agonistic patriliny that we have seen in many warlike tribal societies. The same sense of a beleaguered manliness prevails, as the men engage in violent feuds and distrust all strangers — all nonkin, that is. Sarakatsani men say that friendship is possible only between kinsmen and that all strangers are untrustworthy (Campbell 1964:101). All loyalty is confined to the kindred, especially agnates; empathy ends after second cousins, being replaced by suspicion. The wives, once again, derive from suspected and distrusted outsiders. The structural context is therefore similar in many ways to African, Melanesian, and Amazonian societies.

The degree and shape of misogyny are also similar. Many Sarakatsani men despise women as inferior, weak, amoral, and treacherous. Their misogyny centers on a semireligious condemnation of woman as the "devil's emissaries" (Campbell 1964:277), whose main purpose in life seems to be subversion of man's good works. From a structural viewpoint, it is significant that "good works" can be interpreted mainly as involving the men's efforts to maintain the integrity, continuity, and honor of the patriline.

First, women impede brotherhood by sowing the seeds of internecine disputes that disperse the kindred. As in Nepal, sisters-in-law tend to argue over the rights of their respective children. These female quarrels, Campbell points out (71–78), are inherent in the structure of the kindred since unrelated women marry into and henceforth live in crowded and uncomfortable quarters. Because of the overweening agnatic principle, these women have little interest in promoting the welfare of their coresident nieces and nephews. In fact, as Campbell writes: "The wives openly admit that they live in anticipation of the day when their husbands will separate the single household and each wife will become 'mistress' in her own home" (78). Thus, women in general are a severe test of brotherly love, a trial and tribulation to the men who are ostensibly trying to preserve and expand their kindreds.

Given this state of affairs, the women are always blamed when the family disintegrates, no matter what the cause. However, as in the case of the Nepalese Hindus, there is a degree of truth in the accusations of disruptiveness made about women: the women readily admit that dissolution of the kindred is desirable and that they go out of their way to stoke the furnace of fraternal enmity. Again, women are the necessary evil that these Greek shepherds, like their ancient forebears, have to endure. Unconsciously aware of this stark ambivalence, the Sarakatsani men like to repeat the proverb, "Women make the house and they destroy it" (Campbell 1964:71). Once again woman gets blamed for the failure of an ideal that is intrinsically unattainable.

Second, as among the Nepalese Hindus, women threaten the Sarakatsani kindred through their antisocial sexuality. The Sarakatsani men, who subscribe to the circum-Mediterranean moral system of "honor and shame" (Peristiany 1965; Schneider 1971), believe that woman's rampant sexual nature endangers the honor of the kindred. Men must guard against immodesty on the part of their women: any taint of indecency or licentiousness would dishonor the males and besmirch their honor in the eyes of the world. "Maidens must be virgins, and even married women must remain virginal in thought and expression" (Campbell 1964:270). Any breach of modesty is anathema for the kindred. Yet, the Sarakatsani, like some of the Middle Easterners we looked at earlier, believe that female sexuality is ungovernable and that woman's "nature" (her sexual attractiveness) leads to disaster. Even fully clothed and modestly comported, she is said to inflame the man. Even unintentionally, she "lures him to disaster without even a glance or a gesture" (Campbell 1964:277). Thus women are, by the very fact of their morphology, antithetical to male health and respectability because they are beautiful and sexually explosive. As a consequence, women are a menace to honor: they must be severely repressed and chastened lest they blow up the patriline (276–77).

Summarizing all these ethnographic data, Campbell seems to agree with Lamphere (1974) and Brain (1996) that certain forms of misogyny often can be traced directly to the patri-agnatic principle of social organization. Campbell himself does not speak of "misogyny" in this context, or pass any judgment on the abrasive gender relations he documents. But he does say:

> The male sex is held to be unambiguously superior not only in power but also in worth to the female, to which the stigma of original sin is closely attached. The female is a constant threat to the honour and integrity of the male and must be disciplined and dominated. In the absence of, therefore, a unilineal descent principle, it is reasonable to suppose that these attitudes and beliefs of the Sarakatsani concerning the relation of the sexes [that is, their intense misogyny] are *significantly connected with the preference for paternal kinsmen.* (57; emphasis added)

Implications

The idea that in many cases misogyny could derive from the very structure of society is distressing because it challenges attempts to palliate the problem by appealing to the moral sense. The above discussion highlights some of the intractable problems faced by those who try to change men's attitudes without also attacking deeper structural issues. In any case, no one knows how to "change" kinship structures anyway. Furthermore, as we have seen, misogyny also occurs in many matrilineal and cognatic societies, where the status of women is high. It occurs in certain clan-endogamous societies, such as the Bedouin of the Sinai desert (Stewart 1994). In southern Mexico, it occurs among many village-endogamous peasant peoples, many of whom are matrilineal.

Next we will focus on the upper stratum of European society, the intelligentsia, among whom other conditions and cultural ideals prevail. Unfortunately, we will see that, as Christine de Pizan observed half a millennium
ago, misogyny has no geographical frontiers, no structural limitations, and no
intellectual boundaries.

She's a woman, Sir, and consequently a Monster.

—William Wycherley, *The Country Wife*

6. The Western Imagination

MODERN WESTERN MISOGYNY differs from that in most preliterate societies because it often takes on deceptively sophisticated, even aesthetic expressions, unlike the biology-based, mystical beliefs we have seen in places like New Guinea. Often subtly reasoned, European misogyny places less stress on notions about magical pollution, bodily fluids, and witchcraft, and relies instead on "scientific" judgments about woman's inferiority. Given the richness of fantasy involved, the Western variant could be called a misogyny of the imagination.

Yet underlying the lofty pose, there lurks the same malice toward women and the same male disillusionment. In this chapter, we look at some misogynistic outpourings from Euro-American poets, novelists, philosophers, and social scientists. "In every society," says Karl Mannheim, "there are social groups whose special task is to provide an interpretation of the world for that society. We call these the 'intelligentsia' " (1964:10). What have our intelligentsia told us about women?

Words and the War on Women

Women-hating in the West begins with the ancient Greeks, whose earliest myths and poems include continual reference to depraved and vicious females. The Greeks were on their guard against the she-demons, enchantresses, Sirens, Harpies, lamias, Furies, and equally horrific, wicked stepmothers. The Greek poet Semonides (seventh century B.C.) has already been cited. Also common in Greek writings are women-induced calamities such as Pandora's box and the Trojan War. These ideas, the centerpiece of a cynical and disillusioned attitude that characterizes the Greek view of life in general (Lloyd-Jones 1975:28), find expression in the literature of the age. Linda Coole (1988:6) argues, for example, that even before Homer's time women were being ceaselessly depicted in oral poetry in the bad-wife mode, even among the gods. She points out that in Plato's *Republic,* woman is linked to bodily functions, to Earth and also to Death (14–15).

Roman writing alludes to the nagging, scheming wife, the shrewish, deceitful mistress, the grasping matron, and other pejorative stereotypes associated with contemporary male folklore (Coole 1993:6–7). A prime example is Juvenal's Sixth Satire, a polemic against marriage and "as virulent a diatribe against women as can be found" (Bloch 1991:72). But most Roman writers, including Ovid, Cato, and Virgil, routinely fulminate against feminine wiles and rail against women's scheming ways and fickleness, as in Virgil's gratuitous insult (*Aeneid* 4.659): "How fickle and capricious is woman." Such relentless carping conjures up what Bloch calls the "cosmic misogyny" of the classical world, a world that includes the terrible figures of the Furies, the Harpies, the Fates, but also domestic termagants and kitchen demons (1991:15).

In the Renaissance and early modern periods, authors continued the vilification of woman as the "dangerous sex" (Hays 1964). Even Shakespeare, although not normally associated with a crass misogyny, reflects contemporary thoughts in derogatory speeches in *Hamlet* and *King Lear.* As Harold Bloom points out (1998:491), Shakespeare shows an evident horror of female sexuality in several telling passages in the latter play: as when Edmund calls the womb "that dark and vicious place" (4.3.169–71), and the King reveals his revulsion at the "sulphurous pit," so full of contamination and bad smells. It must be said, of course, that it is hard to tell whether Shakespeare is expressing the views of his characters or his own. In *Cymbeline* ("Could I find out / The woman's part in me!") and in the gruesome figures of Lady Macbeth and the Three Witches, Shakespeare seems to regret that mankind has a female side to bedevil him. At various places in the tragedies, as Rogers persuasively argues (1966:119–20), the Bard seems to regret that, being born of woman, man retains a female element of influence within.

It seems that Shakespeare was, at best, somewhat ambivalent about woman's worth and sexuality. However, even a glimmer of tolerance is hard to find among most of his literary contemporaries. Ben Jonson, for instance, was much more overtly and contemptuously antiwoman. After all, Shakespeare gave us many sympathetic and even heroic female characters, such as the noble Portia in *Merchant of Venice* and the saintly Cordelia of *King Lear*. Often using scheming women to illustrate the vices of avarice, wrath, and deceitfulness, Jonson wrote many implacable tirades against women in both verse and prose, couching all in the conventional wisdom of the day. *Epicœne; or, The Silent Woman* (1609) is a collection of misogynistic charges: the subtitle is an indirect jibe at female garrulity; the male characters in the play denounce women frequently and in volcanic terms. Indeed, such violent misogynistic expostulations were a staple of Jacobean literature, especially drama, in an age when Christian dogma still blamed woman for original sin. In his acerbic comedy *Volpone* (1606), about a dying man about to be robbed by golddigging heirs, Jonson portrays women as more venal than men.

Elsewhere, Jacobean drama takes a dim view of females. In the tragedy *Bussy d'Ambois* (1604), George Chapman puts so many misogynistic speeches into the mouths of so many characters, both villains and heroes, that one can reasonably conclude that the diatribes express his own attitudes. Both sympathetic and unsympathetic characters in the play repeatedly denounce woman's deceit, her ungovernable passions, and her destructive power without any contradictory evidence, as though expressing truths so obvious that no further evidence were needed (Rogers 1966:121). For example, the character Monsieur, who has been betrayed by a woman, soliloquizes:

O the unsounded sea of woman's bloods,
That when 'tis calmest is most dangerous!
Not any wrinkle creaming in their faces,
When in their hearts are Scylla and Charybdis,
Which still are hid in dark and standing fogs,
Where never day shines, nothing ever grows,
But weeds and poisons that no statesman knows:
Not Cerberus ever saw the damned nooks
Hid with the veils of women's virtuous looks.

One particularly mordant example of Jacobean misogyny occurs in the work of another of Shakespeare's contemporaries, the louche playwright John Webster. In his grim plays *The White Devil* (1609) and *The Duchess of Malfi* (1612), Webster compares women with leprosy and gangrene; using grotesque images of decay, he warns against the pleasures afforded by female flesh, comparing the kiss of a beautiful woman to a "dead man's skull" (*Duchess of Malfi*, 3.4) and a woman's body to a "poisoned garden" and a "burial plot" (*White Devil*, 1.2). Like some of the premodern misogynists we examined (and like Chapman above), the morbid Webster identifies woman with physical and moral rot and introduces a series of revolting montages to get the message across: putrefying flesh, skeletons, dripping poison, skin-withering syphilis, and "monstrous desire" (Callaghan 1989:140). Although much of this invective specifically targets loose women and courtesans, the haranguing is so continuous that it attaches by degrees to all femininity. For Webster, women are "sweetmeats which rot the eater; in man's nostril / Poisoned perfumes: they are cozening alchemy" (cited in Rogers 1966:124).

The hero of *The White Devil* succinctly says, "Women are like curst dogs" (2.2). Vittoria, the white devil herself, confesses, "O my greatest sin lay in my blood" (5.6) — that is, her sex. The fact that Webster reviles woman in abstract terms as poisonous rather than in the crude biological idiom of men in New Guinea seems less noteworthy than the striking convergence of tropes and psychological associations, especially the linkage of woman with dirt, poison, decay, and death.

John Milton similarly included blatantly misogynistic rhetoric in *Paradise Lost*; at one point Adam asks why God created woman:

O! why did God,
Creator wise! that Peopl'd highest Heaven
With spirits masculine, create at last
This novelty on Earth, this fair defect
Of Nature? And not fill the World at once
With men, as Angels, without feminine?
(*Paradise Lost*, 10.881–89)

Milton's misogyny has been the subject of numerous critical studies, in particular Philip Gallagher's *Milton, the Bible, and Misogyny* (1987), which traces the poet's antifeminist ideas to early Christian antecedents. Like the patristic fathers of the Middle Ages, Milton continued to hold woman responsible for original sin.

In later centuries, the British, Irish, and American poets maintained a negative view. I have already mentioned the scatological visions of Swift, Yeats, and Pound. In Europe the French philosophes and essayists of the seventeenth century, such as Montaigne and La Rochefoucauld, expressed similar ideas in intellectualized rhetoric, as critic Ruth Abbey points out (1996). Their supercilious, pseudo-rational tone is more elevated than that of the British Swiftians but no less contemptuous. These French thinkers almost always depict woman as disruptive and self-centered, as immoral coquettes and fickle connivers who always stir up trouble and strife. "Women," sneers La Rochefoucauld, "are always somewhat averse to complete rectitude" (cited in Abbey

1966:251). The literary scholar Vivien Thweatt calls attention to the "rabid and inimitable anti-feminism" that mars La Rochefoucauld's work (1980:20), which she finds to be common currency in French writings of the period. Rabid, yes; inimitable, no.

Phaedra

A striking confirmation of Thweatt's indictment comes from Jean Racine's tragedy *Phèdre,* a classic of French theater. Based on ancient sources including works by Euripides and Seneca, Racine's version was first performed in Paris in 1677. This popular play integrates many of the separate misogynistic threads we have discussed and merits a brief digression.

In the play, the widowed king of Athens, Theseus, brings a new wife, Phaedra, from far-off Crete (the dark, mysterious home of the devouring Minotaur, slain earlier by Theseus). The beautiful Phaedra, who is actually half-sister of the Minotaur (structural alienation again), is the headstrong daughter of Minos, king of Crete, who, after death, was made one of the judges in the underworld. Her mother, Pasiphaë, loved a bull (Poseidon's punishment of Minos for not following directions) and gave birth to the half-bull, half-man Minotaur. Having grown up in such a dysfunctional family, it is hardly surprising that Phaedra falls madly in love with her stepson Hippolytus. Headstrong and impetuous, she declares her passion to the young man one day while Theseus is away at war and presumed dead. Outraged, the celibate and virtuous Hippolytus spurns her adulterous and incestuous advances.

The description of Phaedra's illicit passion echoes some key misogynistic motifs already described in other contexts; both Hippolytus and Phaedra constantly use such words as "pollution," "poison," and "contamination," to refer to her character and to her effect upon the kingdom's welfare (Ted Hughes's 1998 translation). Indeed, there is much in Racine's vocabulary and metaphoric style that is similar to the idiom of feminine *contamination* used by many preliterate peoples and some Jacobeans, like Webster.

Returning to *Phèdre*: the old king, after many foreign adventures, returns to Thebes at last. Arriving at his palace, Theseus is immediately confronted by Phaedra, who, to protect herself, accuses Hippolytus of rape. The blameless boy flees from his father's damnation, but is intercepted by the god Poseidon who, answering Theseus's supplication, sends a sea monster to kill the virtuous boy.

Eventually the king learns the awful truth from a loyal servant. Distraught,

Theseus realizes that not only is he responsible for the death of his only son, but his actions have endangered the commonweal of Athens by destroying its future ruler. With the death of Hippolytus, the king's patriline comes to an end. Tortured by unendurable guilt, Phaedra, the instigator of these calamities, poisons herself and dies. The old man is left to contemplate the ruins of his life.

This seventeenth-century tragedy clearly shows both the continuity of male attitudes and their power to fascinate audiences throughout the centuries. The character of Phaedra exemplifies not only the evil-stepmother motif but also that of the foreign in-marrying woman who treacherously destroys the patriline. From a moral-religious perspective, she also personifies corrupt female nature, which "poisons" and "pollutes" the otherwise orderly world of men. These familiar misogynistic themes are dramatically highlighted by the contrasting nobility of the men: King Theseus is high-minded and brave (if naive), and Hippolytus, who is wise and virtuous, suffers a tragic fate caused by a woman's misbehavior. Phaedra's only saving grace is that she recognizes and is horrified by her own innate wickedness. So repelled is she by her own behavior that she commits suicide (by poison).

It all adds up to the ageless paranoid delusion: *mulier venenata,* "poisonous woman," the lurking female always polluting the well. This image of woman as poison continues to haunt the minds of many modern-day literary misogynists in America and Europe, affecting men of every possible sexual orientation and attesting to a specific anxiety that transcends time, place, and sex. For example, in a recent memoir, Norman Podhoretz (1999) describes the misogynistic rhetoric of Beat Generation writers Allen Ginsberg, Jack Kerouac, and William S. Burroughs. The omnisexual Burroughs warned his bisexual friend, Ginsberg, to stay away from women. Podhoretz writes:

Knowing . . . that Allen, as a result of his yage [hallucinogenic] experiments, had decided he should be kinder to women, Bill would go off on long, wicked antiwoman routines, repeating his theory that women were extraterrestrial agents sent by enemies to weaken the male species. They had "poison juices dripping all over 'em," Burroughs said, and if Allen . . . knew what was good [for him, he] would stay away from women. (43–44)

Other Countries, Other Misogynies

Misogyny also finds expression in other forms of literature. Two centuries after Racine's *Phèdre,* and a century before Burroughs warned against female poisons, the Germans were developing their own brand of philosophical antifeminism. Teutonic misogyny has a highly metaphysical and sociological focus; its main proponents are the philosophers Arthur Schopenhauer and Friedrich Nietzsche, both of whom wrote frequently about the danger woman posed to society. Schopenhauer berated women at every turn, making them the villain in his starkly pessimistic view of humanity, reflecting a common masculine sense of disillusionment and betrayal.

A student of Schopenhauer, Nietzsche held a blistering contempt for women, especially in the book *Beyond Good and Evil* and in the essays "Human, All-Too-Human," "Ecce Homo," and "Daybreak." In these works, all written in the 1870s and 1880s, he never missed a chance to vilify the fair sex as weak, dependent, shallow, deceitful, frivolous, immoral, and stupid, even if this required a lengthy digression from his main point. He was especially critical of woman's supposed duplicity, claiming that the only "art" she can produce is "the lie" (1969:519). Woman, he laments, is constitutionally incapable of honesty, truth, or rectitude.

Nietzsche's view of women took on political overtones. He believed that women, like the mass of inferior men, should be excluded from politics because of their moral and intellectual defects. His worst jibe is to compare them with his other pet peeve, his fellow Germans, with whom, he believed, they share a hopeless shallowness: "You can scarcely ever fathom their depths — they haven't any" (1967:322). Over the years, Nietzsche has been described in increasingly critical terms as "showing prejudice about women" (Kaufmann 1950:63), full of "misogyny and sexual disgust" (Shklar 1984:viii), and an "unabashed misogynist" (Detwiler 1990:15).

The tradition of what might be called Nordic misogyny took on new, melodramatic form in the work of expressionistic German playwright Frank Wedekind (1864–1918). In a series of gloomy dramas, the "Lulu plays," Wedekind breathes new life into the familiar figure of the malevolent, man-devouring femme fatale. The arch-criminal, Lulu, is the apotheosis of feminine depravity, luring men to their doom and relishing the results. She is a supreme example of the dangerous sex portrayed in twentieth-century incarnation, not as a witch or demon but as a serial murderess and master criminal. Emphasizing Lulu's femininity as the source of her perversity and making her a warning against Everywoman, these misogynistic plays had a powerful appeal to contemporary audiences. Lulu and her experiences were resurrected in an eponymous opera composed by Anton Berg.

In the same melodramatic tradition, one might cite early twentieth-century films, some of which focus on vicious females. Examples are *A Fool There Was* (1915), by English director Frank Powell, and two German films, *The Blue*

Angel (1930) and *The Devil Is a Woman* (1935), both directed by Joseph von Sternberg. Each centers on a heartless femme fatale who, like Wedekind's Lulu, lures innocent men to destruction. In the silent thriller *A Fool There Was,* Theda Bara appears as a depraved temptress, identified only as "the Vampire woman," who entices a young man into her clutches. As the story unfolds, the Vampire woman effectively strips her victim of judgment, restraint, dignity, finances, and friends. Soon, however (being fickle, of course), she abandons him for a new beau. Distraught and alone, a pitiful shadow of his former self, the hero stumbles about drunkenly in his town house, abandoned and despised even by his once obsequious servants.

Another popular celluloid vamp, Marlene Dietrich, established her fame in *The Blue Angel,* a tragedy in which Dietrich uses her powerful sex appeal to destroy a once-respectable professor, twisting him into a whimpering degenerate. The alluring Dietrich continues her abominable depredations in *The Devil Is a Woman* with much the same outcome. The title says it all.

This theme of devilish womanhood had powerful political repercussions between the wars in Germany. In an absorbing study of nascent fascism in interwar Germany, Uli Linke (1997) sees the image of the soul-destroying vamp reappearing in a particularly vile form in militaristic right-wing propaganda. Railing against the internal enemies of postwar Germany, early Nazi and Freikorps propaganda is characterized by an abundance of "dissolution" or "liquid" imagery showing the dangers posed by femininity to "hard" upright males who turn to jelly when subjected to feminine wiles. An enemy of the manly Reich, Woman represents voluptuousness, softness, immoral weakness; she is the Pied Piper of degeneracy, turning men into mewling, cringing cowards. Seduced by women, the demoralized, transformed weaklings are easily manipulated by Jews, communists, or foreign enemies.

Exploring this imagery of female "overflowing" and "swamping," Linke shows how Nazi propaganda in the 1930s used the image of yielding female flesh as a metaphor for national spinelessness and lack of self-discipline, for "Jewish" betrayal — for the enemy within. In the propagandistic material, images of a corrupt "soft, wet" femininity got scrambled with those of Jews, Reds, and internationalists — all potential traitors eager to seduce and weaken the Germans: "the soft and liquid female body, a quintessential negative other, lurking inside the male body," a subversive source of contagion that had to be expunged or sealed off (Linke 1997:568). The analogies to the magical misogyny of preliterate peoples with its fear of contagion and magical liquids are pronounced.

The curious emphasis on deliquescent imagery, on liquidity and melting, is reminiscent of other misogynies as well. The Nazi male had to fight this treacherous feminine "flood" lurking within the nation's soul. The propaganda of the time portrays him as a stalwart hero shoring up a dam against the surging waters of immorality and defeatism. The symbolic construction of the dangerous female other, and her eventual obliteration, served as a mechanism of self-cohesion for the endangered Reich. Threatened by imaginary floods, torrents, and raging waters, the men stood firm "against these onslaughts of surging womanhood" (Linke 1997:563). The linkage between femininity and political decadence was originally pointed out by critic Klaus Theweleit (1987) in his compelling study of political masculinism among the proto-Nazi Freikorps in Weimar Germany.

In Britain the theme of the death-dealing, soul-destroying woman appears not so much in such political nonsense as in soulful romantic poetry. In this context the culprit is not the woman-Jew, but the cruel and beautiful bitch-goddess, from whom the male victim cannot escape and who drags him down to despair. This motif, focusing on erotic frustration instead of politics, animates Keats's lyric poem "La Belle Dame Sans Merci," which describes a typical callow youth wasting away under the spell of an implacable siren. A similar theme is found in the oft-used Lady of the Lake myth common in British fantasy fiction, featuring an enchanting nymph who drags men down to a watery grave — (water once again).

The Victorian poet Algernon Charles Swinburne, who wrote musical, often erotic verse in which he attacked the conventions of Victorian morality, also wrote about "soul-destroying women" who suck the life from their male victims (Dijkstra 1986:235). The theme of suffocation or captivation by malevolent women forms the core of Somerset Maugham's novel *Of Human Bondage* (1915) in which the shy, club-footed hero is callously taken for all he is worth by a heartless vixen. D. H. Lawrence writes about men trying to find "a refuge from powerful women" who would use them, suffocate them, and spitefully destroy them (Nixon 1986:9).

Perhaps the classic woman-hater among European fiction writers, however, is the Swedish dramatist August Strindberg. Strindberg's play *The Father* is essentially a screed against the destructiveness of women and their exploitation of men. The entire action is a prolonged fantasy of conspiracy and symbolic castration in which the Captain's wife and daughter gang up to rob him of his dignity, his money, and finally his life. In this play and others, such as *Dance of Death* and *Miss Julie,* Strindberg shows an almost pathological hatred of women. But as Hays puts it, Strindberg's hatred is only a "caricature" of the most prevalent nineteenth-century male attitude (1964:256).

Social Science Misogyny

All this artistic misogyny fits in with nineteenth-century "scientific" denunciation of women that the criminologist Cesare Lombroso expressed as a "latent base of immorality that is found in every woman" (cited in Harrowitz 1994:31). Social and political scientists of the day believed that this latent badness inclined women toward atavistic perversity and criminality, endangering male ideals. In his works on social evolution, for example, Herbert Spencer, the founding father of social Darwinism, speaks of woman as having a lower level of development than man; he seriously proposes that there is an "earlier arrest of individual evolution in woman than in man" (cited in Kestner 1989:8).

The theme of woman's intellectual as well as moral inferiority finds expression throughout the nineteenth century under the guise of sociological study. Woman has a "smaller brain" and she is nothing more than an "intellectual cipher" compared to man, according to George J. Romanes, in his popular scientific paper (1887) "Mental Differences Between Men and Women" (cited in Kestner 1989:7–8). William J. Fielding, author of numerous and highly influential books on sex, published a pamphlet on "Woman: The Eternal Primitive," in which he speaks confidently of the "primitive feminine mind" (cited in Dijkstra 1996:4). Kestner cites voluminous evidence to show that this was a majority view in the formative sociology of the late Victorian period.

Sociological misogyny perhaps reaches its apex in the semihysterical work of Otto Weininger, who, before his obsessions drove him to suicide at age twenty-three, wrote an influential book about the dangerous female, *Sex and Character* (1903). In this prolonged tirade, Weininger denounced woman as a "social parasite" who must be repressed for the good of the race (102). Rather than being dismissed as a crank, Weininger won many adherents, especially among anti-Semitic propagandists.

Even the respected French sociologist Emile Durkheim, founder of modern social science, was not immune to the misogynist virus. In his influential book *The Division of Labor in Society* (1893), Durkheim writes: "The volume of the crania of man and woman, even when we compare subjects of equal age, of equal height and equal weight, show considerable differences in favor of the man, and this inequality grows proportionately with civilization, so that from the point of view of the mass of the brain, and correspondingly of intelligence, woman tends more and more to be differentiated from the male sex" (1933:56).

The cultural anthropologists of the period expressed similar suspicions about women. For example, Johann J. Bachofen, a German anthropologist, supported the commonly held idea that females were not only inferior to males intellectually, but lower on the evolutionary scale, less spiritual and more materialistic. In *Das Mutterrecht* Bachofen writes: "The realm of the idea belongs to the man, the realm of material existence to the woman" (1861:150). Proposing that social evolution progresses toward civilization through sequential stages, including an earlier matriarchy and a later, more advanced patriarchy, Bachofen contended that woman was an atavism: humankind's moral and intellectual progress cannot proceed until "patriarchy" is established and "matriarchy" overthrown. Like the novelists and artists we have looked at, Bachofen believed that women represented a real danger to contemporary civilization and had to be repressed for the good of all humankind. The pseudo-history in this book simply repeats the myth of matriarchy popular among preliterate peoples in scientific jargon. There is virtually no substantive difference between the mythology of the Melanesians and the Amazonians and Bachofen's anthropology.

Other anthropologists continued to champion such views throughout the nineteenth century. For example, Scottish John McLennan, author of *Primitive Marriage* (1865) and *Studies in Ancient History* (1876) and coiner of the terms endogamy and exogamy, held that women were "less useful to society" than men were. John Lubbock, in *Prehistoric Times* (1865), wrote that women were weak and dependent and contributed little to civilization. In a book published in 1864, the jurist and amateur anthropologist Carl Vogt claimed that "woman is a constantly growing child, and in the brain, as in so many other parts of the body, she conforms to her childish type" (1864:31). Vogt concluded that since woman's brain was smaller than man's, she must be intellectually inferior, similar to the lower primates. Even Charles Darwin was not above this sort of thing. In *The Descent of Man* (1871) he speaks often of woman as representing a past and lower state of civilization.

So woman is depicted by the world's most benighted and most enlightened as inferior, less evolved, and more bestial than man, an anomaly and a danger to civilization. For many fin-de-siècle thinkers, not only does woman represent an atavistic residue, an evolutionary laggard within the human race, but her physical allure exerts a regressive pull on man. Bram Dijkstra writes in his study of misogyny in late Victorian painting: "Thus, woman became a nightmare emanation from man's distant pre-evolutionary past, ready at any moment to use the animal attraction of her physical beauty to waylay the late-nineteenth-century male in his quest for spiritual perfection" (1986:240).

Jungle Queens and Serpents

The theme of the evil seductress luring man into the primitive past finds rich expression in late nineteenth-century English adventure novels, especially those involving explorers on the Dark Continent. In this genre, authors inter-twine those dual Victorian icons of primitivism — woman and darkest Africa — into flamboyant images of female perversity. Such hybrid tropes flourish pro-fusely in novels like Joseph Conrad's *Heart of Darkness* (1902), H. Rider Haggard's *She* (1887), and various "Tarzan" works by Edgar Rice Burroughs. In these fantasies African women are used as metaphors for bestiality, licen-tiousness, and regression. For example, Conrad's powerful novella, which is about civilized man's descent into chaos and savagery in the colonial Congo, conjures up the spectacular vision of a savage native woman, the embodiment of the call of the wild. His vivid description is worth quoting in full:

> She walked with measured steps, draped in striped and fringed cloths, treading the earth proudly, with a light jingle and flash of barbarous ornaments. She carried her head high; her hair was done in the shape of a helmet; she had brass leggings to the knees, brass wire gauntlets to the elbow . . . bizarre things, charms, gifts of witch-men, that hung about her, glittered and trembled at every step. . . . She was savage and superb, wild-eyed and magnificent; there was something ominous and stately in her deliberate progress. And in the hush that had fallen suddenly upon the whole sorrowful land, the immense wilderness, the colossal body of the fecund and mysterious life seemed to look at her, pensive, as though it had been looking at the image of its own tenebrous and passionate soul. (Conrad 1983: 100–101)

In this vision, woman and brute nature are one. The barbaric Black Woman is the symbol of Africa, which is in turn the embodiment of the overripe rendered throughout in the idiom of pathetic fallacy.

The Jungle Queen extends her arms invitingly to the narrator, Marlowe, inviting him to join her in celebration of the lustful animality of the jungle. Distantly glimpsed amidst rotting vegetation, the archetypal siren represents all that is eerie, uncanny, atavistic: that which is beyond understanding, the Dark Continent itself, unknown rites, the occult, tropical fecundity, cannibalism, savagery. As Marianna Torgovnick says, the circularity between the concepts "female" and "primitive" is so complete in Conrad's work "that it is difficult to tell which set of tropes influenced which" (1990:156).

H. Rider Haggard in his fantasy novel *She* also creates an African totem-queen to symbolize the sinuous, sinister forces of nature. (Both Freud and Jung thought the two-thousand-year-old heroine perfectly epitomized the feminine impulse in nature [Dijkstra 1996:95].) The nameless goddess is referred to symbolically as "She Who Must Be Obeyed," thus implying a tyrannical feminine archetype reminiscent of primitive matriarchy myths and Bachovenian anthropology. With reptilian imagery predominating, "She" is presented as something between human and animal. The majestic "She" is a tall, beautiful woman, but, as the narrator says, "with a certain snake-like grace." She is described as not only resembling a serpent but moving like one: "When she moved a hand or foot her entire frame seemed to undulate, and the neck did not bend, it curved" (Haggard 1976:149). No longer is Eve seduced by a snake; Eve *is* a snake.

Later the bemused narrator ruminates about this snake-woman's influence over him: "This woman had confounded and almost destroyed my moral sense, as indeed she must confound all who looked upon her superhuman loveliness" (239). It is not enough that she terrifies and fascinates him; the snake-woman also debases his moral sense and clouds his reason. The critic Nina Auerbach (1982) calls this serpent-woman theme one of the defining icons of the Victorian male imagination (1982:8–9). In fact it can be traced to the Medusa of the ancient Greeks, the she-demon with vipers for hair, whom Freud saw as the archetype of the dangerous, poisonous female. Torgovnick notes the enduring linkage of primitive animality with female throughout the history of the Western tradition. "What struck me most in this material," she writes (1990:17), "was the way the gender issues always inhabit Western versions of the primitive. Sooner or later those familiar tropes for primitives become the tropes conventionally used for women."

Victorian Painting

Even the medium of painting reflects these misogynistic motifs. In *Mythology and Misogyny* (1989), the art critic Joseph Kestner surveys misogynistic Greek and Roman themes in British classical-subject painting of the Victorian period. Both Kestner and Dijkstra find a remarkable continuity between the pictorial arts and the written word in the expression of antiwoman sentiments in fin-de-siècle Europe. Dijkstra calls Victorian theme painting the "iconography of the battle of the sexes" (1986:217). He provides a wealth of evidence to show how the same misogynistic fantasies that enliven the otherwise dry scientific texts of the day appeared in living color in period art. Victorian art gave dramatic shape to male prejudices about woman's iniquity and degradation. Dijkstra analyzes literally hundreds of paintings, posters, and sketches on classical themes, fairy-land romances, surreal and dream landscapes, and even mundane domestic scenes rendered with symbolic import. In these classically based paintings of cavorting fauns and nymphs, he shows, the male figures are always represented as half beasts: Pan figures, centaurs, satyrs, and so on. Beguiling, voluptuous, and irresistible — the women in the pictures, however, are always perfectly formed human figures shown in provocative poses.

Observing that the mythic males are always presented as being enthralled or entrapped by these gamboling voluptuaries, Dijkstra argues that the underlying motif here is the idea that women by nature are lascivious and with their blandishments turn men into beasts. It is the "viraginous bacchantes" (the women) who cause the men to become satyrs — another variation on Circe. Given the artists' use of the female to represent temptation, their moral vision resembles that of a medieval St. Anthony or St. Jerome; women had become the personification of the sins of the flesh (Dijkstra 1986:221, 253).

Another turn-of-the-century painting genre depicts a heroic male either being dragged down into the depths of the sea by a mermaid or stalked by a demonic temptress whose goal is to strip the hero of his manly virtue. A classic example is the breathtaking canvas by the Pre-Raphaelite Edward Burne-Jones, *The Depths of the Sea* (1886). A haunting, dreamlike scene taking place entirely under water, the painting shows a voluptuous fish-woman dragging a naked youth to the ocean bottom. Around her sensual lips there plays a triumphant, lascivious smile, really a smirk, as she stares brazenly at the viewer; she seems blissfully unaware that the handsome young man in her grasp has already drowned.

Given the Victorian concern for sin and for spirituality, homiletic metaphors of the age depicted human life as a battle between the higher and lower elements. In fantasy painting, as in the poetry and social science of the period, man is higher and woman lower. Depictions of women are symbolically fixated on her physical beauty as a falseness, a trap, that tricks men into lowering themselves. In this way, Victorian visual art duplicates contemporary "scientific" attitudes toward woman's lower place in evolution, her moral inferiority, and, most important, the danger she poses to masculine spirituality. The anxieties evoked by this imagery duplicate those found in early Christianity, Buddhism, Islam, classical antiquity, and all the other times and places we have mentioned.

Kestner sees much the same misogynistic impulse in nineteenth-century British classical-subject painting. Especially common is the use of woman as a pictorial metaphor for depravity and licentiousness. Kestner also sees symptoms of what he calls "gynophobia," man's fear of the female body as a deadly lure, which he regards as a continuation and a reaffirmation of the negative attitudes toward women found in classical antiquity. In British mythological painting, women are again depicted as sirens and sorceresses, driving men to vice. As in the classical antecedents, women are shown as deceiving, licentious, dependent, and atavistic. Kestner concludes:

Nineteenth-century classical-subject painting depicted women in mythological situations to universalize masculine attitudes prevalent in the culture's misogyny and gynophobia. . . . The pictorial ideograms of the classical-subject artists, an associational amalgam of gynophobia, misogyny, and anxiety, conveyed a persistent ideology about women. (1989:63,355)

Iconographic use of the female to represent disorder and destruction, as well as sexual depravity, did not originate with the Victorians. For example, in northern Renaissance painting, such as that of Hieronymous Bosch, the female was often used to symbolize violence and chaos. One frightening example is Bruegel's *Dulle Griet* (1562), which depicts the Spanish occupation of his native Netherlands. The centerpiece of this terrifying picture is a huge-armed unseeing woman, Mad Meg, the artist's emblem of devastation, disorder, brutality, and death.

Divers in Deep Seas

Negative attitudes about women are also found in the work of the contemporary art critics and belletrists, whose writings both reflected and shaped public opinion. For example, John Ruskin in *Munera Pulveris* (1885) takes the moral measure of woman, comparing her to falseness itself, to "the deceitfulness of riches." He cautions about the "deadly Sirens" and enchantresses allied with the "great enemy" (Satan), who, representing "pure animal life," lure men away from higher things (cited in Kestner 1989:28).

Ruskin's contemporary, the essayist and aesthete Walter Pater, gives us an eloquent, if unsettling, rhapsody on the *Mona Lisa* in his disquisition *The Renaissance* (1873). For Pater, as for many others, da Vinci's mysterious portrait represents the Eternal Feminine, with preternatural ties to the unknown in nature and the ocean's murky depths. In a particularly revealing passage, Pater stresses the unworldly and sinister aspects of the *Mona Lisa*:

> The presence that rose thus so strangely beside the waters is expressive of what in the ways of a thousand years men had come to desire. . . . It is a beauty wrought out from within upon the flesh, the deposit, little cell by cell of strange thoughts and fantastic reveries and exquisite passions. . . . All the thoughts and experience of the world have etched and moulded there, in that which the soul with all its maladies has passed . . . the animalism of Greece, the lust of Rome. . . . She is older than the rocks among which she sits; like the vampire, she has been dead many times, and learned the secrets of the grave; and has been a diver in deep seas. . . . Certain Lady Lisa might stand as the embodiment of the old fancy, the symbol of the modern idea. (1986:150)

The modern idea she embodies is the same one we have seen among the ancients: woman the vampire, siren, changeful, protean, diver in unknown seas where no man can live. She exemplifies animal life itself, the unknown, frightful surmises, Freud's "uncanny," all that man most desires and fears.

Two Accidental Misogynists

Misogyny blossomed in the late Victorian imagination, inspiring luxuriant growths. So pervasive was the antiwoman hysteria during the later nineteenth century that some enlightened men unintentionally reflected the overwhelming prejudices of their age. We might call these accidental misogynists, since their uncharitable feelings were spontaneous and would have been denied by them as unworthy if brought to their attention. By looking at these cases, we may learn something about the causes of the male malady, especially among the European intellectual elite.

Two cases I would like to consider are Sigmund Freud, the founder of psychoanalysis, and Johannes Brahms, the greatest composer of the later part of the century. Judging by what we know now about them from contemporary accounts, both of these greats were unsurpassed geniuses in their fields; in their personal lives, both were gentle, ethical, kind, tolerant, and notably free of the ethnic and racial prejudices that swirled around them. By all historical accounts, both men maintained enduring and mutually rewarding relationships with women — in Freud's case, with his wife of fifty years, Martha Bernays; in the case of Brahms, with Robert Schumann's widow, Clara, a friendship which probably remained platonic. Nevertheless, both men were dyed-in-the-wool misogynists who said and wrote terrible (and embarrassing) things on numerous occasions — Freud in his scientific work and Brahms in public asides and in letters. In particular, both expressed vitriolic contempt for what they saw as women's deficiencies in morality and intellect.

Freud's misogyny is recognized by feminist writers and is the subject of heated debate in academic psychology (see Chodorow 1994 for a review). Here I want to stick to a few indisputable and overt references Freud made to the inferiority of women rather than get lost in the complexity of his theories. His low opinion of women comes across in no uncertain terms in two sets of published observations. The first is the phallocentric argument about penis envy. Freud famously declared that women envy the male organ because it is somehow better than the female genitals. Women are not mistaken in having low self-esteem and a somewhat masochistic life orientation since they are equivalent to defective ("castrated") men. But the second observation is perhaps more condemnatory: Freud's claim that women's sense of morality is less developed than men's, that women are innately less ethical, more narcissistic. This idea finds unmistakable expression in *Civilization and Its Discontents,* where Freud actually says that women are "hostile" to civilization (1931:51).

Freud's argument is that the source of the moral sense is the superego, or conscience, which comes into existence with the onset of the Oedipus complex, that is, the child's sexual desire for the opposite-sex parent and wish to eliminate the same-sex parent. Men's Oedipus complex is much more traumatic than women's because only men can experience the terror of castration anxiety. Ipso facto, men's superego is more highly developed than women's; consequently men are capable of much deeper and higher scruples than are women, who remain mired in shallowness and hedonism. A corollary view is that, in terms of culture and civilization, men are progressive and creative, women are regressive, infantile, and chaotic. In Freud's words, originally written in 1931:

Furthermore, women soon come into opposition to civilization and display their retarding and restraining influence. . . . The work of civilization has become increasingly the business of men, it confronts them with ever more difficult tasks and compels them to carry out instinctual sublimations of which women are little capable. Since a man does not have unlimited quantities of psychical energy at his disposal, he has to accomplish his tasks by making an expedient distribution of his libido. What he employs for cultural aims, he to a great extent withdraws from women and sexual life. His constant association with men, and his dependence on his relations with them, even estrange him from his duties as a husband and father. Thus the woman finds herself forced into the background by the claims of civilization and she adopts a hostile attitude towards it. (50–51)

In his vision of female intellectual inferiority, Freud comes very close to the kind of cosmic misogyny that includes the moralistic elements and that we have seen before: he sees women as an atavistic or entropic force that seeks to drag men down. Freud sees woman in advanced civilizations as not only alienated from, but also hostile toward order and progress. He again places woman in the role of the treacherous, backward Eve who threatens collapse of (masculine) civilization. Such ideas certainly place Freud within the mainstream of the misogynistic culture expressed in the art and literature of the time. The images of the snake-woman and the enchantress are merely replaced by a feminized id.

An enlightened liberal, Freud would have been appalled by the charge that his thoughts undeniably resembled the cramped theology of the Middle Ages. Still, Freud supported many women in psychoanalytical careers, and formed close supportive ties to many female disciples. In his study of misogyny in Freud, Samuel Slipp (1993) argues that this ambivalence about women's worth was the central problem stemming from Freud's unresolved Oedipal fixations. Slipp suggests that Freud warded off his incestuous longings for his own mother through a distancing and a denigration of the female, thus becoming a prime example of his own theory about "the degradation of the love principle." As far as it goes, this is no doubt true, but Freud's obsession with woman's inferiority seems to include a suprasexual dimension in which females become synonymous, as in Schopenhauer and Nietzsche, with all the regressive forces that challenge man's intellectual progress, such as narcissism, frivolity and shallowness.

The musical genius Johannes Brahms presents another psychological problem: that of blocked libido. Unlike Freud, Brahms never married and was apparently unable to sustain a sexual liaison with a woman of his class, resorting to anonymous prostitutes instead. His music shows absolutely no trace of antiwoman sentiment. Brahms never wrote an opera and he scorned the fashionable "program music" of the time, so he left no scripted allusions to female villainy. There is nothing in Brahms to compare with the evil Kundry of Wagner's *Parsifal* or the dissipated Venus in *Tannhäuser*. Yet, within this blank screen of pure melody lies the conundrum.

One might say that Brahms's music qua music actually suggests the nonverbal contrary of misogyny. His sensuous scores may be said to show a ten-

dency toward empathy with the feminine. Sweet and caressing, Brahms's ro
mantic compositions seem almost to show that he was not averse to exploring
the tender possibilities that music was capable of, revealing an emotive gener-
osity that some men of his age might have considered feminine. I refer to the
sentimental, occasionally lachrymose quality of Brahms's later compositions,
especially the intimate chamber music.

Although the issue is really one of taste, Brahms's lyrical pathos suggests
to some musicologists an almost maternal sensibility; this quality is pronounced especially in the violin and clarinet sonatas and the horn trio, as well
as in the brooding Alto Rhapsody. There is definitely a melting, sighing quality
in these intimate works that, if not "feminine," certainly seems languidly intro-
spective and tender, qualities the age identified as feminine. Contemporary
critics, for example, spoke of the "sighing quality" of Brahms's late sonatas,
especially those written for "Fräulein klarinette" (Swafford 1997:573). The
famous *Brahms Lullaby* epitomizes this caressing, almost maternal, sweetness
even more openly.

Yet, despite all this, Brahms was capable of very nasty insults to women.
His notebooks, discovered after his death, contain many caustic misogynistic
entries: women are "shallow and senseless," given over to coquetry; even a
good woman is a "treacherous harlot, without her even being aware of it"; a
woman is worthy "only of disdain and ridicule"; her mind is "something un-
palatable to anyone with the least appetite for thought" (Swafford 1997:121).
And Brahms carefully underlined, apparently with approval, passages in his
copy of the Qur'an that chastened and condemned women. At the end of his life,
while attending a dinner in his honor, an inebriated Brahms branded all women
"with a word so shocking that it broke up the occasion and nobody would
repeat it" (547). Brahms's friends and admirers tried to excuse these outbursts
as a reflection of the prevailing Viennese culture, but most of them admitted
that Brahms's case of misogyny was, even so, a "virulent" one, surpassing the
norm, that there was something wrong with the great man on this point (430).

All this is surprising because it is so much at odds with Brahms's otherwise tolerant personality. Tolerant and liberal, Brahms rejected all forms of the
fashionable anti-Semitism of German-speaking Europe at this time. He said
once publicly that "anti-Semitism is madness" (Swafford 1997:599). In fact his
utter disdain for ethnic bigotry and his close association with many Jewish
musicians earned him the ire of anti-Semites like the Wagnerians, who tried
to portray him as a Jew-lover or, on at least one occasion, as being Jewish
himself (505).

Adding to the contradiction, Brahms idolized some exceptional women, such as Clara Schumann and, later in life, the amateur musician Elisabet (Lisl) von Herzogenberg. And he courageously championed the careers of many talented female performers at a time when women musicians were often disdained because of their sex, defending many against the very same misogyny he himself spouted. For instance, at the end of a spirited performance of his own violin concerto in 1885, he vaulted from his balcony seat and panegyrized the female soloist, Marie Soldat, making a pun on her name: "Isn't the little soldier a hell of a fellow? Couldn't she hold her own with ten men? Who could do it better?" (504).

Jan Swafford's interpretation of this curious anomaly in Brahms's personality takes a psychological bent. He claims that when Brahms was a vulnerable lad, his father forced him to play the piano all night (for money) in the tawdry whorehouses bordering the Bremen waterfront. From Brahms's cryptic statements in later life, it appears that he was sexually abused by the prostitutes and forced to watch unspeakable and disgusting things. Traumatized by this premature exposure to sexual perversion, he subsequently associated sex with filth and fell into a defensive posture as an adult by refusing relations with any "decent" woman, never marrying, and being able to function only with "dirty" prostitutes.

There may be some truth to this. Brahms himself answered, when asked about why he never married, that he had "some ground left to be a little frightened by the fair sex" (Swafford 1997:413). We will never know the source of Brahms's fretful feelings, but they do reflect an extreme example of the typical Victorian "good girl, bad girl" dualism. The key to both Freud's and Brahms's accidental misogyny is apparently an intense and a heightened ambivalence about their own fantasies about women, an ambivalence based on an inner conflict about their own needs, both Oedipal and pre-Oedipal, both sexual and nonsexual dependency needs, and a fixation on their long-dead mothers as suppliers of such polymorphous needs.

What this comparison shows is that the misogyny of even great men includes different emotional fixations, and cannot be reduced to any single psychological cause, nor to sexual frustration alone. Freud represents the kind of philosophical or existential misogyny, in which woman is blamed for the inevitable failure of masculine ideals, that we have seen among the ancient Greeks, the Sarakatsani, the Nepalese, pessimistic German philosophers like Nietzsche, and so many others. Even for men with a satisfactory sex life (as Freud apparently had), women is the scapegoat who gets blamed for life's many disappointments and certainly for the imperfections of human nature, especially shallowness and narcissism. This is typically a response of misplaced negativism that may derive from the disillusioned man's own narcissistic injuries, especially the desecration of his childhood dream of the perfect mother, a self-sacrificing, nurturing caretaker who gives food and nonsexual love in equal measure — a scenario which may have been relevant, as Slipp argues implicitly, in the case of Freud, who was always fulminating in his works on femininity about woman's inherent narcissism; that is, her hermetic self-involvement and her consequent turning away from, or lack of response to, male needs. On the other hand, Brahms's distrust and fear of women seems to have its origin in early sexual dysfunction and erotic frustration. Men of their times and men for all times, Freud and Brahms exemplify the complexity of the male malady, each in his own way.

Now we shift gears and make a broader comparison. What common elements unite such diverse misogynists as the New Guinea highlanders, Amazonian aborigines, Jacobean dramatists, Greek shepherds, Johannes Brahms, and Sigmund Freud? We consider this question in the next chapter.

If all the harm that women have done

Were put in a bundle and rolled into one,

Earth would not hold it,

The sky could not enfold it,

It could not be lighted nor warmed by the sun.

Such masses of evil

Would puzzle the devil

And keep him in fuel while Time's wheels run.

                —J. K. Stephen, *A Thought*

7. Commonalities

NOW THAT WE HAVE LOOKED at the "masses of evil" attributed by men to women, from polluting tribesmen in New Guinea to scaring Johannes Brahms out of his wits, the time has come to put the various images and fantasies of woman-hating into some sort of logical framework. Then we can perhaps identify the common denominators. The point of this exercise is, first, to show that misogyny is not monolithic but is comprised of numerous beliefs, fears, and misconceptions, all having something in common. Second, by teasing out the various emotive ingredients that constitute misogyny as a generalized feeling-tone, we can identify unifying threads and motives in the men's behavior and mental states. After this, we review the major theories proposed to explain the phenomenon of woman-hating.

We begin by noting that woman-bashing, like many other moral systems, produces a formal dualism. On one hand there is a body-oriented misogyny (e.g., the Melanesian-Amazonian variant) that obsessively focuses on corporeal functions, physicality, sex, and the senses. This variant shows a preoccupation with woman's reproductive biology: vaginal exuviae, glandular cycles, breast milk, genital morphology. On the other hand, there is a spiritual-intellectual misogyny, which is not necessarily sexual in focus, and which attacks woman for her supposed willful destructiveness, for subverting God's will, and for corrupting boys and men and dragging them backward (e.g., the Buddhist, Muslim, and Western aesthetic variants). This more sophisticated kind of misogyny, although equally obsessive, is less concerned with magical dangers than with moral impurity.

A further distinction involves the scope and breadth of the male anxieties revealed by misogynistic discourse wherever it occurs. Some men fear the influence of woman over their bodies or minds, others her ruinous impact on their immortal souls. Still others have elevated their obsession into an apocalyptic fear not for their own persons but for civilization itself. When misogynistic fears are obsessively organic, they tend toward the fetishistic and the symbolico-magical focusing on menstrual blood or the minacious vagina itself; in other instances these fears lack a somatic correlative and resemble a generalized anxiety disorder with distinctively paranoid elements. In the carnal variant of misogyny, the most compelling ingredient is a hysterical terror of female fluids, which take on a metaphorical life of their own as a morbid fetish.

Some observers have explained the obsessional organic fetishism, specifically of vaginal *blood*, from a Freudian standpoint as castration anxiety, the blood representing the flow from the cut penis. This does help explain the universality of menstrual taboos, since both misogyny and such taboos appear with isomorphic frequency. However, as should be clear by now, like most anthropologists I think castration anxiety by itself is a necessary but not sufficient explanation. Logically, there must be some other variable at work, since the preoccupation with menstrual blood varies greatly from the mild "aesthetic and hygienic" distaste among modern Europeans (Freud 1931:46) to the hysteria of many New Guinea and Amazonian peoples. It is possible, of course, that the difference is based on the level of scientific knowledge in the society (modern Europeans have also been more concerned about woman's supposed mental and moral deficiencies than some preliterate peoples). Given these pronounced quantitative variations, there must be some other, parallel, factor at work, aside from castration fear; for logically, a *variable* (the strength of menstrual taboos) cannot be explained by reference to a *constant* (castration anxiety). Besides, castration anxiety seems supererogatory in cases where menstrual taboos are less onerous than in Melanesia — for example in the modern West.

Purity and Pollution

Most forms of misogyny, both organic and spiritual-intellectual, involve some concept of purity and pollution. All misogynists are alike in viewing woman as contaminating or corrupting both to man's body and to his morality. Some ascetics fear woman as exuding a spiritual toxin and therefore as a kind of human bacillus. In some agnatic societies, this amorphous female hazard is felt specifically in kinship terms: she is dangerous to the integrity of the "community of brothers." Sometimes the pollution fears implicate woman as doing evil consciously by using her powers to defile or diminish man, his descendants, or his ideals. Woman may do this in a diabolical, furtive way (witchcraft), or by making a shambles of family (male) relationships through her sexuality or selfishness. Or she may seduce virginal young men and corrupt their souls. In any case, misogynists regard woman as seeking to subvert the orderly, harmonious world created with great effort by men. Libido is perhaps the most deadly of all woman's sins, but certainly not the only one: there is also venality, disruptiveness, failure to nurture, selfishness, and frivolity.

Visceral Misogyny

Looking at the gynogenetic-toxin metaphor more closely, we ask: what is the concrete focus of the biological pollution fears? First, there is the common idea of feminine-induced defilement, which, as often as not, entails fantasies of noxious substances intruding into the body and doing invisible but insidious and deadly damage. The organic origin may differ, but these noxious fluids and substances are almost felt to enter the male persona and destroy him. The consequence of the violation is inner contamination; the man's body weakens and rots from within. Women "send out" such poisons, intentionally or not, but the somatic displacement of this consternation usually takes shape in tropes of magical invasion by which the pollutants penetrate the male body, with consequent wasting diseases, all requiring powerful masculine (i.e., cultural) prophylactics, such as repetitive rituals of purification, prayers, and purgatives.

A sexual element is of course clearly involved: misogynists fear being turned into the passive partner in a scenario that resembles a parody or inversion of sexual intercourse. The misogynist is afraid of being put into the woman's position and being "penetrated" by powerful forces. The consequent inner rot may even be interpreted as a nightmare pregnancy fantasy: something alien is "growing" inside the man's body. This is clearly part of a fantasy of bodily possession, suggesting a generalized homosexual panic, a fantasy of being turned into the passive "acted-upon" partner.

We have seen this fantasy most clearly in the thaumatological conceptions of some preliterate peoples about the lethal power of female substances to "get under" the man's skin and cause magical transformations. But in the European tradition, the invasive theme often took on a pseudo-medical idiom, for example in the Spanish treatises on preventive medicine, which portrayed woman as a pestilence (Solomon 1997). Witchcraft has much the same etiology. The female witch magically intrudes some noxious material into the victim, who sickens and dies. This basic invasion model reappears in sophisticated Western science, in refined art, and in modern political philosophy, as fears of the phallic, sexually aggressive woman who puts something "under the skin" of males in order to destroy them. At another level, the fantasy resurfaces not so much as a preoccupation with enchanted intrusions but rather in terms of *self-betrayal.* The fantasy shifts from a magic attack on the person from an exterior source to encompass the concept of a preexisting and debased substratum that bubbles and writhes *within* his own body and that erupts under the stimulus of woman. In this sense, woman is an incitement that brings out the worst in man. But the sense of woman as a trap presupposes at a deeper level the cognitive recognition of a willing aggressive or primitive instinct that is there to be stimulated by a woman.

The hidden lava-like substratum may be felt as lust, or as regressive return-to-the-womb tendencies, but it may also take the form of an intellectualized primal chaos in a more general sense, or of some other equally frightening antisocial impulse (as, for example, among fraternally oriented peoples, who blame women for the squabbling that destroys the holy unity of brothers). Regardless of symbolizations, most of these male fantasies conjure up some potent negative *force,* which, endowed with cunning, waits in hostile anticipation of an opening. No matter how this hostile entity is conceived (in biological, moral, or metaphysical terms), it is always mysteriously in league with, anthropomorphized as, or at the call of women. Synonymous with the id, base animality, the libido, regressive instincts, or whatever, this sinister (and crafty) force is normally in abeyance, suppressed by an overlay of inhibitions — that is, masculine discipline. But, more than other people, misogynists seem to distrust the barriers that men have erected against this primal force.

Downfall

The core imagery always seems to include fear of intrusion, of possession, and of moral collapse. The actual metaphor is of being attacked by powerful and inimical forces (from both within and without). This two-pronged attack on the self is followed by loss of control and by disintegration of the ego, often symbolized by drowning or "poisoning." What follows this moral surrender is a submerging into formlessness, literally a falling to pieces, devolution and relapse to some primitive state. This is a particularly regressive fantasy and is often symbolized by drowning and the other aquatic imagery we have seen or by imagery of *downfall* — not only the allegory of the Fall, but also everyday metaphors used to describe debilitating passion: falling to pieces, going backward, falling head over heels, inversion, descent into murky waters. Here, the watery tropes and all the metaphors of moral degeneration intersect in the theme of descending or dissolving and clearly have some connection to return-to-the-womb fantasies.

There are of course other common elements. Paranoid fears of being attacked by hostile forces and being diminished reach hysterical pitch in the various castration terrors. These include the *vagina dentata* that bites off the penis; the Medusa that turns men to stone; Mad Meg and the goddess Kali, female devils who kill and maim; legions of sprites who enchant and transform; and many other supernatural figures who wield frightful weapons to cut and mutilate. If these she-demons are not changing men into some low beast or infantilizing them, they are depicted as bloodying men, piercing their bodies, or disfiguring them usually by beheading (castration anxiety displaced upward? [Freud 1940:273]). The same underlying fear of diminishment is also manifested metaphorically in the figure of Circe, who by turning men into pigs removes their reason (their heads, minds?) and thus turns the spirit, once again, into gross matter, nothingness.

Annihilation fears like these have other psychic corollaries aside from decapitation, castration, and death. An inherent *vulnerability* within the male psyche, a specifically masculine susceptibility perceived as a kind of inner corruption or disgusting weakness (pulpy mushiness, softness), often abets powerful inimical forces. This unacceptable inner flaw is often linked to a lingering residue of femininity *within* the man. This inner femininity is the sensual impulse, the same as "softness," "weakness," the vulnerability to sensuality itself, regressive impulses of going back in time, devolving, turning the clock back, returning to a prior, formless, childlike state, expressed often as a sense of being changed into something worthless. It is clear from all this that regressive fantasies are as powerful a motive in misogynist rage as are the easily identifiable sexual ones. Regressive wishes seem to be felt as a return to a primordial premasculine state, to infancy — that is, to a condition associated with femininity.

The recurring metaphor of poisoning that we have seen so often is also germane to the motif of warding off this dangerous and omnipresent female principle within and without. More to the point, the poisoning imagery is also oral imagery, the swallowing of fatal substances and other metaphorical poisons suggesting a nightmare travesty of breastfeeding. In the misogynist imagination, the breast becomes a poisonous vessel instead of a cornucopia of life. The "flooding" of instinct repeats this motif abstractly: milk, the liquid of life, becomes the stuff of death. As we have noted above, witchcraft, menstrual terrors, other misogynistic phantasms carry the same connotation of being invaded and manipulated by insidious and hostile forces that, through imbibing, enter the male stomach or bloodstream like a noxious liquid. Equally pervasive as the bibulous imagery is the fantasy of being entwined in the serpent-woman's slimy coils or enclosed in the femme fatale's fatal embrace, engulfed, suffocated, as by the omnipotent mother of childhood.

Diagnosis: Paranoia

Taken together, these tropes, passions, terrors, and images could be diagnosed as a paranoid delusion. Individually and in aggregate, misogynistic fantasies amount to a form of psychopathic hallucination in which an invasive evil, originating outside the body in a woman, is identified with alienness, and which, insidious and irresistible, penetrates the self, establishing a beachhead, conquering the male host's moral faculties, flooding reason, corrupting the soul, destroying manhood. The overriding emotion is a fear of collapsing or imploding ego boundaries, forms, and structures and a return to nothingness. Thus, formally, misogyny is similar to any obsessive, unrealistic fear of a conspiratorial, omnipresent enemy who wishes to do these terrible things; it has all the earmarks of a typical phobia, with somatic displacements and fears focusing on woman, who is demonized as the implacable, omnipotent foe who enacts man's worst fears about himself.

Freud's psychology (among others) tells us that such phobias are projections, attributions to others of one's own repressed wishes. These phobias are either projections of the repressed wishes or they are displacements by which inner conflicts find objectification in scapegoats. Phobia formation is what psychoanalysts call "the defense mechanism of *externalization*" (Spiro 1997:155). In the case of misogyny, what is being projected onto woman is man's own peremptory libido and regressive wishes, his own unacceptable impulses, most importantly sexual passion and return-to-the-womb fantasies.

Depletion Once More

A corollary to this multi-tiered paranoia is the theme of masculine *depletion,* which represents a recurrent objectification of misogynists' vague sense of imminent annihilation by predatory women who leech their vital substances. One way that women can destroy men is by stealing their energies. In misogynistic fantasies, women, like succubi, suck men dry, use them up, exploit them, and then cast them aside like desiccated husks. In New Guinea, for example, rapacious women make men shrivel and dry up by "sapping their juice" (Brown 1978:150). The desiccation motif is a constant in the Western imagination; Dijkstra calls it the "Preying Mantis" theme. He refers to the widespread portrayal of woman as the "predatory sex" and as a "social parasite" in Western folklore and art, the spider woman or vampire woman motifs, for example (1996:68,246). The calculating gold-digger and the designing-woman stereotypes also fit this mold of female bloodsucker.

The depletion theme is conveyed poignantly in two formal representations: the idiom of semen loss and the metaphor of financial ruin. The latter we have seen in Western folklore and in dramas, such as Ben Jonson's *Volpone,* Strindberg's *The Father,* and Wedekind's *Lulu,* in which female sociopaths siphon off money and other valuables from pathetically vulnerable males. These themes are replete with a masculine sense of betrayal, helplessness, and disillusionment. Fears about debilitating semen loss are a particularly acute and almost universal male terror, occurring at every level of society and in most cultures. For example, depletion anxiety figures in the Burmese fear of "diminishment" of the man's powers through ejaculation (Spiro 1997:27). Seminal fluid anxiety occurs in the medieval Iberian doctors' notion that sex equals a "depletion of fluids" that damages, dehydrates, and "withers" (Solomon 1997:35). This belief is given credence by the Hispano-Jewish philosopher Maimonides (1135–1204), who wrote that male strength resides in the seminal fluid and "its loss is weakening" (Lederer 1968:52).

The same belief crops up in contemporary Europe. In Spain, for example, men fear the debilitating aspects of sex, which they believe deprives them of valuable semen and saps their manly strength (Brandes 1980:84–86). The body weakening through semen loss motif occurs in "virtually all" preindustrial peoples of the world (Shapiro 1996:6). Another example is the intense fear of seminal-fluid loss in rural Hindu culture (Alter 1996). Among Indian peasants, "loss of the seed is a kind of death," and copulation is lethal if too frequent (Doniger 1980:31). Countless other pseudo-scientific beliefs and phobias equate ejaculation with weakening and diminishment. In modern American culture, one could point to the figure of General Jack D. Ripper in Stanley Kubrick's apocalyptic Cold War movie *Dr. Strangelove*. The deranged general initiates nuclear holocaust to prevent the Soviets from stealing our "vital fluids" (semen). Such fears of depletion dovetail with the paranoid delusion of being invaded and captured. Although portrayed as a certified lunatic, General Ripper is treated as a kind of parody of the military (that is, the hypermasculine) mind.

We thus see a curious symmetry in misogynistic grievances. The misogynist's fear of being invaded has its obverse: fear of being despoiled by a greedy, rapacious female who, while "putting in" something bad, simultaneously melts him down and "takes away" something valuable. Hence the double-barreled anxiety among preliterate peoples that during sex a woman will not only steal the man's semen and weaken him but introduce something into his penis and thus his bloodstream so that he sickens. As men fear the intrusive scourge of femininity, a woman's power to "get under the skin," they fear equally her evacuative powers; she is a hellish cannibalistic siphon. In both fantasies, the misogynist attributes to woman preternatural powers to break down the barriers of man's defenses. Again, there is a possibility that such fears stem from men's identification with woman, especially the fantasized nurturing mother, and that his terrors about depletion represent a wish-fantasy of being both the mother who is being sucked dry and the infant who is sucking.

Liquidity

Water imagery figures prominently in most misogynistic discourse. Such tropes are so pervasive that one is hard pressed to avoid speculating on some primal connection between woman-hatred and hydrophobia. On the one hand, man fears that women will steal his semen and vital juices (or cash, which is psychologically the same: liquid assets). On the other hand, man fears that nautical she-demons will rise from the depths to drag him down as mermaids and sirens dragged the voyagers of antiquity down to a magic underworld in which we cannot live. The same imagery of floods, lapping waters, and drowning appears in the Brazilian *bota* (demon she-dolphin) tales and in Germanic mythology about the Lorelei, a typical riparian siren (Lederer 1968:236), as well as in Icelandic myths in which women are portrayed as "rivers of poison" where men drown like flies in honey (Linke 1996:138).

What Solomon calls the "uncontainable fluidity" associated with women's bodies (1997:78) is exemplified by the amphibious sirens and mermaids, who drag men down into swirling waters, but also reflects a common metaphor for drowning in impulse or sensuality: floating in a warm blissful sea, sinking in oceans of depravity, returning to the womb, and so on. These regressive humid tropes are irresistible and terrifying to misogynists, who appear to be tortured by severe conflicts about the swamps of pleasure conjured up by lubricious or lactating women.

Where does all this wet Weltschmerz come from? The deliquescent imagery could be inspired partly by male fears of and fascination with the female "flow," menstruation. The uterus "melts" and the body "leaks." There is probably also an unconscious reference to the vagina's lubrication during arousal, equally stimulating and horrifying to prudes. There is also a regressive longing for the milky bliss of infancy. These soggy images unite all such feelings and are an effective visual representation of generalized *moral* anxiety in terms of liquidization: melting of the will, liquification, floating away. All these terrors seem to be embodied by images of moist femininity.

Additionally, the gushing, spurting tropes invoke a curious hydraulic motif: woman's body causes a dangerous buildup of pressure in man, leading to an explosion. As well as threatening to flood resistance, the hydraulic images conjure a sense of Freud's "oceanic feeling" (1931:11). He describes this ubiquitous sensation as masking a longing for oneness with the natural world, the intellectualization of primary narcissism, the wish to return to the watery bliss of the womb. Oceanic, aqueous, and regressive images are consonant not only with fears of engulfment, regression, and death, but also with loss of masculine hardness or tumescence. Here the softness and limpness inherent in fluid imagery takes on the special agency of femininity which equals the overthrow of manhood and its degeneration into something worthless and flabby. The regressive aspects of this fantasy are all too evident.

Civilization at Risk

At a higher level is an abstract peril represented by women to society and to carefully cultivated (adult male) institutions. In some societies this cosmic, rather apocalyptic misogyny appears as a vague but familiar fear about "riot" (Bloch 1991:4), the end of civilization. In others, like New Guinea, the concern is about body fluids and secretions dripping down into the underworld and uniting with evil forces that threaten to engulf society (Godelier 1986:60). In still other tribal societies the fear of female-induced social collapse and anarchy adopts a more concrete form involving women's impact upon the continuity of society's building blocks: its patrilines. This fear of genealogical extinction among men living under existentially agonistic conditions creates several different kinds of worry about feminine treachery, mixing the strategic with the occult. But whatever the symbolism, woman's unruly "nature" is again represented as a human solvent, a poison, that wrecks the integument of society, if unchecked by male control, and returns man to a primitive (child-like) state.

One of these male worries is embodied, as we have seen in Melanesia and Amazonia, in the in-marrying "enemy" wife who undermines the solidarity of the brothers by fomenting strife (Meggitt 1958). In Nazi propaganda, also, woman represented the "enemy within," the soft, degenerate part of the self that, like the Jews, worked to undermine Aryan superiority. A similar stereotype is that of the wicked or lascivious stepmother, who, like Phaedra, comes from a distant place and disrupts fragile male structures by her egregious misconduct. Woman is once again the alien, the interloper who undermines carefully constructed restrictions. Men fear her literally as a foreign body, a cancer or "poison" that wrecks illusions and subverts order.

Such male panic is not confined to preindustrial societies. We have seen the same fear of woman's power to wreck society in more sophisticated terms in modern philosophy and sociology and in turn-of-the-century academic psychology. D. H. Lawrence bemoaned woman's tendency to use "subtly diabolic" wiles against man and faulted her as an "inevitably destructive force." In terms reminiscent of the New Guinea or Amazonian aborigines, Lawrence warned against the "colossal evil of the united spirit of Woman" that was "sending out waves of destructive malevolence which eat out the inner life of a man, like a cancer. It is so, it will be so, until men realize it and react to save themselves" (cited in Rogers 1966:246).

We have seen similar anxieties flourishing in the world's many religions. All the great faiths castigate woman to some degree as the cause of disorder and decay. Christian scripture holds woman up as "the devil's gateway," the riotous and depraved sex; in Islam she is *fitna,* chaos; in Buddhism the female sex is composed of wickedness and guile; in Hinduism woman is disorder, discord, subversion, licentiousness, and deceitfulness rolled into one. Thus in misogynistic fantasies about social destructiveness, woman is equated with subversiveness and devolution as negative principles. Allied not only with Sex, but also with Chaos, she represents an elemental, inimical force of nature that implacably undermines whatever restraints men have erected to keep the flood of bedlam at bay. She is the apotheosis of all that opposes order, corrupts, subverts, derails the spiritual quest.

Paralleling these fears of the antinatal woman is the ascription of a malignant primitivity to the female, whom misogynists regard as the unevolved laggard who drags man back to earlier stages of development. We have seen this charge of atavism again and again, not only in preliterate societies in which women are labeled "closer to nature" (Ortner 1974) and are likened to witches and other chthonic, nonhuman forces, but also in modern Western art and literature. In virtually all cultures, men accuse women of being less evolved, less spiritual; men disparage women as regressive, the embodiment of low nature, as using animal magnetism to waylay the male in his quest for spiritual perfection (Dijkstra 1986:240).

This derogatory stereotype is so ubiquitous that no correlation can be detected to the technological sophistication of society, to any particular economic system, or to any political arrangement. The most enlightened and refined Western artists, as well their preliterate counterparts, have depicted women as "savage atavisms both mad and bestial" (Kestner 1989:7). In nineteenth-century European folklore (encompassing ancient archetypes), women were also portrayed as intermediate between men and natural forces (Bottigheimer 1987:115). Most religions — monotheist, animist, and pagan — belittle woman as the main distraction from man's higher quest; in virtually all of man's philosophies, cosmologies, and countless and varied moral schemes, woman is considered lower down the evolutionary ladder than man; she is ruled from "down below" (N. Davis 1978:148).

At the psychological level, such Manichaean judgments inspire overtly paranoid projections couched in morbid etiological idioms such as contagion, disease, and putrefaction. The moralistic worry about civilization "degenerating" or society "disintegrating" is at this deeper level an intellectualization of the fear of *bodily* ruination, which psychiatrists call a conversion symptom. Psychiatrists in Freud's day and long after often identified such psychosomatic symptomatology — ironically — as the chief diagnostic trait of the particularly *feminine* psychosis of hysteria. But given the pervasiveness of misogynistic ravings, it would appear that a far greater number of hysterics are men than women.

Another curious misogynistic expression of man's fear of collapse and ruination that is not strictly sexual in origin is the attribution of *antiprocreative*
impulses to women, the nefarious opposite of motherhood. This allegation
occurs mainly in preliterate tribal societies where structurally abetted misogyny is common. Among many patrilineal peoples who consider wives aliens,
men fear that their wives conspire to prevent pregnancy, working diabolically
against their husbands' desires for sons. The women do this supposedly to
thwart the men's ardent hope for heirs. If unchecked, such female perversity
would of course lead to the extinction of the society. The men thus see women
as the undoers of God's design (to be fruitful and multiply).

This belief in female antibirth perfidy is apparently widespread in the aboriginal New Guinea, where men are obsessed with fertility and procreation as a
way of shoring up their reputations and political power, which depend upon
ownership of pigs, yams, and other foods for lending. They also want many sons,
who will work for them and protect them (Paula Brown 1978). Fears of wifely
betrayal lead to further hostility between the sexes in New Guinea, but the same
misgivings burgeon in other tribal societies in equal measure. It was pointed out
earlier that many Brazilian Tukanoan men, as reported by Jackson (1992, 1996),
believe that their in-marrying wives practice clandestine and magical birth control, secretly abort fetuses, and refuse sex when fertile, all in order to frustrate the
husband's fervent wish for sons. While most pronounced in the tribal societies of
New Guinea and Amazonia, this same perception of female iniquity is found in
the patriarchal Judeo-Christian and Muslim traditions. The biblical scholar
Jacob Lassner, in *Demonizing the Queen of Sheba,* speaks of an underlying fear,
in both biblical myths and Arabo-Muslim texts, that women, given a free hand,
will rescind the covenant of motherhood, defying both their husbands and their
God by abrogating His decree to propagate. The implications of this course are
made self-evident in the texts that warn about women refusing motherhood,
"humankind will not be able to sustain the species and in time will become extinct" (1993:34–35). Some of the same extinction fear of female birth-nihilism
can be observed among contemporary antiabortion zealots in the United States.

Many Misogynies

While misogyny has many guises, there are definitely some common motiva-
tions, affects, and fantasies. Because of the variety of expressions these take,

however, it might be useful to break down the wider concept into its formal components. This implies, also, a brief semantic and typological effort.

First, there is the catch-all category "misogyny," the *horror mulieris* in all its forms. Within this general heading, however, there is a specific focus on the dangers of woman's body and its biology, a focus we might call "gynophobia" (Kestner 1989). This fear centers on the reproductive organs. Fear of the female genitalia gives rise to the antivagina complex that Shapiro (1989) describes as prevalent among Melanesian peoples, which leads to so many male fantasies about dirty crevices, gnashing teeth, and nasty effluvia. Such gynophobic beliefs also appear in Western art and literature, as in Swift's visceral disgust with women's bodies and King Lear's characterization of female nether parts as a dark and vicious place. The *vagina dentata* motif is virtually universal. Gynophobia gives rise to certain complexes of its own, one of which Shapiro (1989) calls "pseudo-procreation," by which he means the fantasy of asexual reproduction.

There is also the fear and hatred of women as mothers, equally widespread and powerful. We might call this, along with Ackley (1992:381), *matriphobia,* or mother-dread. Under this category we would have to include not only the Swiftian revulsion at reproduction (the "monstrous mother" theme) but also the fear of the devouring, punishing mother, found in the cult of the Indian goddess Kali and in so much modern Western literature about the "bad mother."

Matriphobic misogyny was rife in the America of the 1940s and 1950s, possibly as a reaction to women's entry into the workplace. An almost hysterical matriphobia characterizes some American pop sociology of the period. Philip Wylie, for example, in *Generation of Vipers* (1942), formalized an attack on predatory, emasculating American matriarchy. Wylie introduced the term "Momism." The monstrous American mom is responsible for the manifold moral and political ills of modern American society, a vicious, parasitical matriarch who enslaves and emasculates her husband and sons. Bloated, tyrannical, and a "perfidious" materialist (Wylie 1942:190), she lowers the cultural level of the nation and despoils the home. In a particularly vitriolic passage, Wylie accuses moms of having brought America to "a new all-time low in political scurviness, hoodlumism, gangsterism . . . financial depression, chaos, and war." Matriphobia is also evident in attacks on surrogate moms, such as the wicked stepmother and the abusive mother-in-law — both ubiquitous in male folklore.

In the jaundiced eye of misogynists, wives fare little better. There is "structural misogyny," which is essentially antagonism toward in-marrying brides. Uxorophobia, the fear and hatred of wives, takes the form of distrust about in-marrying women's loyalties, their adherence to ideals of the agnatic community, and, especially, their sexuality, which, if flaunted, can destroy a man's honor in an instant — a continuous problem for Mediterranean men (Stewart 1994:108).

Uxorophobia is linked closely to misogamy, or fear and hatred of marriage. The two antifemale phobias often coincide, as, for example, among nervous New Guinea bachelors who bolt from matrimony. Satirists and poets of antiquity, such as Juvenal and Ovid, wrote tracts about the marital trap (Wilson and Makowski 1990), and medieval holy men like Tertullian gave moral counsel against tying the knot (Bloch 1991). Misogamy resurfaces in modern philosophy and literature. It is the central theme in Tolstoy's *Kreutzer Sonata,* whose slightly cracked hero, Pozdnyshev, wants to abolish marriage and sex altogether.

Finally, there are ideological forms of misogyny, wholly political in focus. These emphasize women's supposed social and mental inferiority rather than her wickedness or the polluted state of her organs. One such form of political misogyny is "ideological masculinism," found among many early twentieth-century European fascists and among some patriarchal chauvinists today (Coole 1988; Linke 1997). Masculinists hold that men must rule because women are intellectually inferior (or morally perverse) and must therefore be excluded from political power. Present among the Sarakatsani and other patriarchal peoples, political masculinism was also favored by Plato and Aristotle, Schopenhauer and Nietzsche, and La Rochefoucauld and Montaigne. It persisted among turn-of-the-century criminologists like Lombroso and social Darwinist Victorian political thinkers — Bachoven, McClelland, Durkheim, Spencer, et al.

The obverse to gynophobia is phallocentrism, the belief that the male organ is better, more natural, more primary than the vagina. As a consequence of an anatomical difference, men are better than women (Slipp 1993). Freud is guilty of this fallacy of "sexual phallic monism" (Chasseguet-Smirgel 1986:10) because of his insistence that the male organ — hence male sexuality — is primal or initial or somehow more important than the female's.

A mild form of political misogyny is what political scientist Glenn Tinder (1997:98–99) calls "patriarchal conservatism" and what Blamires (1992:9) refers to as anti-feminism. Not denouncing women as inherently evil, this viewpoint contends that men and women are vastly different in abilities and needs. Although neither sex is superior, women, because of the demands of pregnancy and childcare, require special considerations, which in turn demand some minimal legal distinctions. Some feminists even take a position that men and women should be treated differently under the law (Tinder 1997:98). This view has none of the visceral hatred discussed earlier, but patriarchal conservatism has some elements of misogyny.

To summarize: misogyny has many forms, sexual, matriphobic, political, structural, aesthetic, moralistic. There are few richer or more florid psychiatric symptomatologies than the misogynistic practices and beliefs we have looked at. Woman has become the scapegoat for virtually all the existential terrors of the male, infant, child, adolescent, adult, and patriarch. Now that we are sufficiently confused, it is time to think about some of the more reasonable theories that have been proposed to explain the masculine malaise.

A Woman is a foreign land.

—Coventry Patmore, *The Angel in the House*

8. Psychological Theories

GIVEN THE PREDOMINANCE and emotional salience of misogyny, numerous theories have been advanced to explain it. Before proposing one of my own, I should describe what other explanations have been proposed. These various theories can be broken down into several inclusive categories.

First, there are psychological and, in particular, psychoanalytic, interpretations, mostly based on what Freud said about male psychology and on recent revisions and refinements in the Freudian theory. These can be further subdivided into Oedipal, pre-Oedipal, and object-relations approaches. Whatever their biases, most of the psychoanalytic explanations account for the frequency of woman-hating by positing some universal experiences, such as the crucial role of the "family romance" (that is, the Oedipal scenario), the experience of the mother as love object, and retention of pre-Oedipal residues from the boy's early psychic development.

Second are explanations based on the structural, ecological, and functional models in the social sciences regnant in the 1950s and 1960s. These approaches typically pay little attention to depth psychology, instead stressing the sociocultural and environmental context of misogyny. Such theories see causation in the "fit" between the belief system and the material context. Structural models themselves are of two basic types: (1) those invoking social explanations — kinship systems, marriage practices, dominance hierarchies, and the like — to account for male behavior; and (2) those invoking *mental* structures — that is, abstract cultural configurations, cognitive patterns of symbolizations, value systems, and ideas "in the mind." Such mental structures are associated mainly with the work of Claude Lévi-Strauss and his followers; this mentalistic approach is therefore sometimes labeled "French structuralism."

A final set of causal models takes a more Marxist and historical-materialist approach and, for lack of a better word, may simply be called political. Its adherents approach the problem from the "cui bono" (who benefits?) perspective proposed by Gelber (1986) for New Guinea. According to this viewpoint misogyny is the ideological handmaiden to sexual oppression and gender hierarchy. Most political approaches regard misogyny as a justifying ideology, an epiphenomenon, a part of "superstructure" — that is, a dependent variable, not an autonomous phenomenon, but one caused by something deeper, something more primary and more important. This substructural factor is usually identified as male domination or unjust relations of production. In this chapter we deal with the psychological-psychoanalytic theories. The next chapter deals with materialist interpretations.

Castration Anxiety

Aside from a few brief comments by Sigmund Freud and Karen Horney in the 1920s and 1930s, explanations for misogyny appear relatively late in the psychological sciences. The first systematic hypotheses appeared only after the feminist movement of the 1960s alerted us to the phenomenon as a problem. Some good early works are Hoffman Hays's synoptic Freudian study *The Dangerous Sex* (1964), Katherine Rogers's pioneering study of misogyny in literature *The Troublesome Helpmate* (1966), and Wolfgang Lederer's Jungian *The Fear of Women* (1968).

One of the earliest psychological theories put forth to explain misogyny, especially its gynophobic variant, derives from Freud's basic premise of "castration anxiety," a concept found throughout his writings. Castration anxiety is the major sequela to the Oedipus complex, which Freud and his followers posited as a *universal* element in male psychic development. A boy's sexual desire for his mother and his rivalry with his father occur at approximately ages four through six. At this time the boy is psychically traumatized by the fear that his father will retaliate for his incestuous affront by cutting off his penis. Freud and other psychoanalysts (e.g., Fenichel 1945:78), regarded castration fear as the basic building block of male personality, and the primary motive for repressing the sexual wishes toward the mother and rebellious feelings toward the father. According to these orthodox Freudians, castration fear is the primary reason that boys, later men, universally fear women, and it explains their fearful preoccupation with the morphology and biology of women's sexual organs. In the immature male imagination, the woman resembles a "castrated," mutilated male. The little boy senses the vaginal crevice as a wound and this frightens him. He finds the female genital horrifying and "uncanny" and its monthly discharge a dreadful talisman of what might happen to his masculine integrity.

According to psychoanalytic anthropologists like Geza Roheim (1950) and William Stephens (1962), who seized on this construct to explore many aspects of gender culture, boys' ubiquitous fear of women's vaginal effluvia and the subsequent misogyny can have no other explanation than castration anxiety, expressed in cultural terms as "disavowal" or "denial" of the female and her defective, bleeding body. The logic of this view is plausible when one considers the abundance of evidence concerning male fears about vaginal effluvia, reflected in the myths and legends of horrible female castrators and Medusa-like mutilators of manhood.

In a recent analysis of masculine psychology and culture, Nancy Chodorow concisely summarizes the issue of cultural projection:

Disavowal also enters the realm of mythology. Medusa's snakes condense signification on the one hand of the mature female external genitals and on the other of many penises, which in turn stand both for castration (because the one penis has been lost) and denial of castration (because there are many penises). Medusa's decapitated head, the castrated female genitals, evokes horror and even paralysis — a reminder of castration — in the man who looks at it. (1994:23)

For Freud, castration fear is the reciprocal of penis envy; it is universal and exclusive to males and an epistemological "given." These features explain why misogyny exists everywhere while antimale phobia does not. Women do not fear the male genital as a minatory symbol of mutilation; they are "already" castrated (Freud 1931b). But Freud argues that only men experience a powerful castration fear for other equally salient reasons. First, the boy's Oedipal conflict is severe, even traumatic, while the girl's Electra complex is mild in comparison because she has nothing to be cut off. Second, "it is only in the male child that we find the fateful combination of love for the one parent and simultaneous hatred for the other as a rival" (226). Consequently, the tendency to repudiate and denigrate the other sex is found "exclusively" in the male (Chodorow 1994:22).

However, when considering the relation of this dread of mutilation to misogyny, the unidimensional fear of father turns out to be only part of the syndrome. Castration fear means that the boy is terrified not only of the father but also, and perhaps even more, of the mother. For in his fantasy of parental retribution, the mother also wants to punish the boy for his incestuous affront. (Freud noted on numerous occasions that the Oedipal-stage boy fears the mother also as a castrator; he suggested in fact that the main castration threat to men came from women rather than from men [Lederer 1968:51].) If it is true that the little boy fears the mother as much as the father, this hypothesis would bear looking at in connection with the fear many misogynists have that dismemberment and dissolution will result from women's implacable malevolence. We can also assume that castration anxiety is a somatic displacement from the penis to the entire body and is a metaphor, or synecdoche, for extinction and death — feelings that have been projected in such rich imagery in male folklore, and have been involved with transformative imagery in which the male is diminished or lessened (i.e., loses something valuable — if not his penis, his reason or his head).

Freud's followers added refinements and corollaries to the basic idea of castration anxiety that elaborate on the boy's experience with the omnipotent mother and his reaction to her alien femaleness in infancy. These neo-Freudian revisions emphasize, as a basic ingredient in the Oedipal phase, a boy's tendency to ward off or deny the sense of *his* own discomforting femininity — a dualism in sexual self-image related to his identification with the mother rather than to the avenging Oedipal father. For example Hans Loewald (1980:xx), in postulating a "negative" Oedipal complex, noted the possibility that castration fears could reflect a *wish* for a female identity — that is the desire to be "like" mother — and not simply a *fear* of punishment at the hands of either parent. Loewald believed that such a wish on the boy's part, that is, to be female like mother (that is, to be castrated, a woman without a penis) represents the psychic equivalent of Oedipal surrender, as well as eroticized love for the father.

Thus the wish for surrender *also* must be repudiated by the boy through contempt and rejection of everything female. So, however one approaches the Freudian concept of castration anxiety, one reaches the same final point: the Oedipal trauma leads to a self-protective impulse to denigrate, repudiate, and deny femininity both within and without in order to protect the vulnerable male body and ego. This leads in later development to a misogynistic distancing as a general orientation of men toward women.

Vagina Anxiety

A slightly different theory is that of the protofeminist Karen Horney, who became interested in gender-identity problems in both men and women early in her career. In her paper "The Dread of Women" (1932), Horney explores the fear of women that exists in so many cultures, and which she found powerfully expressed by so many of her male patients. She concludes that these feelings are linked to the boy's anxiety, during the Oedipal period, that his penis is too small for his mother's huge, engulfing vulva. Terrified and humiliated, the boy then anticipates that he will be scorned by his contemptuous mother; he therefore needs to denigrate all women in self-defense.

The fantasy of being "too small" never goes away but escalates into his fear, as a grown man, of being sucked in or engulfed during intercourse by the encompassing vagina (Lidz and Lidz 1989:74). Although it seems bizarre, this theory, if valid, would certainly help explain one of the most common themes we have observed in misogyny: the terror of being sucked down, pulled in, drowned, and overwhelmed by the devouring, engulfing, amorphous, liquefying female orifice. This idea, for example, seems relevant in the case of the sexually-dysfunctional Semai groom, in all other respects normal, who was so terrified of his wife's "big-as-a-house" vagina on his wedding night (Dentan 1979:63).

Maternal Betrayal and Mother Dread

Another wrinkle on this Oedipal theme is brought out by psychoanalysts like Lederer (1968:5–7) and Spiro (1997:152). They argue that man's anger at women is partly due to the little boy's feeling of rage at the mother for her rejection of him during the Oedipal period, his disillusionment at the unhappy denouement of the family romance. When at the end of the Oedipal period, the boy is forced to give up his incestuous longings, he senses his mother's loyalty to her husband — the boy's father — as a humiliating rejection and an unforgivable betrayal. This sense of being cruelly betrayed by the treacherous Oedipal mother damages his self-esteem irreparably and cripples his masculine narcissism to the extent that he comes to fear unconsciously that all other women will treat him equally deceitfully. Thus he thinks, woman = betrayal. If true, this would explain many men's otherwise inexplicable belief that *all* women are treacherous, faithless deceivers who inevitably betray men to their enemies. This theme does indeed run through misogynistic representations. The boy's Oedipal attachment to his mother, an attachment which she must inevitably frustrate in favor of another male, helps to explain why so many men have reproached women for faithlessness and fickleness, for failure to respond to their love.

All these Oedipal theories, of course, take for granted the basic Freudian premise that the boy's relationship to his mother sets the tone for all future relationships with, and feelings toward, women in later life. If we accept this basic premise, then most of the theories make sense in explaining both the origin of the male malady and its ubiquity. These mother-centered psychoanalytic theories would also help explain the frequently encountered "matriphobic" form of misogyny, for they are all founded on the proposition that the boy's feelings toward mother are fiercely ambivalent and that she is always perceived in starkly dualistic terms: as both engulfing and nurturing, seductive and castrating, and consequently as good and bad. Since these indestructibly dualistic feelings are repressed by boys and later by men, and pushed into the unconscious to protect the mother, it makes sense that men would seek surrogate females such as mothers-in-law, stepmothers, and, to a certain extent, their sexual partners, upon whom to vent their unconscious resentments.

All these theories are built on standard Freudian axioms, although Freud himself did not propose them in so many words. Freud did, however, offer an interesting explanation for misogyny in two short papers specifically about male sexual dysfunction and object choice, first published in 1910 and 1912 (1910:165–75, 1912:177–90). Freud starts with the plausible proposition that many men never resolve their Oedipal feelings toward the mother and, as a consequence, suffer lifelong sexual dysfunction because they are unable to accept a sexual woman as distinct from mother. For such a conflicted man, later sexual life is distorted by psychic associations of eros with the incestuous object of childhood, the child's primary object choice (1912:180). For such a conflicted man, sex always remains illicit, incestuous, and frightening, for he regards the sexual act basically as something degrading, "which defiles and pollutes not only the body" but also the spirit (1912:186).

In order to obtain erotic release, therefore, these neurotic, sexually conflicted men must demean the sexual object. By doing so they compartmentalize their sex lives and rescue the mother (1910:168) from the pollution of their own Oedipal cravings. Thus, all potential sexual partners in adult life — that is, all nubile and unrelated women — must be denigrated as "worthless" and "dirty." This debasement of the sexual function goes hand in hand with an overvaluation — in fact, idolization — of the mother as pure and sexless, and therefore the exact opposite of a sexual woman. And thereby is enacted a psychic contrast and separation of love objects, the psychic "splitting" between mother and sexual partner that gives rise in cultural terms to the madonna-whore complex of Catholic Europe and the good girl-bad girl double standard of Victorian morality, with all the misogynistic stereotyping that must inevitably ensue from such a dichotomous vision.

The Pre-Oedipal Mother

Subsequent to Freud's formulations on the Oedipal complex, other psycho-analysts have emphasized different aspects of a boy's relationship with his mother to account for woman-dread. Some of these researchers find the pre-Oedipal period, from birth to age four, of more importance than the Oedipal. One such theory points to the omnipotence with which the boy endows his mother in this earlier stage of life before the Oedipal complex, in fact during breastfeeding. The mother, not the father, controls all the resources the boy needs and wants — food and love. She therefore looms largest in his tiny consciousness; she is the only recognizable external locus that feeds and caresses him, and also frustrates his desires, punishes his instinctual behavior, and controls him. Mother looms larger than all other objects in the world; she is the primal omnipotent mother, all-powerful comforter and punisher.

Being so completely dependent upon and in awe of her, the boy develops powerfully ambivalent feelings toward this fantastically omnipotent figure. On the one hand he has feelings of love; on the other hand he has surges of hate and resentment. Both young boys and girls experience this ambivalent response to the all-powerful mother. However, men express it in later life through their vindictive feelings against women and by degrading everything female. In comparison, unable to find a sexual "other" upon whom to affix blame (mother being also a female), some women do the same thing through a stance of self-punishing masochism.

Object Relations and Misogyny

Another hypothesis flowing from neo-Freudian and object-relations theories in psychoanalysis is based largely on Melanie Klein's pioneering work on infancy, and especially on the work of Margaret Mahler (Mahler et al. 1975). This theory holds that all children at age eighteen months or so develop an identification with their primary caretaker, normally the mother. Many boys in patriarchal societies — if not *all* boys — feel this irreducible core feminine identity as a threat to their masculine self, an inner softness or weakness, a deficiency lurking within. It must be repudiated so that the boy can later develop a manly identification consonant with cultural expectations; that is, the boy at some point must "dis-identify with the mother" to become a true male as defined by convention (Greenson 1978).

The process of *disidentifying* with mother takes on an all-or-nothing character, which among other things, always includes an often violent rejection of everything feminine, so that masculinity becomes defined as the opposite of, and a distancing from, femininity. The idea of a psychic disidentification with mother also figures prominently in the feminist psychology on gender, especially as developed by Nancy Chodorow (1978, 1989, 1994). Chodorow argues that a psychic turning away from the mother is less necessary for girls than boys during childhood, because most girls grow up with a feminine identification anyway, which they model on their mother (1978). The male's switch in identity is made even harder for most boys, especially in androcentric societies where the sexes are segregated, if the father is often absent from home at the stage of life when disidentifying is taking place. At the same time, the housebound mother is always available for the girl, who can readily identify with her. As a result of these basic gender differences in growth and development, the boy, lacking an immediate model for a satisfying manhood, tends to construct a kind of fantasy masculinity based upon the psychic defense of reaction-formation: a fierce denial of all femininity, a categorical rejection of all that is associated with mother.

This position is summarized by Samuel Slipp in his useful book on misogyny in Freud: "To develop masculinity, boys need to distance themselves from their pre-oedipal mothers and identify with their fathers" (1993:89). Slipp notes that since fathers are so often unavailable to their young sons — for cultural if not emotional reasons — many boys develop an exaggerated style of hypermasculinity that takes root in a rigid denial of all feminine qualities, a machismo that denigrates women — which we call misogyny.

On-the-Ground Applications

Empirical applications of this disidentification theory are legion in psychological anthropology. For example, it has been proposed to explain certain puberty rites in tribal societies. In many societies, young boys are forcibly taken away from their mothers in early adolescence and subjected to harsh, bloody, or otherwise stressful puberty rites administered by their fathers. Such rituals of passage often include sadistic beatings, violent flailings, scarification, and bloody circumcisions without anesthetic, all of which the boys must endure stoically to show they are worthy of "manhood."

The disidentification-from-mother theory holds that these tortures and terrorizations are the culture's efforts to wean the boys from a culturally unacceptable femininity through a toughening-up process that makes "men" of little boys who are still too identified with their mothers (that is, retain a feminine sense of self [Whiting et al. 1958; Lidz and Lidz 1989:68–69]). The same process could be found until very recently in the British public-school system, still in vogue in some elite quarters, in which boys at age eight or nine are sent to boarding school where they are terrorized by their elders (Chandos 1984:170–73). The violent puberty rite hastens the supposedly necessary rupture with the mother and their "masculinization."

Many boys in tribal societies are taught to despise everything that smacks of femininity as a threat to masculine status. In later life, this depreciation translates into a mild misogyny, which may in middle age become occasional wife-abuse or mother-in-law baiting. It also may become a full-fledged violent complex, as in New Guinea or Amazonia, depending upon other cultural variables. Interestingly, harsh male rites of passage occur with extreme violence and bloodshed in those societies described as being hypermisogynist: New Guinea, Amazonia, and some parts of sub-Saharan Africa.

Regression

A related theory also relies upon the concept of an omnipotent Oedipal mother who must be repudiated by her son for him to gain autonomy. This theory posits that owing to psychic residues, the boy, and later the grown man, experiences a powerful unconscious wish to regress to infancy, to reunite with the mother and return to the bliss of nursing (Stoller 1974a, 1974b). This regression theory holds that all children experience this anaclitic longing, felt as a wish to merge identities with the all-encompassing, all-flowing breast. Psychoanalyst Janine Chasseguet-Smirgel sees this regressive longing as a basic and deep-seated impulse in both sexes: "The hypothesis I would put forward is that there exists a primary desire to discover a universe without obstacles, without roughness or differences, entirely smooth, identified with a mother's belly stripped of its contents, an interior to which one has free access" (1986:77).

Others argue that the boy, more than the girl, has a powerfully ambivalent response to this universal regressive wish. On the one hand he feels it as a pleasurable symbiosis with the mother—a recapturing of the carefree, prelap-

sarian world of infancy — but on the other hand he senses it as dangerous
backsliding that is as terrifying as it is pleasurable, for it means extinction of
masculinity. Psychoanalyst Robert Stoller puts it this way:

> While it is true the boy's first love object is heterosexual [the mother], he must perform a
> great deed to make this so: he must first separate his identity from hers. Thus the whole
> process of becoming masculine is at risk for the little boy from the day of birth on; his
> still-to-be-created masculinity is endangered by the primary, profound, primeval one-
> ness with mother, a blissful experience that serves, buried but active in the core of one's
> identity, as a focus which, throughout life, can attract one to regress back to that primi-
> tive oneness. (1974a:358)

Frightened by this powerful ambivalence, the boy decides at some point to end
the struggle by repudiating the regressive side of the equation: he rejects the
mother and adopts a mask of hatred and contempt for femininity. "Some of the
uneasiness men feel about women . . . reflects the need to raise this barrier
against the desire to merge with the mother" (Stoller 1974b:170–71). In this
view, women are indeed "dangerous," for they represent the living embodiment of the boy's regressive fantasies: the infantile "home." It has been my
contention all along that regressive conflicts and maternal identification are as
important in misogyny as sexual and Oedipal issues, so this regression hypothesis is one that I find particularly useful. However, it also cannot stand alone.

The Olfactory Hypothesis

One final hypothesis about the mother-infant relationship adds an interesting
twist. In a psychoanalytical study of "masculinization" in New Guinea, Theodore and Ruth Lidz (1989:68–69) propose that one of the causes of the male
aversion to menstruation and therefore to women's bodies stems from a sensual
childhood experience with the mother, but one unrelated to either breastfeeding
or the hypothetical psychic merging of identities. Their idea is, rather, that the
disgust stems from the child's acute sense of smell. They believe that menstrual
taboos arise because of a retention of the child's early disgust at the mother's
odors during menses — and the child's consequent "dysphoria." This olfactory
dysphoria, they suggest, is something to which the nursing child is especially
susceptible (at least among peoples who do not have access to modern internal
protection during their periods). To the child, they argue, the mother's odor
provides a sense of security and attachment. But the menstrual odor displaces
the customary smell and disrupts the sense of comfort and security, perhaps to a

frightening degree. The dysphoria produced by the menstrual odor may well persevere into adulthood in the male, and be reinforced by a shift, from the woman's usual odor that attracts sexually, "to one that many men find repulsive" (68).

But why should this olfactory revulsion affect the male child so much more dramatically than the female, so that it leads to misogyny? The Lidzes do not answer this directly, but rather direct the reader to Freud's comments on the subject. These appear in a brief but important footnote about the sense of smell in *Civilization and Its Discontents.* Freud says there that in the course of evolution the human male sexual response has shifted from a periodic olfactory stimuli (that is, estrus in the lower mammals) to a permanent visual stimulus (appreciation of female physical beauty). The consequence of this evolutionary shift is that males experience an "organic repression" against vaginal smells as a defense against an earlier and superseded stage of evolution:

The organic periodicity of the sexual process has persisted, it is true, but its effect has rather been reversed. This charge seems most likely to be connected with the diminution of the olfactory stimuli by means of which the menstrual process produced an effect on the male psyche. Their role was taken over by visual excitations, which, in contrast to the intermittent olfactory stimuli, were able to maintain a permanent effect. The taboo on menstruation is derived from this "organic repression," as a defense against a phase of development that has been surmounted. (Freud 1931a:46n)

While not a sufficient explanation of misogyny, the idea of olfactory dysphoria during nursing is useful in trying to understand gynophobic hyperbole about rotting, decay, and pollution, all of which carry both moral and sensate connotations for misogynists. It also helps us understand the seemingly gratuitous disgust that some ascetic men experience at women's bodily secretions, as well as men's obsession with vaginal odors and effluvia. It would also explain why the vagina cannot be "above" a man's nose in highland New Guinea, and why the female sexual organ is regarded as capable of sending out malignant emanations into the air (after all, smell is a response to airborne particles released by decaying objects).

Paleolithic Periods

A variation on the aroma theory contends that menstrual taboos originated among hunting peoples in the Paleolithic era as a means to facilitate the hunt. Vaginal odors supposedly drove away game (some of which are repelled by human smells), which led to severe restrictions on the movement of menstruating females. Some anthropologists have extended this hypothesis into a theory that menstrual taboos are most stringent and numerous among hunting peoples today. However, empirical research on menstrual odor, taboos, and hunting has been informal and inconclusive, and no direct correlation among these variables can be proved either archaeologically or ethnographically (see Buckley and Gottlieb [1988b:21–23] for a review of these ideas).

The inference one must draw from all this is that the common putrefaction imagery in the male malady stems from this "organic repression" of the olfactory sense as it relates to vaginal secretions, to which men are acutely susceptible, and thus to women and their bodies. For some students of misogyny, then, woman-hating is not culture-bound at all, but is part of our evolutionary biology, deeply related to our gonadal organization and firmly embedded in the mammalian heritage of man. As Warren Shapiro suggests, "this ambivalence [about women] is by no means culture-specific but has instead something to do with Homo sapiens as a mammal with an unusually long period of infant/ mother interaction" (1996:11–12). If true, this is indeed unfortunate, because such an evolutionary "mammalian" origin makes misogyny all the more intractable, since there is no getting away from being a mammal.

Psychic-Dependency Theory

Another interpretation stresses boys' physical rather than psychic dependency on women as the starting point for misogynistic rage. In infancy the boy depends completely upon the mother, not only for food but also for protection, comfort, warmth, and love, and, indeed, virtually all physical pleasure. Many grown men retain this infantile sense of utter neediness at the unconscious level and come to associate it with the wife or another significant female. Their abject dependency upon women is exaggerated in most patriarchal societies because men are not supposed to cook or serve food, to wash or clean, or indeed to care for themselves. Men in such societies (most societies) do depend upon women for their comfort and indeed for their very existence.

Psychology tells us that when people are so utterly dependent upon others for the basics of life, they feel endangered. Thus they often come to regard the caretaker with resentment and even rage (Spiro 1997:17–18). In this way many vulnerable men develop a sense of antagonism toward women in general, whom they see as indispensable not only for their pleasure, but also for their very existence, and therefore overly powerful. These men see all women as, like mother, controlling their pleasure, frustrating their desires, threatening their masculine autonomy, thus cruelly dominating and abusing them.

Psychic-dependency theory has been invoked by a few anthropologists to shed light on misogyny in specific cultures where men do indeed feel especially dependent upon women. Gelber (1986:150), for example, says that highland New Guinea men are so dependent upon their women that they cannot help but resent it. The New Guinea men know that the role of women "is crucial to nearly every activity of men, from the basic activity, such as eating, to the most highly valued symbolic activity, competition for prestige." Since the men refuse to do the requisite "woman's work" involved in sustaining daily life, the wives are forced to do everything. The men, when pressed, will admit that "women are the hands of man" (Lindenbaum 1976), without whom they cannot function or even survive. The men deeply resent this paradoxical situation (for which of course they are totally responsible).

Jackson (1996:117) also invokes this "inept male" theory to explain why the men in Amazonia are so angry at their wives. The focus is more on offspring than on food and sex: the men eagerly want heirs to continue their line. But the women, as we have seen, are much less eager to get pregnant, and the men, who cannot reproduce by themselves, feel not only helplessly dependent upon, but also dominated by their antinatal wives. This frustration breeds outrage, leading to misogynistic outpourings. In Burma, likewise: the husbands are dependent upon their wives both instrumentally and emotionally, for virtually everything in life (Spiro 1997:18). This utter lack of independence from female or maternal figures leads to an enraging belief that women are not only are too important in their lives, but that they "dominate" men.

Ethnographic Applications

Some writers have used a combination of Oedipal, pre-Oedipal, and dependency theories to explain empirical cases of misogyny. Among the groups subject to such multiplex theorizing are the New Guinea highlanders and the Amazon aborigines, whose misogyny, as we have seen, is a test case in bigoted hyperbole.

Along with their olfactory hypothesis, for example, the Lidzes stress gender-identity conflict as a casual factor in New Guinea misogyny. They argue that it is not disgust at menstruation alone that causes the New Guinea men to despise, fear, and abuse women, but disgust in tandem with the psychic battle against the feminine identification. Basing their ideas upon field data collected by Herdt (1981, 1986) on the Sambia, the Lidzes make a case for viewing ritual aspects of Sambia misogyny, such as male puberty rites in which men mock femininity, as products of the inner conflict over gender identity: "It seems clear enough that Sambia men as well as those of many other Papua New Guinea peoples are concerned that the female aspects of their personalities will gain the upper hand, and it seems very likely that the severe rituals they must undergo to assure their masculinity and the need to denigrate women so severely reflect such concerns" (Lidz and Lidz 1989:101).

A similar theory figures in Thomas Gregor's discussion of the antifemale beliefs of the Mehinaku Indians of central Brazil. The Mehinaku men, as we have seen, are very misogynistic, calling the vagina "dirty," abusing women as being of no account, and so on. It turns out that these men experience a very prolonged period of intimacy with the mother, which comes to an abrupt end only after they are forcibly removed by adult men from the mother's embraces. On the basis of Mehinaku male folklore and their rather macho sexual ideology, Gregor argues that the men harbor a deep, lingering identification with their mothers and longing for mothers' nurturing. At the unconscious level, these regressive feelings are incompatible with the culturally appropriate image of men as tough, strong, and independent. Thus, Gregor argues, they experience a conflict between the macho image and the tenacious woman-identification (Gregor 1985:197). According to Gregor, the man's conflicting feelings of anger and dependency are generalized to all women "and become the basis for devaluating women and accepting the culture of masculinity" (182).

Robert and Yolanda Murphy arrive at a similar interpretation concerning the Mundurucú Indians, also of the Brazilian Amazon (Murphy and Murphy 1974; R. Murphy 1977). Like their neighbors, the Mehinaku, the Mundurucú men are very misogynistic and macho, very concerned about their male privileges and jealous of their manhood, which must never be contaminated with anything feminine. These men also experience a prolonged period of intimacy with their mothers, sleeping with them, and nursing until age five.

Reviewing this material, the Murphys argue that much of the Mundurucú antifemale ideology stems from their psychic struggle to detach from the mother. These Indian men, they say "are born of women, nurtured and loved by women, protected and dominated by women, yet they must become men" (1974:226). The greatest threat to their manhood is their own regressive fantasy about a return to maternal symbiosis. The Murphys extrapolate from their Brazilian data to men everywhere and argue that there is in every male a struggle between his maturation and his status as a man, on the one hand, and his return to passivity on the other (1974:226–27). We have indeed seen that the fear of "re-

turning to nothingness" figures strongly in many misogynist fantasies and phobias and tends to assimilate to a fear of extinguishment and death in many men.

Does Misogyny Recapitulate Phylogeny?

These various ideas, although perhaps insufficient in themselves to explain all
types of misogyny everywhere, do help us understand the ubiquitous male fears
of extinction, helplessness, drowning in women's embrace, paralysis, and returning to "nothingness." Regarded as a whole, one underlying concept links
these theories: the idea that maleness is a fragile pose, an insecure facade,
something made up, frangible, that men create beyond nature. Linked to this is
the notion that this masculine artifice has to be defended against an encroach-
ing, elemental, "dependent" femaleness in the same way that civilization has to
be defended against entropy.

This concept has been further elaborated in ontological terms by a number
of neurobiologists to include a genetic, as well as psychic, component. The
genetic hypothesis of male fragility, rather grandiose in its evolutionary implications, points to the fact that the human fetus is in fact anatomically female
until masculinized through the action of certain late-appearing hormones. That
is, the primal state of the human organism in the womb is classically female not
male (*pace* Freud). Thus, in order to differentiate somatically, the male fetus
has to enact a permanent separation from a prior state of femaleness — a primal
female state that is always "there" in submerged form. This inner femaleness
threatens to reassert itself, subvert the superimposed "cover," and take over the
organism. Thus, the state of being male, the condition of masculinity itself, as a
cultural construct, and psychic condition, is a parlous artificial state of being, a
thin veneer over a deep and abiding femaleness.

Slipp summarizes the bioneurological basis for this notion:

the mammalian fetus has feminine structures during the earliest stages of its existence.
Genetically, the male fetus has a YX set of chromosome, while the female has XX.
Because of the Y chromosome, the male fetus is differentiated structurally from the
female by the release and action of the androgen hormone, testosterone. This occurs, in
humans, from the sixth week to the third month of life. . . . Essentially, the female is the
primordial or basic form of the fetus. Within the Garden of Eden of the womb, it is Adam
that arises out of Eve, and not vice versa. (1993:173)

Intrigued by nature's "masculinization project," Slipp and other theorists extrapolate from this, apparently on the basis of the analogy about ontogeny

recapitulating phylogeny, to conclude that the powerful rejection of femaleness in so many men may be a genetic response to the uncertain state of their own identity as male.

This concept is useful in explaining certain aspects of misogynist feelings. For one thing, it gives us insight into the intense fear that most misogynists have of some powerful force that lurks within the male self, waiting to usurp their manhood, take over their bodies and minds, and hurl them down into some soft, wet, feminized miasma. There could be no better metaphor for the man's desire to return to the "liquidity" of the womb. Clearly, many misogynist men must harbor inordinate hatred for this regressive impulse within themselves. Similarly, the sense of being poisoned or corrupted by some female-induced pestilence could also be interpreted as a psychopathological somatization of this sense of inner defilement; hence all the sickness and contagion imagery. What is rotting is one's own defenses against the self.

Also, the abstract moral sense that women pose a threat to civilization also may be seen as stemming from the same regressive impulse. For if all men gave in to this infantile desire to regress, civilization would indeed disappear, because there would be no men to do the work to support civilization. I made just this point about this "extinctionist" male fantasy in a global study of masculinity codes (Gilmore 1990). In that study, I concluded that manhood cults, such as machismo, are not simply ways of brutalizing women, but are often built up as barriers by cultures against men's regressive feelings, as a way of inducing men to be brave and strong in the face of adversity. Misogyny may be seen as an unfortunate epiphenomenon of these heroism codes.

Frustration-Aggression, or Sour-Grapes Theory

The final universalistic explanation for misogyny derives from work done in the behavioral school of experimental psychology. The idea is relatively simple, stemming from the bioneurological differences between male and female sexual arousal and their social consequences. This "frustration-aggression" theory of misogyny, as I will call it, views misogyny as the social product of male sexual frustration.

As many studies have shown (summarized in Symons [1979] and Konner [1982]), and as common sense tells us, the male's sexual response is more peremptory than the female's. Men are more easily and more frequently aroused by simple visual stimuli than are women (Freud noted this is an aspect of evolutionary biology). Men also (perhaps as a consequence of the visual-stimuli arousal) tend to be far more sexually promiscuous than women. Psychological studies have shown that the average American man thinks about sex about ten times more often than the average woman does and has many more fantasies and daydreams about anonymous sexual encounters. Gregor summarizes:

The anthropology of sexual behavior has established that sexuality is astonishingly plastic and variable in its expression from culture to culture. No purported universals in sexual behavior are unquestioned, and only a few seem reasonably well documented. Among the best established of these is that males have a higher level of sexual interest than do females. Evidence in favor of this proposition includes men's higher levels of androgens, which are connected to the sexual drive in both male and female, the suppression of the orgasm in many sexually dysfunctional women, and the lower level of sexual stimulation required for male arousal. (Gregor 1985:3)

The differences in sexual response between the sexes are both qualitative and quantitative, and they go back to the basic physiology of reproduction. After puberty, the male gonads (the testes) produce sperm constantly, putting relentless pressure on the man for release, as occurs for example in involuntary nocturnal emissions. Although there are equally imperative emotional and social pressures involved in women's sexuality, there is no equivalent neurobiological, or *physiological,* pressure for frequent orgasm. Consequently, given the peremptory power of male libido, men probably experience a greater degree of sexual need and therefore frustration than women. If so, this would help explain the constant male obsession with sex and the polymorphous erotic fantasies that all men constantly have. As we all know, and as the experimental psychologist John Dollard and his followers proved long ago (Dollard et al. 1939), frustration in the mammals, human beings included, leads to feelings of anger toward the inhibiting object and then usually to acts of aggression toward it.

From this stimulus-response angle, we might interpret misogynistic hostility as an affective offshoot of the inevitable frustration that most men experience in their attempts to achieve complete sexual fulfillment. Complete sexual fulfillment for males is simply unlikely to occur given the social, moral, not to mention legal prohibitions that exist in all cultures about promiscuity. Complete fulfillment is also probably unobtainable for purely psychodynamic reasons, as Freud argued in "On the Universal Tendency to Debasement in the Sphere of Love" (1912:189). Most men, Freud claimed, can never find full satisfaction in their erotic life because the residue of Oedipal fixations makes sex always a substitute, never a completion: "as a result of the imposition of the barrier against incest, the final object of the sexual instinct is never any longer the original object but only a surrogate for it." Always dissatisfied to some extent, then, and frustrated by woman's limited accessibility, most men are simply angry at "Woman" for being sexually arousing and beautiful, and at the same time frustrating.

Anthropologist Thomas Gregor has actually invoked such a frustration-aggression formula idea in trying to explain the misogyny of the Mehinaku Indians of Central Brazil. As well as being notoriously misogynistic, most men are paradoxically obsessed with sex, saying they can never get enough of it. Often dissatisfied with the quantity, if not quality, of the sex they get from their rather disinterested wives and their often calculating mistresses, the men criticize women for being less interested in sex than they are. The consensus among the Mehinaku men is that women are "stingy with their vaginas" (Gregor 1985:33), cruelly withholding. Following the sour-grapes theory, it is probably not surprising that these same men vilify the hard-to-get vagina as dirty, uncanny, and polluting.

In the next chapter, we introduce companion and competing theories that confine themselves to specific cases and rely more on the various structuralisms, sects of Marxism, and varieties of feminism.

From the start, the gods made woman different.

—Semonides, *Woman*

9. Structural and Materialist Theories

PSYCHOLOGICAL AND GENETIC THEORIES that emphasize such factors as castration anxiety or olfactory dysphoria help to illuminate some of the many constants in misogynistic behavior — for example, menstrual fears and taboos. But they do not help very much when it comes to understanding the variables, such the intensity of horror associated with the bodily effluvia or terror of the vagina. Theories that attempt to explain the variation and the local differences in empirical cases might be called structural or materialistic theories: they emphasize stimulus-response rather than "innate" intrapsychic dynamics, and they look beyond the psyche, to impinging "outside" factors, to account for the male attitudes.

Structural-Functional Theories: Melanesia

It seems axiomatic that some psychological factor is involved here. But many anthropological theorists reject psychology altogether and see misogyny as performing a material or political "function" in society. Most traditional anthropologists, for example, see misogyny as having the function of contributing to male hegemony — keeping women down. However, we have already seen some other structural-functional interpretations that take a more "value-neutral" position, seeing misogyny as performing some sort of adaptive role in "fitting" the society into its environment. These ecological approaches are especially prominent in New Guinea and Amazonia.

Given the proliferation of misogynistic attitudes and their lurid ritualization in highland New Guinea, where people are still close to nature in the sense
of relying on Neolithic technology, anthropologists working there have been
unable to resist functionalist and ecological explanations. The intrepid Australian Mervyn Meggitt (1958), for example, attributes highland sexual antagonism to the practice of intermarriage between warring groups: men marry
women from groups they fight, and in-marrying wives are therefore considered
antagonists. As a consequence of these marriage patterns, these women are
(perhaps unsurprisingly) distrusted and feared, and held in contempt as inferior
and foreign. Others have weighed in with further refinements in this general
approach.

Langness (1967) takes a slightly different perspective on the issue, although he also concludes that sexual antagonism is directly related to the
warfare endemic to the highlands. His argument is that a small population, like
those of highland clans, is faced with a constant threat of annihilation under the
warlike conditions that prevail. Such groups urgently need a powerful and
motivated army to defend them. In order to attain the degree of male solidarity
to support such an army, the males must separate from the women physically
and emotionally and find some unifying cause to rally around. Thus, misogynistic scapegoating can be seen as an indirect means of achieving male bonding
needed for survival. The ideology of female pollution provides a symbolic
justification for spatial segregation and thus ensures the necessary physical
conditions for masculine unity. Stated more succinctly: despising the women
creates male esprit de corps.

The ethnologist Marilyn Gelber (1986) offers a more recent interpretation.
Taking a structural-functional view combined with a Marxist stance about the
functions of "ideology," Gelber says that like patrilineal peoples everywhere,
the men of the New Guinea highlands live in agnatic local groups and uphold
descent in the male line. However, these agnatic local groups are unusually
mixed and fluid demographically owing to the frequent population movements,
asylum seeking, and refugeeism that characterize the highlands as a result of
chronic warfare. In order to function effectively under these unstable conditions, the men need moral unity to compensate for the structural disunity. To
survive as a coherent group, they have to reassert whatever ties that bind and
counteract genealogical diversity. The ideology of woman-bashing serves this
unifying purpose.

Gelber's case rests on the premise that whenever one interprets an ideology, the first question to be asked is "cui bono": who benefits? To what "use" is
a specific ideology being put (151)? Her answer: "The quality of being male, as

opposed to female, is something which all men of the local group obviously have in common. Elevating this distinction to a principle of inclusion and exclusion and endowing it with a mystique may help the men of the locality to disregard or minimize their own conflicting loyalties and statuses" (58).

Gelber thus corroborates the Meggitt-Langness hypotheses, using a wider set of data. Bashing women is the only group enterprise uniting the men in both a moral and a physical sense (because the men live in all-male men's houses for fear of their wives). The men derive two specific benefits from this practice. First, they achieve a group coherence otherwise impossible. Second, they can go off and fight their enemies with enhanced psychological vigor. Thus, to take this to its logical conclusion, the entire society benefits, not just the men, since the men are better fighters and can protect everyone from attack. Curiously, such circular functional interpretations find latent benefits in misogyny for the women who bear its brunt. This paradox, of course, does not sit well with feminists.

In another stab at finding adaptive value in New Guinea misogyny, Lindenbaum suggests that Melanesian ideas about female pollution help keep the highland population under control. When they were first discovered, in the 1930s and 1940s, the native highland populations did seem, according to current estimates at that time, to be approaching the maximum carrying capacity of the land given the limitations of aboriginal horticultural practices. Populations were dense, and there was already crowding along the valley walls, driving neighbors into frequent skirmishes as the people expanded their gardens. It is true, of course, that the men's fears of women did keep the frequency of sexual intercourse low, as we have seen. (Lindenbaum suggests that New Guinea misogyny might have been "an effective cultural barrier to human reproduction" [1972:248] — that is, an indirect form of birth control.)

To be fair, none of these theorists falls entirely into the usual functionalist trap of teleology. That is, none of them confuses cause and effect: Gelber does not contend that the men hate women "in order" to achieve solidarity; nor does Lindenbaum claim the men ran from women "in order" to keep the population down. Rather, they see male bonding and the resultant social or demographic effect as consequences or unintentional sequelae of the ideology. In any case, it is clear that the misogyny can be "explained" as having a useful function, even if this function is latent and unconscious — an epistemological position that most anthropologists today, not only feminists, find objectionable.

From a psychological viewpoint, it is nevertheless not surprising that the highland New Guinea men would elaborate their anxieties about the alien women in their midst into a series of paranoid beliefs and institutions about women. These beliefs and practices about female pollution can be seen as a utilitarian metaphor for a very real fear of women's capacity for betrayal. The contamination of betrayal simply gets restated in a symbolic idiom of magical pollution. This reworking of a social phobia into a magical belief system is a common enough distortion among people anywhere — indeed, an intellectualization not too different from what we have seen in Europe.

Sex Ratios

Another theory that emphasizes demography bears mentioning. Based on global data rather than New Guinea or any other specific place, this explanation is offered by sociologists Marcia Guttentag and Paul F. Secord in their book *Too Many Women: The Sex Ratio Question* (1983). The authors propose a statistical correlation worldwide between the sex ratio in any given society (that is, the numerical proportion of men to women) and the valuation and status of women. Using statistical data from many past and present societies, from primitive to advanced, they argue that when adult women outnumber adult men in a given society (when there are "too many women" due to war, male migration, or other demographic causes), the men will tend to depreciate and ill-use the women, who represent an overabundant and therefore cheapened resource. Conversely, when women are in short supply, the men will hold women in higher esteem and will be less misogynistic. The authors make a good case for medieval Europe, where women vastly outnumbered men and where misogyny did indeed reach a kind of apex, as we have seen. However, their hypothesis fails in many tribal contexts in which women are both scarce and devalued at the same time.

For example, among the Yanomamo Indians of Venezuela, men outnumber women due to violent spousal abuse and female infanticide (Chagnon 1997). Yet the Yanomamo men, as we have seen, are among the most misogynist males on the face of the planet, treating their wives like slaves. So, once again, we have a useful explanation in a few specific cases, but one that, despite the authors' assertions, has limited applicability.

Some Feminist Views

There is wide disagreement among functional theorists about what purpose misogyny performs and who benefits. However, most of these theories begin with pretty much the same interpretive position concerning ideology and politics: the basic premise that an ideology such as misogyny is always a response to real social and political threats. The threat may be to the very existence of the entire group, in the case of egalitarian societies under conditions of warfare, or the threat may take the form of a challenge to the hegemony of the elite group. All the political theories we will peruse owe something to the Marxist-Gramscian notion of hegemony — that is, the belief that the ruling ideas are the ideas of the ruling class (or sex) and are specifically designed to justify the oppression of the subordinate groups.

Another approach to the function of misogyny is purely feminist, leaving out any reference to social class and other Marxist tenets. For some radical feminists, misogyny is the ideological handmaiden to patriarchy, which is the major form of inequality worldwide and the basic engine of world history. Many of these feminists see world history not as the unfolding dialectic of class conflict, as in Marxism, but as stages of gender conflict. For these theorists, misogyny is a carefully cultivated prejudice intended to debase women and thus to legitimize their oppression in society. For some feminists, such as Katherine Anne Ackley (1992:3) and most of the contributors to her edited volume of misogyny in literature, this male ideology is not premeditated, but simply the product of male nature and an uncomplicated, if nasty, masculine wish to dominate. Men are all in the grip of a "basic gynophobia" stemming from innate aggression caused by their endocrinology.

A variation on this reductionistic and sexist view is found in the recent work of some male feminists (perhaps "antimasculinists" would be a better description), like R. W. Connell (1995), Miguel Vale del Almeida (1996), and Matthew Gutmann (1997). These writers believe that misogyny is entirely socially constructed. It is the ideological spinoff of male cults like machismo, which demonize women as a means of subjugating them. Consequently, to cure themselves of misogyny, these theorists urge men to get rid of "traditional" manhood, "hegemonic" masculinity, or "heroic manliness" (whatever these terms may mean). They argue (paradoxically, very belligerently) that a gentle, pacifist androgyny is the only solution to the male malady; in other words, why can't a man be more like a woman? Connell, in particular, is vitriolic, almost violent, in his hysterical denunciations of "traditional masculinity," which he wants stamped out everywhere.

Empirically, these antimasculinist views find some support and some opposition. The idea that misogyny is a by-product of the culture of manhood seems relevant for "macho" warrior societies like those of New Guinea. The more macho men are and the more wars they fight, the more seemingly misogynistic they indeed are. But the same theory fails utterly in cases like the Semai, the Yurok, the Nepalese Hindus, the Buddhists, and the Bushmen, among whom the lack of a warrior code goes hand in hand with ample evidence of the *horror mulieris* in one form or another. These gentle peoples do not engage in warfare, and all of them are in fact devoted to nonviolence as a way of life. Neither do they have a masculinity code that depreciates women. Yet they harbor some crippling anxieties about menstrual blood, and most of them entertain myths and legends about a dangerous female who entraps men and boys. Even the relatively androgynous !Kung San Bushmen of Botswana believe that female bodily functions like menstruation and childbirth are polluting (Lee 1979:451). The lack of machismo in such a society indicates that machismo and misogyny cannot be functionally linked in all cases.

Feminist Literary Theory

Katherine Rogers (1966) studied misogyny in Western literature from the ancient Greeks on and basically concurs with the feminist views described above, but she adds some multidimensional depth. Like Ackley (1992), she believes that antiwoman beliefs derive from a "patriarchal" feeling that all men have: "the wish to keep women subject to men" (271). However, she regards this patriarchal wish not as a product of male "nature," but as a response to a very real male fear of the potential *power* of women — in other words, as a defensive maneuver against anxiety: "The fear that the woman who is freed from restrictions will become man's master, lies at the root of patriarchal insistence on her subjugation." Rogers acknowledges the probable psychological genesis of such a fear, saying it may be traced ultimately to the mother's power over her son (275). Rogers has the subtlety to entertain the idea that male behavior may derive from inner conflicts rather than from a genetically induced and inherent male megalomania. Whether these inner conflicts are "curable" is a question she does not attempt to answer.

Some other feminists take a slightly more focused view of the functions of misogyny in patriarchal society. Noddings regards misogyny as the consequence of keeping women sequestered in the house and denying them their rightful place in the wider realm of society. Misogyny is a "moral-theological justification" for male superordination in the public (i.e., political) realm of life (Noddings 1989:36). Noddings regards this political-spatial subjugation as the basis of woman's worldwide disenfranchisement.

Certainly the degree to which misogyny sparks the seclusion of women indoors and out of sight would tend to lend credence to this idea. At least it seems relevant in many Arabic and Muslim societies, the Latin-Catholic Mediterranean societies, and those other preindustrial cultures in which ideas of honor and shame govern sexual relations and where women are either veiled or segregated in the home.

Historical Materialist Approaches

The views described above, although they look to specific contexts, nevertheless have a fairly global scope. Oppression and male dominance are after all nearly universal, varying only in intensity. Other students of misogyny, however, argue that misogyny is a variable phenomenon that cannot be attributed to the nature of man or woman, but must instead be located in the particular historical and cultural *context*. After all, some societies are more patriarchal than others, so each case has to be examined individually.

This ad hoc approach, sometimes called the "historical materialist" viewpoint (Bloch 1991:83), obviously has strong Marxist affinities, but also partakes of Marxism's academic heir, the currently fashionable postmodernism. For many postmodern theorists, woman is not a "thing" defined by her "essence" but an endlessly negotiable "text to be read," and thus to be appropriated in any given situation (Bloch 1991:47). Like literature, the female text has a variety of meanings depending upon the political intentions of the reader. Men see what they want according to the dictates of their own material interests, which are, in turn, set by local conditions of time and place. The postmodernists claim that to attribute misogyny to inherent traits of either men or women is to take an "essentialist" position: an a priori assumption of immutable qualities.

However, there are problems with this position. A major drawback is a lack of grounding in the physical sciences. Without sound knowledge of biological and genetic sciences, the postmodernists can blithely claim that man is the one animal whose body has no inherited genetic load and whose evolution has no noticeable effect upon his current behavior. In their view, man is thereby excused from membership in the animal kingdom, courtesy of rather mystical invocations about the evils of essentialism.

Despite such drawbacks, some of the more enlightened of these theorists have done some excellent work on the origins of misogyny in specific periods and cultures; outstanding examples are those of Howard Bloch (1991) on medieval Christianity; Peter Brown (1988) and Elaine Pagels (1988) on late Roman and Dark Age Europe, Michael Solomon (1997) on early modern Spain, Bram Dijkstra (1996) on Victorian Europe, Steven Derné (1994, 1995) on Hindu India, and Tonglin Lu (1995) on Communist China.

Bloch's work is an erudite and concise exposition of the best in the historical-materialist and postmodern positions. Taking his cue from Jack Goody's work on early Church social policy (1983), Bloch argues that medieval misogyny could represent the ideological dimension of a patristic attack on women as threats to the power of the Church: the early Christian dualistic split in the representation of women (that is, the split between the angel in the house and the lascivious devil out of it) permitted the patriarchs to domesticate women, to infantilize them, to keep them out of the public life, and in so doing to gain control over their bodies, their children, and their property (Bloch 1991:81–83). Bloch argues that the ecclesiastical hierarchy wanted to get its hands on the property that women and families controlled, as well as the reproductive capacity of women. So, during the formative period of the Catholic hegemony, the Church elders — all men — promulgated a philosophy that demonized women, thereby making it easy to deprive them of legal rights. Bloch's view is that medieval misogyny, far from being determined by the immutable biology of sex or by innate male psychology, is caused by deeper cultural currents determined by material forces and interests that cannot be confused with nature and which he identifies as "family structure, patterns of inheritance and control of patrimony" (177). But how such fleeting legal norms as control of patrimony and patterns of inheritance got to be deeper than biology and sex is anyone's guess.

Historian Peter Brown has made a similar argument about the role of the formative Catholic Church. To simplify somewhat, Brown's argument is that the early Church seized upon sexual asceticism as a unique form of worship that could set the Christian faith apart from all others and achieve a special form of identity for it as well as hierarchical control over the Christian priests. Sexual puritanism served as the unifying focus that could define the struggling new faith and encourage its internal social and moral cohesion. Since sexual renunciation was also a renunciation of woman, misogyny became a kind of self-defining ideology that made the Church a unified body of thought and a unified body of men.

Thus the studied misogyny of much ascetic literature did not reflect merely a shrinking away from women as a source of sexual temptation. It was mobilized as part of a wider strategy. It served to contain and to define the place of the ascetic movement in late Roman society. . . . The leaders of the churches in Egypt as elsewhere, fell back on ancient traditions of misogyny in order to heighten a sense of sexual peril. In so doing they ensured that their heroes, the monks, remained in the prestige-filled, and relatively safe, zone of the desert. In fourth-century Egypt, fear of woman acted as a centrifugal separator. (Peter Brown 1988:243)

Later, as the Christian faith became the official state religion in Europe, this kind of "separating" asceticism continued to serve as a justification of men's domination over women, largely through St. Augustine's reading of the scriptures, and as a buttress for women's seclusion.

Historian Elaine Pagels takes a slightly modified view. She sees the parable of the Fall in the Bible as a moral statement about the human propensity to do evil, a propensity inherent in the sexual instinct. As the early Church sought to control all human behavior within its growing realm, the Old Testament implication about human ungovernability inherent in the parable of the Fall could be used, as it was initially in the teachings of Paul and later by Augustine and other ascetics, as a justification for institutional control over the individual. This reading of Genesis was later seized upon by both Church and state leaders to legitimate imperial rule. The repression of the sexual impulse thus became the prototype of all varieties of governance, political as well as moral and spiritual. Naturally, since it is woman's body that inspires the evil that men do, it is woman who must be removed from sight and kept in bondage.

In his analysis of the antiwoman medical texts in early modern Spain, Michael Solomon takes an even narrower view of misogyny's function in Christian Europe. Taking the usual cui-bono approach by presupposing that misogyny is always consciously or unconsciously directed toward gaining some contiguous material advantage, he asks: "What do men hope to gain by their anti-woman diatribes?" (1997:3). Solomon concludes that antiwoman ideology worked to keep women out of the lucrative curing professions so that men might monopolize them. By associating women with disease itself, the male doctors could more easily justify barring them from the "authorized system of health care" (172–73).

Again, this Machiavellian thesis may work in the case at hand, but it cannot be extrapolated to, let us say, Melanesian or Amazonian misogyny, where *horror mulieris* has negative institutional effects upon the men as well as some positive effects. Melanesian misogyny denies the men much sexual gratification and even more egregiously leads to painful rituals of propitiation. It also limits the men's movements and terrorizes them with taboos and magical prohibitions. In other words, some forms of misogyny do not seem to help so much as hinder men, which makes the "cui-bono" model less useful. How can the masochism be explained — the self-mutilations, prohibitions, self-flagellations, denials?

Turning to more modern times, Bram Dijkstra concludes that in Victorian Europe aesthetic women-bashing was caused by the exigencies of burgeoning late nineteenth-century capitalism. This regnant capitalism needed to desexualize labor, so its leaders turned sex (and by extension women) into a threat to be repressed. This same expanding capitalism bred European imperialism, which in turn demanded that women stay home, repress their sexuality, and mind the children. It also codified bourgeois cultural hegemony, which taught men to be chaste so they could save their energy to do the dirty work of the empire (Dijkstra 1996:58–59). A sexist ideology that kept women in the house and promoted male heroism was the logical outcome of a cultural environment in which the "evolving male" was expected to combine socioeconomic belligerence with an ideal "of personal continence in the service of worldly success" (Dijkstra 1986:235).

Thus, for Dijkstra, Victorian misogyny is the product of a certain kind of late-monopoly, imperialist capitalism. While this theory is again quite useful for the case at hand, it does not seem too relevant for understanding New Guinea menstrual taboos, Hindu she-demons, early Buddhist misogynistic exhortations, or the Qur'an's denigration of female sexuality. Imperial capitalism cannot be branded the villain in all these cases. Besides, misogyny seems completely compatible with many other forms of economic and political relations; the bourgeoisie has no monopoly on misogyny.

Curiously, Communism has also been blamed for misogyny. In a study of male attitudes in contemporary mainland China, the literary scholar Tonglin Lu regards institutional misogyny as the result of conscious Communist government policy, especially in the workplace. Her explanation is that it stems from anxiety within the Communist male hierarchy about losing primacy of place to strong women. Chinese women-bashing is, therefore, "largely motivated by fear" (Lu 1995:8), fear of women's growing influence in the factories and other places of production. Lu sees this sexist policy as a last-ditch attempt of the ossified Communist leadership to find a scapegoat for the failures of the past decades. She regards this as typical of late-Communist culture: "Like the nationalism dominating most Eastern European countries, the misogyny prevailing in contemporary China can be explained by the need to search for a different and oppositional Other onto which the source of all social problems can be projected" (Lu 1995:9). So late-monopoly Communism also seems to breed misogyny.

Turning to India, not exactly either capitalist or communist, we have a quasi-Marxist interpretation of Hindu misogyny. In two highly focused studies, ethnographer Steven Derné interviewed a large sample of Hindu men, mainly of the upper castes, in the northern Indian city of Banaras. Without being accusative or challenging, he gently solicited their own ideas about why they held women to blame for so many of society's problems. He found, not surprisingly perhaps, not only that the men were quite conscious of their masculine privileges and violently jealous of them in regard to the inroads made by females, but also that many of them openly acknowledged that their misogyny served to buttress their position and to keep women in servitude. Derné reports: "many of the men I interviewed also recognize the advantages they gain from women's subordination, and they seek to maintain their superordinate position" through the manipulation of misogynistic caricatures (1994:221). The men were simply (and admittedly) "using" misogyny as a way of maximizing their power and privileges. Putting women down made it easier to justify their subordination.

Honor and Shame

Another "contextual" explanation for the mistreatment of women derives from the ethnographic study of the Mediterranean "honor-and-shame" complex found in the traditional Mediterranean world (Peristiany 1966; Schneider 1971; Gilmore 1987). This particularly circum-Mediterranean value system has been proposed as the reason for negative attitudes toward women and for the seclusion and veiling of women. We have seen that in many of these areas, both Christian and Muslim, a man's "honor," or reputation before his peer group, depends in large part upon the sexual comportment of the women in his family. Wives, mothers, daughters, and sisters must tread the straight and narrow and are constantly watched. If a woman strays even once (and is found out), her transgression can ruin the family's reputation (that is, the man's honor) in a flash. Therefore the women loom large in the men's imagination as powerful dangers to be contained (and confined). Woman's sexuality is, once again, explosive and ruinous, like gunpowder or fire.

In the anthropological literature on the Mediterranean, honor is shown to be a male attribute (Pitt-Rivers 1977:21). Frank Stewart (1994:107–8), writing about the Bedouin, states simply and categorically that Bedouin women do not have honor, and that only men can lay claim to it. Women, instead, have the reciprocal of honor, which is "shame," that is, sexual modesty (Pitt-Rivers (1961:114).

In the value system of traditional Mediterranean societies, male honor derives in large measure from the struggle to maintain intact the shame of their kinswomen. This struggle renders male esteem insecurely based upon the behavior of their women, who indeed have the awesome power to destroy the carefully cultivated honor of the men. The particular native concept of "honor," then produces a precarious inverse equation of moral obligations in which women unintentionally become the weak link in the chain of manly virtue and the vulnerable point in family status. In a sense, woman's shame, or shamelessness, is once again perceived as a kind of danger or contagion: "Dishonour is contagious, through women," as John Davis says for southern Italy (1973:160). Woman's sexuality, and by extension, women themselves, therefore exercise tremendous power over men and their patrilines, and this power to damage is associated with a contagion that must be contained and isolated. Women can corrupt or "poison" reputation, in typically misogynistic terms of desecration and social destruction which must be fought with all means, including killing. In the contemporary Muslim Middle East, men are still occasionally aroused to violence by their women's sexual misconduct. As late as 1999, between January and July, eleven women were murdered by their kinsmen in Jordan for sexual offenses (*New York Times,* 13 August).

By referring to honor and shame, anthropologists help us understand why women are said to be dangerous and are devalued in some parts of the world — and hence why they must be dominated and hidden, kept indoors, veiled, and heavily chaperoned. But naturally, this interpretation is empirically limited to some Mediterranean and Middle Eastern societies, mainly in earlier times; and although there is some evidence that other cultures still place some emphasis on honor and shame, this explanation has not been seriously proposed for any other part of the world. It is clearly not relevant where females are not secluded and where sexual shame is not an important cultural issue — for example, among sexually liberated peoples like the Mehinaku and many modern Europeans.

Some Summary Thoughts

Although useful, all these political theories fail in one important way: they do not tell us why a political ideology of male supremacy should necessarily include magical elements, a terror of the vagina, anxieties about the loss of honor and phobias about mermaids, feelings of disgust and revulsion about blood, zoomorphic transformation fantasies, and concepts of pollution and contagion. By comparison, consider how capitalist hegemony functions to oppress the workers (in Marxism). Marxists believe that the oppression of the poor is facilitated by bourgeois notions of superiority-inferiority. This seems reasonable. But even dogmatic Marxists would probably admit that such notions rarely include hysterical accusations that the poor are magically polluting the rich, or that the workers are intrinsically evil or have frightening sexual organs or sinister chthonic powers emanating from their bodies.

As I argued in the introduction to this book, antiwoman feelings are usually driven by an irrational emotionality that is not the same as the simple expediency that characterizes political oppression or economic exploitation. Oppressing someone does not necessarily lead the oppressor to create a justifying ideology attributing pollution and magical danger to the oppressed. There must be some other, more visceral, more emotive element involved. The factors above demand a psychological dimension. As Ward Goodenough puts it: "there is no logical reason why male dominance should be associated with . . . ideas that women are impure and defiling and hence dangerous to men" (1996:192).

Mental Structures

Finally, there is the "French" mental-structure interpretation, which focuses not on sociopolitical context but on alleged cognitive structures that exist in the mind. In a series of publications, Claude Lévi-Strauss developed and elaborated a theory of mental functioning based on the notion of binary oppositions, which he believes underlie the structure of all human cognition. To simplify somewhat, his analyses treat all mythic themes as metaphors that oppose such linked polarities as culture-nature, raw-cooked, domesticated-wild, man-woman, left-right, safety-danger, good-evil, high-low, sacred-profane, and so on. Acting as a kind of metalanguage for ordering experience, these binary scales provide a normative grammar for ordering the world into categories and thus making sense out of the threatening cosmos. Although Lévi-Strauss himself nowhere says so in so many words, such bipolar schemes are usually developed by the males of any given society (since males control culture). These schemes also always have a value referent. Since men make up the schemes, they naturally place themselves in the category that includes "good," "right," and "pure." And since women are the opposite of man, it stands to reason by a process of homologous reasoning that they should be placed in the other pole representing "bad" and "polluted."

Thus misogyny may be interpreted as stemming from the bipolar working of the male mind (as well as its inherent egoism). Proposing a different kind of "innateness," then, this Lévi-Straussian theory does not indicate a good prognosis for the male malady — which, however, is beside the point. Also, Lévi-Strauss's claim for the universality of his binary pattern seems to be supported, since misogyny does seem to be at least near universal. But this "mental-structure" explanation fails to tell us why some societies are *more* misogynistic than others. Again, other factors must come into play to either mitigate or exaggerate innate misogynistic tendencies, if such exist.

Now it is time to take a more systematic look at the other side of misogyny — at man's unquenchable love for and glorification of woman — and to confront the question of what this seismic ambivalence means for the life of man . . . and of woman.

The Eternal Feminine

Draws us ever upwards.

—Goethe, *Faust,* Part 2, 4.7

10. Gynophilia

IF THEORIES ABOUT MISOGYNY make an impenetrable thicket, so do men's feelings. Like so much having to do with men and women, misogyny is only one piece of the puzzle. To be sure, many men hate and fear women, but just as many also love and revere them. It is obvious that two edges of this mental sword are related in some labile fashion and share origins in the ancient touchstone of the primitive male cerebellum.

"Woman" has the uncanny power to frustrate man's noble (but unrealistic) ideals, to subvert his lofty (hollow) ends, and to sully his (deluded) quest for spiritual perfection; but she also, and not coincidentally, provides him with the greatest pleasures of his earthly life. These pleasures are not just sexual release, but also other life-sustaining comforts that only a woman can provide (based on the organization of most societies): food, tenderness, nurturing, and heirs. It is not surprising that the men who most deplore and distrust women are the same ones who most admire, want, and need them; the most histrionic and poignant rituals of woman-adulation occur in the same societies responsible for the most egregious and sordid examples of woman-bashing.

Equally powerful and equally ubiquitous, this other side of man's torturous mental coin could be called (following the practice of using the Greek root) "gynophilia" — an admittedly monstrous neologism offered reluctantly in the absence of any other acceptable term. Like misogyny, gynophilia is kind of male neurosis, for it stems from the same unresolved conflicts and it has both a carnal and a spiritual manifestation with the usual repetitive rituals and inventive folklore. It is an overvaluation existing side-by-side with misogynistic vilification in a parallel universe, as it were.

The two sides of the equation are destined to coexist eternally, each stimulating and exacerbating its opposite. Let us start with a detour back to Melanesia.

Woman-Loving Melanesia

One of the traits that first fascinated anthropologists working in the New Guinea region is the strikingly *ambivalent* male attitude. On the one hand there are endless rituals by which men combat female pollution; on the other there are equally numerous and bizarre rituals by which men honor women by emulating them. These emulative rituals seek paradoxically to bring men and women closer together, to break down the walls between them erected by the men while in misogynist mode, and to bestow upon the men a mystical simulacrum of femininity.

The most extravagant of these female-impersonation rites is what anthropologists call "male menstruation" (Tuzin 1997:165) or "imitative menstruation" (Lindenbaum 1976:57). These are periodic ritual bloodlettings specifically designed to emulate the women's monthly flow. By doing this, the men believe they can capture not only the potency but also the fertility that nature bestows upon women. The men want this sexual transfiguration desperately because they feel that men are weak and need women's attributes to thrive.

Anthropologist Anna Meigs, who studied sexual ideology among the Hua people of New Guinea for eighteen months, writes: "although males denigrate females as ignorant and treacherous in the social sphere, they admire and laud their magnificent biological powers within the arcane enclave of the men's house. Through the imitation of menstruation . . . the men attempt to stimulate their lagging growth and to recover their waning vitality" (Meigs 1984:131–32). Meigs continues, speaking about the Hua people specifically, but in terms that could just as well apply to Melanesians: "Males label female organs and fluids as disgusting and dangerous, and yet also view them as the awesome sources of life itself" (73). Thus, despite their anxieties about female pollution, the men "become" menstruating women in a curious ritual mimicry of the very same biological event that instills anxiety and even hysterical fear.

The first anthropologist to report systematically on this practice of men ritually imitating women in order to capture their essence was the Australian Kenneth Read, who studied the Gahuka-Gama people of the Asaro Valley in the central highlands. His earliest work dates from about 1950, a time when the Gahuka-Gama were still almost a Neolithic society with unadulterated rites. He found that these people practiced a secret male cult, called *nama,* in which youths were forced to undergo bloodletting from their noses every few years as part of a long initiation into manhood. (In the following description I use the present tense, although many of these rites are now extinct.)

In this *nama* ritual, the older men surround the younger ones gathered near a river and thrust razor-sharp leaves back and forth in the boys' nostrils until the blood gushes forth. This bloody event is greeted with shouts of approval from the nearby throngs (Read 1952, 1965:167). The men say this simulated menstruation helps the boys grow and gives them the "natural" powers of women. The men openly admit to envying the women's biological powers and want their boys to have them.

But imitative bleeding is not always part of an initiation ceremony; nor is it confined to youths in need of growth magic. Ian Hogbin, who worked on the island of Wogeo, off the New Guinea coast, was startled to see men cutting their tongues and penises in conscious (and stated) imitation of women's periods. In *The Island of Menstruating Men* (1970), he describes the male bloodletting in chilling detail. The men do it because they believe it ritually bestows upon them some of the advantages women have from nature.

Although the Wogeo men, like other Melanesians, abhor woman's menstrual blood, or so they say, they also, and without conscious hypocrisy, regard it as a useful and powerful magical substance that makes women potentially healthier and enables them to "grow" stronger than men. Since Wogeo men do not menstruate naturally, they do not have access to the same power women have; nor can they cleanse their bodies of accumulated filth as the women do through nature. They must do so through magical (ritual) means. Male menstruation accomplishes both tasks at once, cleaning out the obstinate male plumbing and giving the man magical female powers.

When feeling the need to menstruate, the Wogeo man goes down to the beach with a sharp stone or razorlike blades of dried palm grass. He then removes his clothing and wades out in the water up to his knees. He stands there with his legs apart and induces an erection. When ready, he pushes back the foreskin and hacks at the glans until the blood gushes. A menstruating woman and a menstruating man are alike called *rekareka* (polluted). They both go into retirement, keep warm, and observe strict food taboos (Hogbin 1970:88). No one may come near either man or women in this liminal state. The sexes are made equivalent through the man's ritual menstruation; the man has, in a sense, achieved a kind of surrogate womanhood. A man says he feels "much better" after his induced "period" is over. His body loses its fatigue, his eyes grow bright, and his skin and hair "develop a luster" (88–89).

Similar practices, especially the nosebleeding (which seems by far the most popular form of male bleeding) are reported all over Melanesia. They reach an apogee in the eastern New Guinea highlands, where misogyny also reaches a climax, and both initiates and adult men participate (Berndt 1962:67–72, 104; Lindenbaum 1972, 1976; Tuzin 1980; Meigs 1984; Herdt 1982a, 1986). According to Terrance and Patricia Hays (1982:221), nosebleeding (and also bleeding of the tongue and/or urethra) may be universal in the eastern highlands. In some societies, like the Sambia, the men use prickly dried leaves, which they shove up their noses in order to rupture the mucus membrane and induce copious bleeding (Herdt 1982a:223–33, 244–46). In other societies, the men use cured cane grass or the sharpened bones of small animals to draw blood (Lindenbaum 1976:57). There are good accounts of nosebleeding or nose piercing for the Gahuka-Gama (Read 1965:167), the Gururumba (Newman 1965:42), the Bimin-Kuskusmin (Poole 1982b:127–29), and the Fore (Lindenbaum 1976:57). Alone among this group, the Bimin-Kuskusmin do not poke the nostrils with sharp objects but instead brutally tear open the nasal septum of boys during their initiation, greeting the flow of blood with whoops of joy. They also say the boys have now had their first menses (Poole 1982b:127).

Like the Wogeo islanders, many of the highland New Guinea peoples cut the penis itself to draw blood. Some tribes use both the penile-incision method together with the more common nosebleeding style to ensure sufficient flow. For example, the Ilahita Arapesh (Tuzin 1982) and the Awa (Newman and Boyd 1982) slice open the glans penis, and the Awa men may also cut wedges out of each side of the glans to increase the flow of penile blood. As well as the excruciating septum-tearing of boys, the Bimin-Kuskusmin also make an incision near the young man's navel to draw blood as though from an imitation vagina (Poole 1982b).

Elsewhere in New Guinea, the men insert slivers of bamboo or wads of sharp dried leaves into the penile urethra; in other places, the backs of male initiates are scarified with nettles to draw blood, and in yet others the nasal septum is perforated so that the blood drips (Lidz and Lidz 1989:63–64). In all cases of bloodletting the male menstruations are said to be strengthening and purifying for men (Lindenbaum 1976:57). The men believe they could not exist without these salubrious aids.

Male Pregnancy

Many men in New Guinea also entertain fantasies (and fears) about getting pregnant. The Hua believe that a man can become pregnant, sometimes as a result of homosexual intercourse, but sometimes through a more ambiguous nonsexual circumstance that is not really clear but has to do with eating proscribed foods or breaking certain taboos (Meigs 1986:46–47). Like some women, many men find pregnancy a constant threat and take precautions against it, usually of a ritual and magical type — for example, eating the proper foods and strictly observing sexual abstinence. Although some more sophisticated Hua men discount the idea of male pregnancy, many others accept it as commonplace, and some even claim to have seen fetuses "after their removal from men's bodies, an operation performed by non-Hua specialists." The surgical procedure: a cut is made in the abdomen, often in the area of the navel, and a bamboo tube is held to the wound. The fetus is said to be carried by the blood into the tube (Meigs 1984:48).

Similar male-pregnancy beliefs have been reported for the Tauna Awa, also of the eastern highlands (Hayano 1974:20). These people diagnose a man's distended stomach by saying that an embryo probably entered through the penis and the man has gotten pregnant. The Gimi people, neighbors of the Hua, believe in a disease called *amusa kio,* or "pregnant disease," which afflicts obese men, as evidenced by their swollen bellies (Meigs 1984: 47). Abdominal swelling in males is also diagnosed as possible pregnancy among the Keraki of the Trans-Fly area of New Guinea. In one case related in 1936 by ethnographer F. E. Williams, a deceased man with a distended stomach was said to have died because he was pregnant and the baby could not get out (F. Williams 1969:201–2).

In addition, New Guinea is rampant with fertility rites in which men imitate female reproduction and try to create vaginas and wombs out of natural materials. In one such rite among the Maring, reported by Buchbinder and Rappaport, the men dig earth ovens and plant certain cultigens in them, imitating impregnation and gestation. These earth ovens and the associated planting ("having a bun in the oven," so to speak) represent, the men say, their own efforts to achieve female fecundity. The little plants are taken out of the ovens when they are "ready to be born." In the anthropologists' words, the men are trying to "assimilate the vagina" (1976:29–30). Other groups practice birthing rites involving smooth stones resembling fetuses, which are buried, plus other kinds of earth burials and retrievals with other fetuslike objects. These fertility rites allow the men "access to some of the fertility and growth-producing powers attributed to females" (Meigs 1984:133).

Some of the New Guinea men dispense with the obvious transsexual symbolism of such burials altogether and go straight to cross-dressing and even to simulated transvestite sex. The Fore people have initiation ceremonies in which grown men dress up as women, grass skirts and all, and enact lurid scenes of copulation with traditionally dressed men (Berndt 1962:103). Apparently, this kind of sexual transvestism is not rare (Lindenbaum 1972:250). The men say, again, that it is good to be like women, for women are powerful and healthy, and imitating them gives men the same strengths.

The Couvade

Additionally, a few groups in New Guinea practice an institution known in anthropology as the *couvade* (from the French *couver,* to "hatch" or "incubate"), also a form of female impersonation, which is most common in South America but has been reported in a few isolated areas in Melanesia (Poole 1982a). The couvade consists of the husband's ritually participating in the wife's pregnancy and childbirth in order to empathize with her, to ease her burden, and to make the baby stronger (Munroe et al. 1973, 1981; Barnouw 1985:143). In a well-reported case among the Bimin-Kuskusmin, the man undergoing couvade may sequester himself in the family hut with his pregnant wife, observing the same food taboos as she does; he experiences sympathetic labor pains, assumes the wife's birthing position, grunts and groans along with her, and so on (Poole 1982a).

In *Symbolic Wounds* Bruno Bettelheim regards the couvade as stemming from a universal male desire to "find out how it feels to give birth" (1954:211). He argues that such transsexual rites and fantasies are expressions of "womb envy" or "parturition envy," a part of which is the male desire "to possess female genitals in addition to their own" (53). Robert and Ruth Munroe and John Whiting (1981) agree, and trace this wish to the male's latent cross-sex identity. Surveying the anthropological literature, Barnouw explains the couvade as "a pattern of variable content in some societies, in which a man observes certain taboos and restrictions in relation to his wife's childbearing cycle. He may rest before or after the birth, observe food taboos, and refrain from such actions as handling knives or sharp implements. . . . A man [in couvade] acts like a pregnant woman" (1985:142–43).

The clearest case reported for New Guinea is that of the Bimin-Kuskusmin of Sepik Province and has been described in meticulous detail by Fitz John Poole (1982a). The expectant Bimin-Kuskusmin father identifies with the pregnant wife: he observes all the food taboos that the wife observes, eating "female foods," which are normally off-limits to a man, and he gets a "female name" to further empathize with the wife. As labor progresses and she takes to her cot, he begins to play a "passive female role," lying around in the hut and being cared for by his kinsmen as she is. Like his wife, he also becomes "highly polluting" to all people except initiated men, pregnant women, and certain female ritual elders. During his wife's labor, he lacerates his body with stinging-nettle leaves, drawing blood, in order to feel and share her pain; his abdomen swells painfully (they say), and he smears it, as she does hers, with a medicinal white pigment.

When the labor pains reach their climax and birth is imminent, the husband assumes the typical squatting position of a woman in parturition; he begins violently contracting his viscera, copying the woman's pelvic contractions. This charade of labor facilitates the delivery for mother and child (Poole 1982a:69). After the birth, he, like his wife, is considered weak, fragile, and prone to postpartum illnesses; both husband and wife are quarantined along with the newborn. During the whole birth process, he is called the "pregnant father" (Poole 1982a:82).

Amazonian Parallels

One may argue, as a general rule, the greater the deprecation of women the greater the unconscious idolization; the stronger the revulsion, the greater the desire and identification. These affective opposites are directly and reciprocally related. The inverse correlation, which I think is close to being universal, is borne out empirically once again when we consider our second example of extreme woman-hating: the Amazonian Indians of South America.

Like the Melanesians, many Amazonians also engage in rites of male "menstrual" bloodletting, and they, too, explicitly liken these rites to women's menses. For example, the Kalapalo of central Brazil have an ear-piercing initiation ceremony for boys in which the first cutting of the ear is said to be like a girl's first period (Basso 1973:66). Also in central Brazil, the Mehinaku people even more explicitly identify the ear-piercing ceremony (called "Pihika") as equivalent to a girl's first menstruation (Gregor 1985:187–88). The boys undergoing Pihika and girls undergoing menarche rites experience the same preritual preparations, observe the same food taboos and fasts, and are carried to and from their hammocks in the same way so that their feet "do not touch the ground," and follow the exact same postritual proscriptions about food, sex, and work.

One of Gregor's male informants told him the boys were having their first "menstruation" in the ear-piercing rite, a parallel perceived and approved by most Mehinaku men: ear piercing, as Ketepe (another Mehinaku man) puts it, "is menstruation." He continues: "The Pihika ceremony is like a girl's first menses" (Gregor 1985:188).

We see much the same thing among the Vaupé Tukanoan Indians of the Brazil-Colombia border. In a form of imitation menstruation, the Tukanoan men rub a red plant dye (*bixa orellana*) over themselves, imitating the loss of menstrual blood (C. Hugh-Jones 1979:107) and thereby assuring themselves of a healthier and longer life. In fact, the ritual male menstruation is seen as inducing a healthful and beautiful skin change in the men, which in turn confers "semi-immortality" (271). In this way the Tukanoan men appropriate "female power" otherwise inaccessible to them (Jackson 1996:104). It is of special interest that women, thought to be "weak" and "helpless," are also associated with long life and robustness.

The Pira-paraná Tukanoans, who were studied on and off by Jean Jackson for years, make the connection between male rite and female menstruation overt, saying that their male rites constitute "imitation menstruation" (Jackson 1996:105). Thus, it is quite clear that, despite their constantly fulminating about menstrual pollution, the Tukanoans most definitely do not see menstruation as entirely negative. Rather it represents themes of life/growth and death/decay. What better metaphor could there be for the ambivalence of man toward woman and her body (Jackson 1996:104)?

Amazonian Couvade

Just as male menstruation may be considered the Melanesian female-impersonation ritual par excellence, the couvade takes pride of place for Amazonian men, among whom it is much more common than in Melanesia and a signature feature of aboriginal culture. In fact, the couvade was first reported by travelers and missionaries from Brazil in the nineteenth century (Taylor 1888), long before the New Guinea highlands were even remotely known, and although found occasionally in other parts of the world, the couvade is first and foremost an Amazonian rite (Rival 1998:629).

An early study of the Siriono hunter-gatherers of east Bolivia (Holmberg 1950:68–70) describes the couvade in some detail. The Siriono couvade consists of a long series of taboos and ceremonies that the expectant father must observe to ensure the birth of a healthy child. The father stays with his wife in the hut and eats as she does, abstaining from any proscribed foods (especially highly desirable smoked meats) that might make the baby weak or deformed.

The Indians believe that both husband and wife are pregnant and that both must watch their diet to promote the health of the fetus. After the birth, in which the father participates vicariously by imitating labor pains, mother and father are secluded and scarified together.

The Mehinaku perform similar couvade rites. The husband, although not actually imitating labor or the rigors of childbirth, follows the same rules governing his wife's confinement. He refrains from eating certain foods during her pregnancy, especially fish; he gives up sex for the duration, and immediately after the baby's birth he goes into postpartum seclusion like his wife. Although the Mehinaku couvade has a variety of meanings, such as dramatizing paternity, the most striking feature is the emphasis placed on the feminine nature of the father's connection to his offspring. Like mother and child prior to birth, the linkage is direct. The father's movements are restricted like those of a woman in an advanced stage of pregnancy; all of his activities are thought to have an direct impact on the health of his child; and, analogous to a woman who has recently given birth, "he assumes the taboos appropriate for postpartum flow of blood" (Gregor 1985:195).

The couvade was practiced in remote parts of the Amazon Basin, where old traditions linger. For example, it was still found in vibrant form among the Huaorani Indians of the Ecuadorian Amazon as late as 1998. As soon as pregnancy is detected by a Huaorani woman, both husband and wife enact a series of shared food taboos, ritual quarantines, and magical observations, all designed to make the gestation period and delivery easy and safe. The man avoids hunting and stays at home as much as possible, preferably lying in his hammock where he spends the night alone.

Gestation among the Huaorani is considered a collective effort of both parents; the father's diet is just as important to the fetus as the mother's. He is a kind of second mother. The period of couvade may continue for six months or more. The husband stays with the wife throughout the delivery, rubs her belly with nettles and magical substances, and then cuts the umbilical cord as further demonstration of the oneness of the experience (Rival 1998:625–29).

Vicarious Femaleness: Couvade-Like Practices Around the World

Although associated mainly with Melanesia and Amazonia respectively, both male menstruation and the couvade are worldwide phenomena, taking on myriad formal guises, but always involving male imitation of female bodily functions. Starting with bloodletting, we see numerous examples and variants throughout both the preliterate and "civilized" worlds, such as phlebotomizing, cupping, and leeching, all involving periodic draining of blood from veins or arteries for health reasons (Brain 1988:312). Long ago, Bettelheim called attention to several cases of self-cutting as imitation, explicit or implicit, of menstruation; for example, some Australian Aborigines practice subincision of the penis, making a longitudinal cut on the underside of the organ that not only draws blood but actually makes the male genitalia resemble the female organ in having a slitlike opening (Bettelheim 1954:173 ff.)

Another psychoanalytically oriented anthropologist, Geza Roheim, notes that the subincised penis in Australia is sometimes called "vagina" in sacred songs. Blood flowing from the cut penis is often referred to in terms meaning "women" or "milk" (1949:324). And in one ritual he describes, a man who has subincised his penis runs backward to a stream and lifts his organ to display the incision. Some central Australian societies even use parallel terms for menstrual blood and the blood that comes from the penile subincision (Roheim 1949:325). This practice of penis mutilation is found mainly in aboriginal Australia, but also occurs among many native peoples throughout the Pacific (Hays 1964:23).

In a review article on medical bloodletting in history, James Brain makes a good case that this practice, as employed throughout Western history from the ancient Egyptians on, has overtones of menstrual imitation. He remarks:

What seems abundantly clear from all the evidence is that the implicit, if not the explicit reason for bloodletting in the Occidental, and probably in the Oriental tradition too, was to stimulate or provide a substitute for menstruation. . . . When we look at what seem to be the bizarre and bloody practices of some of the so-called "primitive" peoples of the world in simulating menstruation in men, we should do well to appreciate that comparable practices were current in the Western tradition from the beginning of written records until the middle of the twentieth century. (Brain 1988:320)

Brain cites copious evidence from Western published and handwritten sources, including Roman texts and medieval and early modern medical tracts to prove his point. A Byzantine book on hygiene written in the thirteenth century, for example, makes claims for the benefits of a "hemorrhoidal flux" in men to equal women's menses. It even instructs readers to follow the phases of the moon in timing this flux — that is, to imitate woman's lunar cycle (Brain 1988:316).

By the seventeenth century, knowledge about the circulation of blood had increased thanks to the discoveries of the English physician William Harvey; nevertheless, the general practice of phlebotomy as a form of ersatz menstruation persisted in Europe (Brain 1988:318). According to Celia Mettler (1947:940), little had changed in medical writings since Hippocrates wrote, "In a woman, vomiting of blood is relieved by menstruation; when not cleared up by menstruation, nose-bleeding removes all danger," and recommended this practice periodically for men in order to remove the "bad blood." Mettler notes that among seventeenth-century physicians a periodic flux of blood was regarded as normal not only for the female after the age of puberty, but for the male: "the hemorrhoidal flux took the place of uterine bleeding. If these fluxes were suppressed and phlebotomy were not employed, trouble was to be expected" (940).

The reference to nosebleeding in the previous quotation from Hippocrates reminds us of the New Guinea rituals of male menstruation. One may also point out in this context that the nose may convey unconscious phallic symbolism; consequently nosebleeding implies a genital flow in men. Allusions to nosebleeding reappear in the most unexpected places in the Western canon. For example, it crops up gratuitously in Webster's *The Duchess of Malfi*, in which the character Antonio, secretly wedded to the duchess, has a nosebleed at a very inopportune time. His blood flows as another character, Bosola, tries to discover whether the pregnant duchess is in labor. Antonio is trying to foil Bosola's curiosity when he is suddenly afflicted with a gushing nosebleed while reviewing some papers on his desk. He expostulates:

> My nose bleeds —
> One that were superstitious would count
> This ominous, when it merely comes by chance.
> Two letters, that are wrought here for my name,
> Are drown'd in blood! (2.3)

The psychiatrist Karl Menninger (1941:63) describes a young male patient as suffering from "vicarious menstruation"; in the clinic the patient developed a profuse, apparently hysterical, nosebleed. The private correspondence between Freud and Wilhelm Fliess (who was, incidentally, obsessed with the psychological significance of the nose) is replete with references to the idea of male menstruation and its manifestation in psychosomatic nasal bleeding (Brain 1988:318).

Further Parallels

On the other hand, the couvade, being so closely linked to "primitive" mentality, with its native Amazonian roots, might seem to defy any analogies in modern civilizations. But such is not the case. Ethnographic studies find evidence of couvade or couvadelike symptoms in at least seventy-four contemporary societies, including many agrarian civilizations and even some modern industrial nations (Barnouw 1985:143). In a study of this phenomenon in Western populations, for example, clinicians Mack Lipkin and Gerry Lamb found that hysterical pregnancies and imitative pregnant behavior were surprisingly common, not only among psychiatric patients, but also among healthy, educated men. Their study found that 225 out of 1,000 expectant fathers had couvadelike symptoms, varying from distended stomachs to "morning sickness." And they note that their sample comprised mainly well-adjusted men. The men were without concomitant disease that might have explained the pregnancy symptoms (1982:112).

The British psycho-obstetrician William H. Trethowan also cites an amazing wealth of evidence drawn from biographies, memoirs, autobiographies, and the like, as well as psychiatric case histories, to show that the practice of imitative male pregnancy was not uncommon throughout Western history. For example, there is evidence that such luminaries as Francis Bacon, James Primrose, and many Restoration playwrights either experienced or witnessed such symptoms. Beaumont and Fletcher, in two of their plays written in the 1640s, *The Custom of the Country* and *A Wife for a Month,* refer to "sympathy pains" in husbands when their wives were in labor. There is also an unequivocal reference to a husband "breeding for his wife" in Restoration playwright William Wycherley's *The Country Wife.* And a clear reference to couvade-type symptomatology is found in a poem (1650) by Robert Heath:

> We observe each loving husband, when the wife
> Is laboring by a strange reciproque strife
> Doth sympathizing sicken; and't may be
> In law they're one and in divinity. (cited in Trethowan 1972:70)

Almost identical phraseology and ideas have been recorded in Germany, Ireland, and China (Trethowan 1972:70).

Male Pregnancy

Similarly, the idea that men can actually become pregnant (not merely imitate the symptoms) is common not only among men's cults in preliterate societies like New Guinea but also in Western literature and folklore. A recent study by the Italian historian Roberto Zapperi (1991) shows how the idea of "the pregnant man" has inspired western and central European folklore since ancient times. Zapperi supplies copious written data, as well as numerous images and photographs, to demonstrate this topos. Traces of this pregnant-male theme, both humorous and grotesque, are found in a wealth of tales from Italy, France, Germany, Finland, and other European countries, as well as in the ancient Hebrew and various Islamic traditions. Personal beliefs in male pregnancy, including imitative and empathetic pregnancy behavior, are also widely recorded in Western clinical and psychiatric literature (Jacobsen 1950).

Indeed, psychiatrist Gregory Zilboorg argued (1944:290) that woman-envy in men is psychogenetically older and therefore more fundamental than the penis-envy theory Freud postulated. And Bruno Bettelheim (1954) noted the similarities between "womb envy" in the boys he saw in his clinic and rituals of men's cults in Oceania. Folklorist Alan Dundes has shown that many preliterate cultures throughout the New World have myths of male partheno-genesis or "anal birthing" in which male culture heroes or gods appropriate women's procreative powers. This culture hero or spirit, usually in the guise of a raven or coyote or some other totem male animal, dives into the earth and resurfaces with some piece of magical dirt, which he then excretes through his anus, giving birth to all the creatures of the world. Dundes regards this common theme of "the mythopoeic male" as an example of a universal womb or pregnancy envy (1962:1038).

Transvestism and Female Impersonation

Transvestite rituals, too, in which men dress as women and act out feminine pantomimes, are also more common than one might expect and are not confined to "primitive cultures." Since antiquity, male cross-dressing has been de rigueur in carnivals in most Mediterranean countries (Gilmore 1998). Anthropologist Carole Counihan (1985), for example, describes transvestite ribaldry in the small Sardinian town of Bosa and notes that man-to-woman cross-dressing is a traditional feature of most southern Italian carnivals. Sex-change imagery has also occurred historically throughout literate Europe, particularly during festivals of inversion or moral disinhibition. The Greek myth of Teiresias, for example, includes a spontaneous sex change during an Attic carnival. Social historians of Europe like Natalie Davis (1978) and Julio Caro Baroja (1965) have documented male-to-woman rituals throughout medieval, Renaissance, and modern Europe. In Latin Catholic countries like Italy, Portugal, and Mexico, such transvestite rituals continue to highlight transsexual burlesque, female impersonation, birthing parodies, and other genres of sexual inversion among men (Rodriguez 1991). A recent study (1991) by cultural historian Marjorie Garber shows that cross-dressing has been an integral part of Western cultural history from the Renaissance to Hollywood's heyday. Wherever transvestism takes place as a cultural theme, male-to-female dressing is far more prevalent than the woman-to-man variety.

One notorious example of man-to-woman masquerading in mainstream America is the all-male Bohemian Club of California, whose members include former president George Bush and former governor Edmund Brown of California. The Bohemians hold an annual meeting in a redwood forest in Sonoma County, during which all members cross-dress, put on jewelry and makeup, and perform comic skits in nylons, pantyhose, and high heels. In one account, a club attorney reportedly described his own stage appearance as a wood nymph: "we wore wings and body-stockings," he reminisced with great delight (Gregor 1985:207). Other all-men's societies and organizations, whether elite political clubs like the Bohemians or noncommissioned soldiers in their barracks, often stage similar though less elaborate productions featuring female impersonations (Gregor 1985:207–8).

As noted above, men apparently do this much more often than women. Both Bettelheim (1954:35–36) and Lederer (1968:215–16) note that men and boys throughout the world seem to enjoy cross-dressing, transsexual dramatics, and pseudo-homosexual horseplay of this sort much more than females do. Stoller (1974a, 1974b), Greenson (1978), and many other neo-Freudians suggest that this means that men generally are more conflicted about their masculine identity than are women about their femininity. Gregor believes that the Mehinaku Indians, like men everywhere, are deeply troubled by remnants of their infantile cross-sex identity with the mother and try to compensate by displays of "pure masculinity," but many are still unconsciously drawn to their inner femininity and enjoy enacting sex-reversal rituals that permit the hidden woman within to come to the fore in a culturally approved, semicomic way. He concludes that "there are continuities of masculinity that transcend cultural differences" in this regard (1985:209).

A Positive Look at Menstrual Taboos

A classic case of male ambivalence about woman is menstrual taboos. Although men in virtually all cultures find menstrual blood repugnant, most have extremely conflicted feelings that include, along with pollution fears, a healthy dose of respect, awe, even adulation for the association of menstruation and reproduction. Recent feminist re-studies of menstrual taboos, in fact, have shown this positive "other side" to be as powerful as the negative, if not more so (Buckley and Gottlieb 1988a, 1988b; C. Delaney 1988; Small 1999). This reinterpretation of menstrual taboos has led to a total revision within anthropology of former assumptions about the single-sidedness of menstrual fears.

For example, anthropologists Thomas Buckley and Alma Gottlieb (1988b:37) speak of the dialectical relationship between negative and positive poles of menstrual rituals. They show that in many cultures, men may regard menstrual blood with revulsion, but this may be tempered by awe and even veneration. Menstruating women are not always denigrated, and may actually be revered and respected if they adhere to ritual prescriptions. Moreover, menarche is usually celebrated with profound honors in most cultures, despite the parallel anxieties. Janice Delaney and her coauthors (1988:18–20) also note the ambivalence with which men relate to menstrual blood and point out that many of the terms used for this blood include elements of *mana* and *sacra* (sacred and God-given qualities).

Perhaps most important in this inversely positive image of menstrual blood is its connection with human fertility. Among the Swazi of the former Bechuanaland in Africa, for example, menstrual blood is considered part of the fetus that grows within the womb. Furthermore, in certain situations menstrual blood is not destructive, but is considered a life symbol or rather a life force (Kuper 1947:107). Even in New Guinea, menstrual blood partakes of this dialectical dualism. Many highland peoples believe that babies are formed from a mixture of uterine blood and semen, so that menstrual blood is tinged with a great amount of positive symbolism, especially as the men so fervently desire sons.

In highland New Guinea, some peoples regard menstrual blood as a beneficial medicinal and protective substance. Both the Siane and the Hua peoples believe that a woman's vaginal blood is a resource that the community "cannot afford to lose," and they ritually recycle it by smearing it on young girls approaching menarche to improve their health and ensure future fecundity (Meigs 1984:132). If handled with care, the blood also makes men healthy and strong and is regarded as a powerful restorative (the men may actually ingest it in potions). Like many Melanesians, the men of these groups are very concerned about fertility and view woman's blood as one of their ideals, a sacred, spiritual substance, without which they could not live. "Women, although themselves purely material, capricious and unpredictable, continually produce spirit in the form of blood and may at any time become purely spirit without men being able to see any difference. . . . They are the ultimate ideal of society" (Salisbury 1965:75). The complete opposite of the taboos and horrors described earlier!

Margaret Mead reports that the Mountain Arapesh actually eat dried menstrual blood as an antidote to sorcery (1940:421–22). Anna Meigs corroborates this medicinal use of vaginal discharge and notes that the highland Hua use menstrual blood and its many symbolic equivalents (all derived from red dyes and natural substances) to cure illness and to promote general good health in males. She summarizes this stark dualism in New Guinea attitudes toward female effluvia: "Menstrual blood and parturitional fluids are viewed as the most dangerous and polluting of all substances. They are also recognized as the most creative" (1984:111). In other words, menstrual blood is both the worst and the best thing in the world.

The notion that a menstruating women can protect or succor, rather than endanger men is found among some American Indians. For example, the Cherokee believe that the sight of a women in her period will protect the men from the dreaded "stone-clad monster," a mythical cannibal creature who kills and eats hunters in the wilderness. The anthropologist Raymond Fogelson (1980:135–36) reports that the Cherokee of North Carolina believe that if seven menstruating women stand in a row between the men and the cannibal, the monster will be paralyzed, enabling the hunters to disable and kill it. In the Amazon, also, as we have seen in the case of the Tukanoans, menstruation is regarded not only as negative. Rather, it represents themes of life and growth (Jackson 1996:106). Other native peoples share this blatantly ambiguous view of menstrual blood. The Ndembu of Zambia regard all blood, including uterine blood, as having both good and bad connotations: "What are we to make of the red symbolism, which, in its archetypal form in the initiation rites, is represented by the intersection of two 'rivers of blood'? This duality, this ambivalence, this simultaneous possession of two contrary values or qualities, is quite characteristic of redness in the Ndembu view. As they say, " 'redness acts both for good and ill' " (Turner 1967:77).

The same mixed reaction to woman's bodily fluids is found in many of the great religious traditions we have looked at, and in the very same faiths that also regard woman's reproductive effluvia as the most polluting stuff in the world. In most religious traditions, one finds, again, a wildly mixed message. For example, in Islam, menstruation is said to be both polluting and sacred, deadly and lifegiving. In the Muslim account of Creation, woman's blood is seen not as a source of pollution but as the substance of creativity: "Recite, thou," says the Qur'an, "in the name of thy Lord who created; Created man from clots of blood: — Recite thou!" Uterine blood, like the menstruating woman in Islam, is *sacra,* both sacred and accursed simultaneously (Delaney et al. 1988:19).

The same ambivalence holds true for Shintoism. One of the Eastern religions that strongly condemns menstruation as defiling, Shinto also venerates the menstruating woman as religiously pure, even sacred. Women may have been considered polluted during the menstrual period, as in later centuries in Japan; or they may have been considered sacred to the gods and therefore unapproachable during this time. "In the latter case, menstrual blood, far from being a defilement, would be a sign of religious consecration" (Smyers 1983:9).

The Ainu people of northern Japan regard menstrual blood as a talisman. When a man sees some of it on the floor of a hut, he will rub it over his chest believing that he will thereby secure success. There is an old Japanese saying: "When a woman is menstruating she is purified, becoming the wife of the *kami* [spirit]." This too hints at a sacred status for menstruating women (Smyers 1983:10).

The same dualism applied in some Hindu traditions. The Nepalese Hindus who loathe and revile a female's blood as noxious and a menstruating woman as dangerous also revere both the blood and the woman as a basis of renewal and growth. Menstruation has positive connotations through its connection with fertility and men in Nepal, like many New Guinea peoples, believe that uterine blood forms the baby in the womb when mixed with semen (Bennett 1983:217).

Sacred Sisters

From the structural point of view, a certain dynamic uncertainty creeps into men's attitude toward women. While men in agnatic-based kinship groups may suspect their in-marrying wives of treachery and even accuse them of trying to poison the men of the patrilineage, the very same men often lavish praise upon the women belonging to their own patrilineages: their mothers, sisters, and agnatic cousins. For example, in New Guinea there is a marked contrast between the image of the wife and the image of the sister. While the wives may be feared as dangerous and polluting, many highlanders say, "Our sisters are our mouths" — that is, as necessary and useful to the man as his own mouth, the route by which a man fills his stomach. While the wife's vagina is poisonous and uncanny, the sister's is "the road along which pigs [i.e., meat] come," because she brings a bride-price payment into the clan for each child she bears (Berndt 1962:151). Lindenbaum (1976:59) reports much the same admiration for sisters as supporters of the patriline and fillers of a man's belly. Among the Maring (Buchbinder and Rappaport 1976:18), the brother-sister relationship is said to be "idyllic," the ideal human relationship. Langness (1976:97) reports that the phenomenon of brother-sister harmony and affection is generally widespread in New Guinea.

The split between "good" sister and "bad" wife, which is so profound in Melanesia that men often say they wish they could get rid of their wives and reproduce asexually with their own sisters (Gelber 1986), mirrors the familiar dichotomy between the madonna and whore in Mediterranean Europe and the good-girl bad-girl contrast found in Victorian and other puritanical cultures. Such a split in the female image occurs as an integral element in many, if not most, misogynistic traditions, attesting again to the deep ambivalence within the male psyche and the masculine tendency to polarize and compartmentalize women into personified moral extremes. The Nepalese Hindus provide an empirical case of this splitting tendency. The following information comes from Lynn Bennett's readable book *Dangerous Wives, Sacred Sisters* (1983), a title that cuts to the quick.

Hindu Sisters

The Hindus of Narikot village, Nepal, are typical misogynists, as we have seen. Yet, to the same extent that the men scorn alien women who enter their community as brides, they praise their own sisters, whom of course they cannot marry. More than anything else in the culture, as Bennett says, this split shows "Hindu ambivalence about the female sex" (1983:316).

To Hindus consanguineous kinswomen (sisters and daughters) not only can escape the misogynistic calumny heaped on wives but can actually attain the status of "sacred," becoming purer, literally closer to God, than any man. This curious paradox devolves from the fact that blood-related women are not permanent members of the patriline but temporary "guests." Rather than threaten the line with dissolution as do the wife and sister-in-law, they can and do add substantially to its wealth and power. They do this first by bringing in bride-wealth when they marry and, second, during their unmarried lives, by performing the critically important religious purification rituals by which their kinsmen, especially their brothers, prosper.

In Narikot, for example, sisters perform a series of calendrical rites that ensure long life and prosperity for their brothers. These occur during the Bhai Tika (or "Brother Tika") festival (Bennett 1983:246–50). Without proper performance of these rites, the men would decline and suffer from divine retribution. After a long series of minor rituals involving the sisters' use of "pure" substances like flowers and cow's milk, the climax of the Bhai Tika celebration comes on the fifth day, when sisters ensure the long life of their brothers by literally worshipping them:

> The brother (or brothers) must sit in the center of a circle while the sister worships Ganes and all the other gods and finally the walnut, which represents Yama. Then she lights the votive lamp in the circle and, taking the spouted vessel in hand, walks three times around the edge of the circle evenly spilling out a little of the water as she goes. Next she makes another triple circumambulation of her brother, this time dripping a steady line of oil from a sprig of kus grass. (Bennett 1983:249)

The brother is literally in the position of a god, the sister like a priestess.

To further compound the paradox, the Nepalese Hindus, like many other misogynists, and without conscious hypocrisy, worship their own mothers and motherhood in general. In addition, they regard mother's milk as the purest substance on earth and indeed worship as holy the flow from the maternal breast and its animal symbol, the cow. Once again, by this polarized contrast with the attitude toward woman's fluids, the men demonstrate the central ambivalence in the Hindu image of the body of woman (Bennett 1983:316). Because it expresses in unusually stark and dramatic ways the male ambivalence toward women, we will consider this Hindu dualism at greater length in the next chapter.

It is clear, however, that misogyny constitutes one pole of a cognitive and affective duality. Powerful ambivalent feelings must lie at the core of the male malady, feelings that touch upon all aspects of womanhood: sex, pregnancy, food, and, in particular, motherhood and the regressive male desire for maternal nurturing. It is now time to explore this fundamental and multilayered ambivalence at greater length.

Woman's at best a contradiction still.

—Alexander Pope, *Moral Essays*, Epistle 2

11. Ambivalences

WHAT THE PREVIOUS MATERIAL SHOWS is that men's feelings toward women are contradictory, labile, bifurcated, and ambivalent — to put it mildly. Ambivalence occurs when one experiences diametrically opposed emotions at the same time: the affected person is drawn in opposite directions, torn by incompatible emotions. He feels anxiety because he cannot reconcile the clashing feelings.

The word "ambivalent" (ambi-valent, having two "valences" or directional charges, as in electrical current) was apparently coined by Freud's contemporary Eugon Bleuler in an article written in German in 1910 (Weigert 1991:20). By coming up with *ambivalenz,* Bleuler was attempting linguistically to capture what he saw as the divided emotional state from which so many of his neurotic patients suffered. By the time of Freud's later career, the concept had already become a basic tenet of the psychological understanding of how the mind works. A powerful heuristic tool, the concept of ambi- or bivalence underlies most other psychological notions such as repression, psychic conflict, and anxiety. When ambivalent affect occurs, the mind often responds by driving the struggle into the unconscious, thereby protecting the ego against paralysis and breakdown. In the prevailing psychoanalytic view, ambivalence is a "stressful condition from which the sufferer seeks escape," often by means of seizing upon an ideology of absolute certainty, that is, by choosing some rigid belief system or delusion, or other mental resolution that provides superficial relief (Weigert 1991:23). The outward signs of this inner struggle are neurotic symptoms, fears, and obsessions (Brenner 1974:100–1).

As the reader will have surmised, it is the basic argument of this book that a series of multilayered *ambivalences* (the term is intentionally plural) in men lies at the heart of the misogyny affliction. At least judging from the material presented in the preceding chapter, and taking Melanesia and Amazonia as prime examples of the extremes to which antifemale prejudice can go, it seems abundantly clear that many, if not most, of men's feelings about women are a hodgepodge of strongly contrasting impulses, starkly contradictory affects and fantasies. Unlike some who have studied misogyny, I believe this tension-ridden state, not simple hatred or a wish to dominate, accounts for men's denigration of women.

This effort stems from the fact that the object of ambivalent feelings produces a fixation unlike any other psychic condition because each side of the affective equation stimulates and exacerbates the other unceasingly, sparking an endless and dynamic tension; as a result, the object looms excessively large in psychic importance. In misogyny the engines of conflicted emotions involved are the peremptory male desire and need for the female and the unconscious discomfort that such feelings prompt on the behalf of the superego, leading to powerful, constant, but ineffective repression. Ambivalence is a supercharged tie because of the ego's desperate attempts to deal with the dynamic tension created between the extremes of feelings and the intolerable sensations such tension produces. This struggle creates the obsessive aspect, the unending fascination and the aggressive response.

The central tension often achieves social expression in a simultaneous series of ritualized manifestations of both disavowal and imitation. We have seen ample evidence of this thesis in Melanesia and Amazonia. In these two hotbeds of misogyny, the otherwise fierce and brave warriors, who are afraid of no man, literally quake in terror before woman. Yet these very same warriors enact lurid rituals of female impersonation in which they go to extreme (albeit gruesome and masochistic) lengths to emulate the female body and its functions. These same men also passionately crave most lecherously the same female bodies, the same vaginas, the same sexual fluids that they outwardly despise as dirty and polluting. It seems that wherever we find misogyny, we also find its diametric opposite in equal measure: and this is the key to misogyny.

One must also point out the tendency toward masochism in misogyny, the pain men inflict upon themselves. Rather than only hurting women, misogyny also rebounds bitterly upon its perpetrators, a common enough psychological outcome when a powerful ambivalence leads to self-doubt and self-hatred. One is tempted to conclude, perhaps too glibly, that men who hate women hate themselves even more. What they really hate (and fear) is the "femaleness" within. So, like many self-destructive neurotics, misogynists cut themselves, draw blood from their veins, inflict painful rituals on their bodies, including mutilation, thereby realizing their own worst fears and fantasies of what women supposedly conspire to do to them. Even the most sophisticated men, who would scoff at the self-inflicted wounds of primitive peoples, often deny themselves a pleasurable sexual life by spurning women. Or else they constrict their own lives with phobias, delusions, and debilitating ritual practices. No man was more hobbled by this paradox than the otherwise brilliantly successful Johannes Brahms.

This said by way of introduction, it is now time to expand our double-edged perspective on misogyny to include a second look at the other societies and social categories we have described above. In each case we shall see, instead of a single-sided negative emotion, an amalgam of extremes: hate and love, side by side at every level, revulsion coexisting with attraction. I interpret misogyny as stemming from man's basic discomfort about his passionate desire for woman in all her guises: not just as a sexual object, but also as the fantasized generous, loving mother, the brimming breast, the selfless comforter, the indispensable omnipotent goddess who nurtures boy and man. The result of men's irreconcilable inner conflict is the proliferation of misogynistic institutions, beliefs, and practices as well as their opposite, gynophiliac practices such as cross-dressing and male menstruation. The latter are less common than the antiwoman manifestations, and are often more disguised because they contradict the admired masculine pose.

Western Ambivalences: Ancient

Even in the ancient Western world, sexual ambivalence was an insistent theme. Although the earliest Greek poets like Semonides called woman *kakon,* the worst of evils, they also called her *kalon,* the most beautiful thing — sometimes in the same breath. An example is Hesiod's comment in the *Theogony* about woman as being the "beautiful evil" (*kakon kalon*). What this rather typical mixed usage shows, according to classical scholar Meagher, is that the Greek view of woman was never pure or one-sided, but essentially dualistic, a "living contradiction" (1995:51). This contrariness is true throughout the Greek corpus involving women: all men would willingly fight for Helen, as the poet says, as well as denounce her or kill her. And the Helen of myth stands for all women, for Woman: she is as desirable as she is dangerous, "fascinating and redoubtable" as well as sexually provocative, the apotheosis of perilous pulchritude (Lloyd-Jones 1975:26). Helen is at the same time object of both adoration and loathing, but she is loathed *because* she is so adored (Meagher 1995:67). The simultaneous but incompatible feelings she arouses are coterminous and inextricably linked.

In her study of misogyny in Western literature, Katherine Rogers (1966: 53–54) finds this same inconsistency in the Roman tradition, and in fact in all men's writing about women, through the Renaissance up to the present day. She summarizes by saying that men's fear, dislike, and contempt for women in the literary canon have always been accompanied by an equally intense "love and respect" for women, bordering on the fanatical. The enduring and chronic nature of this bitter inner conflict and the lack of a viable resolution are due to the eternal power of the extremes, for the more intense the relationship, the more it is likely to engender ambivalence. And the ambivalences so engendered are, in turn, infinite.

Rogers regards the Latin attitude about women a prime example of this paradox. The remark by Catullus, *odi et amo* ("I love and I hate"), in relation to one of his mistresses, accurately sums up this attitude among Roman men of letters (46). Latin love poetry, for example, rhapsodizes ecstatically about the charms and beauty of women, their lifegiving qualities, as well as their moral flaws, sometimes within the same work.

Early three-dimensional art, even before the Greeks, also expresses the theme of sexual dualism to a surprising degree. Dijkstra finds the theme already well developed in Egyptian statuary imagery, as in the paradoxical conglomeration of female features found in the hybrid figure of the Sphinx. "The Sphinx, soft-breasted mother and steel-taloned destroyer conjoined, was only one of the many Chimeras of womanhood expressive of the . . . extreme dualistic mentality" that characterizes man's response to woman (1986:333). The mythical female figures that so terrified the ancients, the lamias, nymphs, hamadryads, and serpentine sea-creatures, were usually hybrids, both alluring and foul, voluptuous and odious.

Western Ambivalences: Medieval and Renaissance

The ancient "oxymoron" (Dijkstra's term) of masculine attitudes toward women continued unabated throughout the Middle Ages. If anything, male attitudes became even more oxymoronic, because revealed religion further inflamed the moral struggle. Although the patristic churchmen reviled femininity as the devil's trap, and in some ways even went beyond the Greek and Roman antipathy toward women by adding a brimstone element drawn from the parable of the Fall, these same clerics rescued women from some of the worst misogynistic abuses. For example, St. Augustine, despite his railings against sin and his unresolved conflicts about sex, also respected and revered women, painting them as purer and more pious than men at their best. In fact, according to philosopher Jean Elshtain, St. Augustine went further toward rehabilitating women than other men of his day and was indeed "one of the great undoers of Greek misogyny" (1981:73). What might seem a minority opinion is seconded by Coole (1993:47), in her review of politics and woman-hating in Western culture. As we have noted, this partial rehabilitation of woman in Christianity, especially in Latin Catholicism, stems in part from the growing attachment to the figure of the Virgin Mary in the high Middle Ages, which reaches its apotheosis in the worship of the madonna, the perfect mother, of the Renaissance.

Although the medieval and early-modern periods in Western history were perhaps the most misogynist of all, as Bloch (1991), Muir (1997), and Solomon (1997) have pointed out, the same time-frame also saw a cultural development in which women were exalted to the greatest extent in Western history, both abstractly and specifically. One has only to look at the theme of romantic courtly love to appreciate medieval and Renaissance gender ambivalence.

Bloch, for example, takes this gender contradiction as the central motivating phenomenon of medieval misogyny, which he calls a "both-at-once" and "bivalent" attitude (1991:67). Reviewing the mass of continental literature of the period, Bloch can only wonder at finding so many positive depictions of women alongside the innumerable negative portrayals (ibid.). He refers specifically to the institution of chivalrous love, which found its highest expression at this same time. In this courtly tradition, balladeers and troubadours, as well as monks and holy men, sang the praises of women extravagantly, devoting their lives to their service and exaltation. Woman represented an ideal of tender purity, fertility, and innocence, through whose worship a man might attain the highest spiritual plane. Men were worshipping woman even as they were casting her into the jaws of hell.

There can be no better manifestation of Christianity's double attitude toward women than this paradox of romantic idealization coexisting with abject degradation. It is no coincidence, then, that the peevish Tertullian, author of many scurrilous antiwoman diatribes, blithely refers to women in the same breath as "The Brides of Christ," simultaneously the devil's agent in human form and the purest instrument of God's grace. Supremely contradictory, symbol of both God and devil, woman was reified as man's damnation but also as his salvation. While her body was an infernal trap, in her passive and sacrificial

maternal goodness woman nevertheless represented a model of spiritual perfection. Rather than corrupt and destructive, she could also be purifying, uplift-
ing, and life-giving.

Later in the Renaissance, the romanticized view of woman as pure and
innocent finds further expression. One example is Edmund Spenser's *Faerie
Queene,* with its exaltation of Queen Elizabeth, whose sagacious rule further
enhanced the reputation of women in England (Rogers 1966:135). Throughout
the late medieval period and into the Renaissance, European knights swore
fealty to a good woman, "mistress," an unconsummated relationship continuing until death; it was a kind of secular holy quest, rather like Dante's platonic
admiration of Beatrice. The good woman became the avatar of the incorrupt-
ible, the holy.

A well-known example of this moral dualism is drawn from European
folklore: "The Beauty and the Beast." In the original French fable, which has
come down to us in so many variants, an honest woman turns a horrid beast
(actually an enchanted prince) back into a handsome man, reversing the usual
order of the woman-induced zoological metamorphosis (Lederer 1968:164).
No longer the "cruel beast" who brings out the animal in men, no longer the
witch Circe who turns men into swine, woman has become the embodiment of
the positively transformative forces of civilization, raising men up from animality rather than casting them down into it.

Nordic Ambivalences

One encounters the same splitting tendency in much Nordic literature, for
example, in old Scandinavian folklore. We have seen examples of Icelandic
mythology in which woman is the icy or poisonous river into which men fall
and drown. On the other hand, as Linke points out, in the same body of oral
literature the figure of woman is split into the "venomous river of ice" and a
"milk-producing cow," a bovine source of warmth and nourishment (Linke
1996:141–42). Mothers and motherhood are portrayed in starkly dichotomous
terms in northern European lore as elsewhere; in Old Norse myths woman is
either a "devouring" destructive monster or else the "all-good" nurturer. Both
the sexual and the nurturing aspect of women are split and bifurcated to an
astonishing degree.

Speaking of northern European folklore, one might mention the ancient
legends that Richard Wagner used in his music dramas, all having strong moral
messages. Although he uses females to symbolize vice (Venus, for example, in

Tannhäuser, who entraps the knight-minstrel in her sybaritic paradise, or the temptresses in *Parsifal*), Wagner also uses them as symbols of purity paving the way to man's redemption. The virtuous maidens Elsa and Elisabeth in *Lohengrin* and *Tannhäuser* respectively both "save" a conflicted man from spiritual ruin through selfless love. Both heroines are paragons not only of virtue but also of self-negation, nonsexual qualities that men of the time regarded as saintly (although Elsa's curiosity about Lohengrin's origins proves fatal in the end). The virtuous Eva Pogner in *Die Meistersinger* plays virtually the same redemptive role, rescuing the conflicted Walther from himself, symbolized by the laurel wreath she places on his head at the end of the opera.

Even more striking in this regard is Senta in *The Flying Dutchman.* In this tale of sin and redemption, the ghostly Dutchman has been condemned by the devil to wander endlessly from port to port. His torment can only be ended by the selfless love of a woman who will prove faithful "until death." In a typical metaphor of spiritual transfiguration, the Dutchman is finally rescued from his cruel fate by the loving Senta, who leaps to her death in the final act shouting, "true to thee unto death." Through her sacrifice, the curse is lifted, the Dutchman redeemed. His satanic ship finally sinks, and he and Senta are seen, transfigured, triumphantly rising toward heaven. In Wagner's dualistic vision, as in most late Victorian literature and art, woman represents both death and eternal life for man, sin and salvation, carnality and purity, debasement and divinity. Her moral "weather" is as two-sided as the North Sea over which the restless Dutchman roams.

Western Ambivalences: Victorian

Throughout the nineteenth century, woman gets royal treatment as well as misogynistic abuse in literature and art. Often compared to angels and goddesses in English poetry, she is praised as "the nobler half of humanity" in the work of the early Victorian poet Charles Kingsley. In his poem "Yeast" (1848), Kingsley suggests that only woman can save man in a moral sense and speaks of the "Triumph of Woman" as leading to the redemption of all humanity (Rogers 1966:189). Rather than dragging man down, angelic woman raises him to lofty heights (the sexual double entendre of the "raising up" or "lifting up" conveys the sexual-moral ambivalence so redolent in sex-drenched Victorian poetry).

For other Victorian poets and artists, woman is "the priceless pearl" who sheds the light of God upon man. In the work of many idolaters, woman is the "finer" and "more noble" sex, more spiritual and more refined than man. For worshipful Victorians, woman is not only the duplicitous temptress who sullies man's fragile ideals, but also the "jewel," the "flower," the possessor of a superior moral power nourishing the weaker and less noble male soul (Dijkstra 1986:8). Tennyson, in a typical prowoman elegy, *The Princess,* praises women in general, especially their purity of spirit, and extols their virtuous example. Tennyson's contemporary Owen Meredith goes so far as to rehabilitate the original Eve and hold her forth as the ideal of mankind rather than the false betrayer depicted in morose medieval theology.

The art critic John Ruskin, who warned in *Munera Pulveris* against women's power to bewitch, also lavished overwrought praise upon the fair sex in the same work. For Ruskin, a good woman turns the family into a sacred place, a vestal temple, and he constantly compares women to fragrant flowers: they are as pure, innocent, guileless, and life enhancing.

The British Victorian novelists incorporated both sides of woman in their work in an even more developed and stereotyped way, furthering the fragmented moral vision. We are all familiar with Dickens's portrayals of such paragons of virtue as Dora (*David Copperfield*), Amy Dorrit (*Little Dorrit*), Little Nell (*The Old Curiosity Shop*), Lizzie Hexam (*Our Mutual Friend*) and so on, all of whom counterbalance his criminal and duplicitous female characters like the heartless Estella and the vindictive Miss Haversham in *Great Expectations.* As in Dickens, the nineteenth-century novelists' image of woman is thus as rudely split as medieval and Renaissance representations, a classic case of the projective power of the inner contradictions within the masculine fear-hate/love-worship complex. Sometimes, as in Dickens's portrayal of the complex Nancy in *Oliver Twist,* the two sides of woman appear within the same individual. Nancy starts out as a willing accomplice of archcriminals Bill Sikes and Fagin and helps them kidnap Oliver. But halfway through the book, she has a characteristically feminine change of heart and sacrifices her life to rescue the abused child. Woman in Dickens, as in much Victorian literature, often has an exalted function as a sort of natural, self-sacrificing priestess, closer to God than man, and a source for him of spiritual strength and encouragement (Slater 1983:307).

One finds this dualistic strain very powerfully in the transcendentalist novels of John Cowper Powys, especially in *Wolf Solent* (1926) and *A Glastonbury Romance* (1932). In these dreamlike narratives, Powys portrays his female characters in almost pantheistic terms as mirroring both the fertile beauty and the wanton destructiveness of nature itself. He constantly compares them to lush saplings, trees, flowers, and other growing things, but also to ugly mushrooms, vegetative rot, windstorms, floods, and fire. Like so many other English novelists of the time (1850–1950), Powys uses "Woman" to symbolize both the best and the worst in nature and in humanity. She is worshipped for the sexual pleasure she gives man and feared for the same reason.

Unlike the Melanesian and Amazonian gynophobias, which emphasize bodily pollution and magical emanations, the Western strain of misogyny often takes on a rather moralistic and intellectual tone ("Swiftian" physical disgust being comparatively rare and confined to certain poets). Rather than being seen as polluting, woman is regarded from an ethical, rather than sexual standpoint, as wicked and destructive or as irrational and frivolous. The danger is *moral* rather than magical or biological. Western religions, the established Christian church in particular, confirms all this cynicism and disillusionment, at least throughout its formative and medieval periods. It is therefore not surprising that in the West the inevitable converse of misogyny, gynophilia, should also reflect moralistic pietism and should elevate woman to the position of salvation's handmaiden, a kind of sexless "priestess" for man: a complete reversal of the woman-as-devil viewpoint.

Oddly, this Victorian idealization of a fragmented female imago has also had its detractors. So pervasive was the moral exaltation of women in the late-Victorian, early twentieth-century period that many, like D. H. Lawrence and Ezra Pound, thought it went too far and so, in a curious kind of dialectic, reacted against it with a counterbalancing antifeminism. In English and American literature this reaction often included a defensive idolization of phallic masculinity. For example, Pound castigates woman as no more than a biological "process," and D. H. Lawrence, in *Aaron's Rod,* implicitly explains some of his fictional character's misogyny (and by extension his own) as a defense against the great, smothering gynophilia of the day. He violently denounces "this great and ignominious dogma of the sacred priority of women" — the belief "that all that is productive, all that is fine and sensitive and most essentially noble, is woman" (1930:186–87).

Ambivalences in the Hindu Tradition: My Mother/My Cow

Let us turn elsewhere for further evidence, to India. To fully appreciate the many dualisms in Hinduistic views of woman, we must return to the earliest proto-Indo-Aryan deities of Asiatic prehistory. In the first stages of the Indus civilization, the archaeological evidence reveals a notable paradox: she appears simultaneously as fertility goddess and destroyer. To sum up, around the Eastern fertility goddess, whom many consider a prototype of Pandora, there is a bundle of associations. On the one hand this goddess is regarded as life-enhancing and all-giving, but on the other hand she is made responsible for the demonic seduction of men, for their death and damnation, as well as being associated with dirt, decay, and the chasm of the underworld. Thus the fundamental ambivalence of life-death, which we have been tracing all along, is once more repeated, as are those of lover-betrayor and nurturer-withholder.

It is noteworthy, from this perspective, that the dreadful castrating goddess Kali, one of the many forms assumed by the protean goddess Devi, has another gentler side as well, a side that connotes not only fertility but blessedness. There is, in fact, no other deity in the Hindu pantheon, male or female, who has such a divided, contradictory persona. On the one hand, the goddess-mother Devi is the bloodthirsty scourge, but another incarnation is nurturing Uma Parvati, the loyal wife of Siva. The terrible side of the Devi is represented by the bloodthirsty virgin warrior Durga and her hosts, who include not only Kali, but also the goddesses Camunda, Mahisamardini, Yogi Nidra, and Ambika — all killers. The gentle side of the goddess is perhaps best represented by Uma Parvati, devoted wife and mother. We might characterize this gentle aspect of the Devi as the pure, faithful wife and the gentle mother of Hindu lore.

The paradoxes of Hindu womanhood intensify at every turn. As Bennett concludes, the fact of her contradictory nature is what makes Devi-Kali so powerful as a symbol of woman as a platonic category and of man's ambivalence toward her. Even the contradictions contain contradictions. The gentle Uma Parvati, although devoted and faithful to her husband, is so erotically stimulating that she is somewhat suspect in the Hindu canon. Even the ruthless killer Kali is closely linked with purity and asceticism, because an ideal of godly perfection drives her homicidal fury. Typical of the protean Hindu deities, they are not what they seem.

Clearly, in the Hindu pantheon, just as in the Christian, woman plays an ambiguous moral role. On one hand, sexual woman is persecutor, seducer, and corrupter of man; on the other, as mother, she is nurturer, comforter, and ennobling influence, both "dangerous" and "sacred" at the same time (Bennett 1983:316). This glaring paradox is best summarized by Sanskrit scholar Wendy O'Flaherty Doniger, who says that woman may be the cause of all evil in Hindu mythology, but "it is she who takes the burden of it away from man" (1976:141). She gives and she takes; she creates and she destroys. The nature of woman (to man) is a dualism, a paradox, a contradiction at every turn.

Turning to the Nepalese variant of Hinduism, we see how the "Hindu ambivalence about the female sex" (Bennett 1983:316) works itself out in a specific empirical case: matriolotry versus uxorophobia in Himalayan culture. We have already seen the negative side of this equation: hatred and fear of wives. The other side is the worshipful attitude toward sisters and, even more so, toward mothers. Just as Hindu misogyny often focuses upon the female's bodily effluvia, especially menstrual blood, Nepalese matriolotry takes the same bodily focus in a curious and typical inversion: the veneration of mother's milk.

Most female bodily functions in the village of Narikot, Nepal, have a negative connotation for the men. The striking exception is mother's milk, which is literally worshipped as a gift from the gods and said to be pure, lifegiving, and holy. Like menstrual blood, breast milk is undeniably linked to sexuality and reproduction, however not with polluting or destroying powers, but, on the contrary, with its equally powerful creative, beneficial, and life-giving side. So deep is the respect for mother's milk that it overcomes the negative aspects of female sexuality and purifies "female sexuality through motherhood" (Bennett 1983:252). Much of this transformation has to do with the religious linkage among three primary symbols in Hinduism: milk, cows, and women.

In Hinduism generally, milk and cows are sacred, and woman's association with them provides her with a counterbalancing aura of holiness that actually neutralizes many of the negative connotations of female sexuality. In a paper on female purity in Hinduism, anthropologist Nur Yalman explains the threefold convergence:

And again it is most appropriate that the "cow," the supreme symbol of the Hindu mother, should also be the most potent symbol (as well as main source) of purity. The cow is sacred . . . the giver of all things. . . . The association between cow and women (especially the mother) is, of course freely made. . . . The cow is sacred because it is like the mother . . . it provides milk. (1963:43)

Thus the stark nature of the misogynistic-gynophiliac split in the Hindu vision: the mother is associated with purity, milk, constancy, devotion, and selfless love; the wife with pollution, "rampant and debilitating sexual demands, menstrual blood and potential unfaithfulness" (Bennett 1983:255).

The veneration for mothers in the Hindu tradition, like the female river in Nordic mythology, tends to overflow its bounds and to touch all women by association. The reason for this excess is that all women are potentially mothers and can change from object of man's erotic desire into paragon of selfless maternal devotion. Through metamorphosis, woman can turn man's carnality into spirituality and can lead all men down the road to salvation. Indeed, the Hindu man can see the very face of God in a woman. Such a revelation is enunciated in the writ of many Hindu holy men, such as Swami Nikhilananda, a famous modern devotee of Ramakrishna:

By seeing God in a woman [man] gradually sublimates his carnal desires. *Carnality,* which seeks fulfillment through the physical union with a member of the opposite sex, is one of the deadly enemies with which spiritual seekers . . . have to wrestle. A woman can easily conquer it by regarding a man as her child. She is, in essence, the mother of all men, no matter what other relationships society may sanction or speak of. A man, too, easily subdues his lust by seeing in a woman the symbol of motherhood. (1962:82)

Buddhism, Yin and Yang

Taking the Japanese variant of Buddhism as an example, we have already seen that a menstruating woman not only might escape polluted status in the Buddhist canon, but can be valued as the opposite and be given a "sacred status" (Smyers 1983:10). In addition, in early Japanese Buddhism, before the condemnatory Tokugawa edicts, women were sometimes seen as exerting a purifying power. Not only were women not seen as inherently polluted beings; they may even have "the power to remove pollution." It is a curious fact that in the *Obaraekotoba,* the ritual prayer for the very solemn semiannual purification of the Japanese nation, "the four kami [spirits] who are invoked are all female" (M. Harding 1971:125).

Furthermore, in classic early Buddhism, woman is granted a positive soteriological role. Buddhism in its origins was above all a pragmatic soteriology, that is, a theory of human salvation that sought to free humanity from suffering and to lead mankind to the exalted state of perfect wisdom. Curiously, rather than a bar to, or diversion from, wisdom, as is often the case in the misogynistic Buddhist texts that condemn woman as diverting men from holiness, in some holy Sanskrit teachings woman is paradoxically given a central and facilitating role in this search for perfection. The concept of wisdom, always a prime Buddhist virtue in the quest for man's liberation from worldliness, has been primarily expressed with a grammatically feminine noun (*prajna/panna*). Implicitly, there is an assertion that there can be no truly liberating wisdom that was not at the same time compassionate. In Sanskrit both of these terms, wisdom and compassion, are represented as feminine.

In the early Mahayana literature, however, the grammatically feminine gender begins to take on firmer psychological grounds when we find the ultimate virtue of perfect wisdom personified in feminine form as "the mother of all Buddhas":

> The Buddhas in the world-systems in the ten directions
> Bring to mind this perfection of wisdom as their mother.
> The Saviours of the world who were in the past . . .
> Have issued from her, and so will the future ones be.
> She is the one who shows this world [as it is], she is
> the genetrix, the mother of the Jinas [= Buddhas]. (Sponberg 1992:26)

As Sponberg points out, the femininity of this prerequisite in the search for liberation is no longer coincidental, and not surprisingly it is readily incarnated in the form of the Himalayan goddess Prajnaparamita, an onomastic hybrid, which translates both as "perfect wisdom" and "the mother of all Buddhas" (Sponberg 1992:26). So, once again, a holy *woman* figures prominently as a moral model in man's salvation, much as does the Virgin Mary in Latin Catholicism, the Prophet's daughter and heir, Fatima, in some branches of Islam, and the sacred mother-cow in Hinduism. In a typical reversal, common in so many religions, women become the path to God instead of the devil's gateway.

There is a parallel in medieval Chinese Buddhism as well. During the assimilation of the Buddha's teachings into Chinese culture, the male bodhisattva (enlightened being) from India, Avalokitesvara, became transformed in local lore into a beautiful white-robed Chinese woman (the reasons for this are not clear). In addition to the sex change involved in this religious diffusion, the accompanying female symbolism of the bodhisattva was enlarged to include female yin symbols, for instance, moon, water, and vase, from the yin-yang polarity of traditional Chinese philosophy (Reed 1992:159). This lovely female deity (Reed 1992:174, fig. 20), often depicted in Chinese painting and statuary art, became the very feminine figure Kuan-yin, who is known today not only to alleviate women's sufferings, but also to have special powers of healing and purifying. In fact she is viewed by some as a "Buddhist savior," with Christlike overtones. Furthermore, she serves both Chinese men and women alike as "a model of piety" and right action (Reed 1992:176).

Islam, or The Prophet's Dilemma

We have presented ample evident of the misogynistic thread in Muslim cultures and in Middle Eastern gender philosophies: woman is compared to chaos, blamed for sin and lust, likened to the devil's traps, and so on. Yet, despite all this antiwoman excitement, which seems more narrowly sexual than elsewhere, there is another, calmer thread running through both the Qur'an and Muslim society in general in all its rich variety. Certainly one may agree with

Arabist Daniel Varisco when he stresses that a single-sided, or monolithic Islam "does not exist" (1995:22). Other scholars have provided good evidence that the picture is indeed complicated. As Barbara Stowasser says, the Qur'an has a "richness and subtlety" (1994:56) in its treatment of women, allowing for many varied interpretations, one of which, of course, is that the Qur'an is a highly ambivalent text when it comes to women. This means that its author, Mohammed, cannot make up his mind, and that as the Qur'an represents it, God's will in this respect is essentially and dynamically dualistic. For Mohammed, "Bivalence is the will of God" (Bouhdiba 1985:7).

First, there is the question of woman's status as a mirror of her supposed inner qualities. We start with the Qur'an's "ethical egalitarianism," which is a building block for most legal and political judgments in Islamic thought. In many of its suras, or verses, the Muslim holy book extends this strongly egalitarian position to women, placing them on equal terms with men; then, as though thinking better of such ideas, the Qur'an contradicts itself in subsequent suras, so that a pattern of contradiction or oscillation emerges. From an ethical point of view, some Muslim scholars argue that the Qur'anic vision of gender is actually at odds with some of the legalistic and pragmatic recipes, which reflect the supposed inherent deficiency of women. "There appear, therefore, to be two distinct voices within Islam, and two competing understandings of gender, one expressed in the pragmatic regulations for society . . . the other in the articulation of an ethical vision" (Ahmed 1992:65–66).

Thus in some passages in the Qur'an (and post-Qur'anic texts) woman is said to be of a "single soul" with man and therefore equal (sura 4:1). At another point, despite all the previous caveats about woman's amorality, they are said to be also equal to men in piety (Haeri 1989:67). The Islamic perception of women, as Haeri finally confesses, is essentially indeterminate, oscillating, "ambivalent at best."

Indeed, some scholars even argue that "a feminist breath sometimes blows through the most sacred texts [of Islam]" and even, in what may perhaps be an overstatement, that "Islamic civilization is essentially feminist" (Bouhdiba 1985:19–20). For example, Bouhdiba points to the exalted status given to such females as Fatima, the Prophet's daughter and to Khadija, the first lady of Islam, whose status is also saintly (20). Bouhdiba says that a man "cannot be a misogynist" if he follows the sacred texts to the letter, for these usually demand respect for women and generous treatment for women at all times (116). Paramount here is the respect offered to chaste wives and especially to mothers. Indeed, the mother once again overcomes misogynistic prejudice and becomes sanctified as the moral model for humanity. Bouhdiba speaks of the "cult of the mother" in Islam (214), which, as one might expect, resembles nothing so much as Marian worship in southern Europe; and he refers to the Middle East as "the kingdom of the mothers" (225), an epithet that would ring true for Spain and Italy as well.

Furthermore, there is some historical and archaeological evidence that Islam's impact on gender has had more than a few positive benefits for Middle Eastern women, despite what many Western feminists may say. This argument is made by such feminist writers as Haeri (1989), Ahmed (1992), and Stowasser (1994). Comparing Islam to pre-Islamic (tribal and pagan) conventions, they point out that Islam banned infanticide (females were the customary victims), limited polygyny, accorded women an ample share in their parent's inheritance (which was denied them previously), and gave them the right to enter into many contracts and to dispose of their possessions according to their own will — all rights restricted or denied under pre-Islamic tribal laws (Haeri 1989:24).

Even the view of female sexuality in Islam takes on a starkly dualistic vision. Woman's sexual allure is bad and chaotic when invoked outside of legitimate marriage, but it is God's will when used for procreation. This subtle prosex message is certainly more audible than in Christianity. In Islam, sex is "highly commendable" and even a "sacred function" when used for procreation: that is, to increase the community of the faithful (Bouhdiba 1985:13–14). Consequently, female sexual attractiveness outside of wedlock may be explosive like gunpowder and as dangerous as the devil's trap, but legitimized by propriety is a holy thing because it leads men to procreate.

Interestingly, some of the ambiguity about sexuality expressed in the Qur'an may be due largely to the strongly virile nature of its author, the Prophet himself. According to contemporary accounts and to what we know of his life, Mohammed was a highly sexed man (and a practical one; he married a rich widow), having many wives and mistresses. He was in fact known to be irresistibly attracted to pretty women and often struggled to resist their spell. For example, there was his beloved Coptic concubine, Maria, who held him "in thrall" with her sex appeal (Mernissi 1987:56). The Prophet never denied or hid his own powerful desire for women, but he did feel his sexual needs as dangerous to his soul. It was a feeling with which he was neither entirely comfortable nor reconciled, as the following vignette reveals.

One day the middle-aged Mohammed went to the house of his adopted son Zaid to pay a social call. At the doorway he was greeted by his son's young and voluptuous wife, Zainab, who was engaged in her toilette and was only half-dressed at the time. Covering her dishabille modestly, she politely invited her stepfather-in-law inside to wait. Feeling a surge of uncontrollable lust for her, the Prophet instead turned and fled in confusion, mumbling prayers. Learning of the episode, Zaid offered to divorce Zainab so that his stepfather might marry her. After some soul searching Mohammed accepted his adopted son's offer and married Zainab. This union led to a special passage in the Qur'an, which was designed to quell the scandalized clamor that erupted among the Prophet's contemporaries about the hasty match, seen by some as too close to incestuous. Verse four of the thirty-third sura denies that adoption creates legal and relational ties between individuals (Mernissi 1987:57).

It is clear from the historical evidence that Mohammed as a man was vulnerable to sexual temptation and fully recognized this weakness as a moral problem. Accordingly, he spent much time wrestling with his own desire, thereby producing a monumental inner struggle that accounts, at least in part, for his ambivalence about women as reflected in the Qur'an's emphasis on the control of lust as a primary duty of the Muslim. As Mernissi puts it: "Fear of succumbing to the temptation represented by women's sexual attraction — a fear experienced by the Prophet himself — accounts for many of the defensive reactions to women by Muslim society" (54).

Once again woman is held to blame for man's inner turmoil, and woman scapegoated for what she is not so much the cause as the object. Seen in this light, Muslim misogyny is really not so much an attack on women as it is a flight from woman "as the source of uncontrollable desires in the male self" (Bouhdiba 1985:116). Islamic misogyny, like all others, is a flight from inner conflict over women; misogyny is the psychic consequence to male ambivalence and turmoil. The reification of this struggle that occurs in Islam is similar perhaps to what occurs in Christianity, Hinduism, and Buddhism, except perhaps for the added biographical ingredient of the Prophet's apotheosis of sexual anxiety into liturgy. One may say that St. Paul and St. Augustine played similar roles in forming Christian theology.

Parallels Elsewhere

This many-faceted male ambivalence about women finds expression in all the cultures we have examined and is usually consciously, if not unconsciously, expressed, in various public institutions, such as proverbs and folklore, and not always in a purely sexual sense. For example, in those agnatic societies where men denigrate in-marrying women as disruptive and traitorous, the same men speak approvingly of these same women's contributions to the patriline. The men especially appreciate and revere woman's reproductive capacity, which is the key to genetic survival and genealogical continuity. Prime misogynists, the Sarakatsani reflect this dual attitude when they say that women both make and break the kindred: a local proverb has it that "Women make the house and they destroy it" (Campbell 1964:71). Throughout Orthodox Greece, as in other parts of the Mediterranean, the men worship a specifically female deity, the Virgin Mary, hold up the maternal woman as the human ideal and revere (female) virgins as holy.

Taking a tribal example, even the Tukanoan Indians of Brazil, who deplore women as treacherous, dirty, and perversely antinatal, also praise them as creating life and thus renewing the patriline, if only by default. "In brief, Tukanoan women are seen as both destructive and creative with respect to the patrilineal clan" (Jackson 1996:96).

Analyzed comparatively and in context, misogyny therefore seems more and more a response to man's limitless responses to his own mixed feelings about woman as lover, wife, and mother rather than a simple negative reaction to the sexual "other" or an attempt to politically dominate women. Misogyny, like most prejudices, is, in the end, a symptom of a wide-ranging inner struggle, an effort to relieve massive self-doubt through scapegoating. Does this mean that a malady as complex as misogyny can be cured or at least ameliorated? We take up this and other issues in the following chapter.

It is high time the people of this country found some other way of loving God other than by hating women.

—Oliver St. John Gogarty in a speech to the Irish Parliament (ca. 1950)

12. Conclusions

IF MISOGYNY IS A PREJUDICE based on uncertainty, then what is most striking about misogyny is how consistent the uncertainty is. Everywhere we look, men are sorely divided in their feelings toward women, but everywhere the repetitive emotional complex in so many males clearly points to some psychogenic factor above and beyond the vicissitudes of social context or environment. Explanations based on politics or economic "systems" certainly cannot do complete justice to the problem, for it seems that all political systems, economic arrangements, and ideological systems are consistent with misogyny. Woman-hating is just as bad under capitalism as it is under any of the various socialisms or under tribal communalism; misogyny occurs in "prestige" economies without money just as virulently as in modern cash-oriented economies.

Certainly neither history or religion can be invoked to explain misogyny. Historical periods in Europe march in and out in a never-ending pageant (for example, classical antiquity, the high Middle Ages, the Renaissance, and the Enlightenment), each with its intellectual paradigms and moral baggage, as do religions, sects, creeds, and schisms. But misogyny remains, perhaps only taking on different coloration to suit the times. Nor is the kinship pattern of the society or its family structure the answer to why this male prejudice crops up everywhere. True, we have seen how agnatic kinship and exogamy *exacerbate* misogyny. But patrilineal, agnatically oriented tribesmen who live in exogamous villages are no more misogynistic than were Victorian gentlemen who lived in tight-knit nuclear families in London, or otherworldly Chinese Buddhists, or celibate Christian anchorites and cenobites, misanthropic nineteenth-century German philosophers, the cognatic Semai, the semimatrilineal Yurok, the fully matrilineal Blackfoot Indians, or the Muslim Bedouin Arabs who live in endogamous clans.

Is an "Explanation" Possible?

The ubiquity of misogynistic feelings, their overdetermined quality, then, calls for a deeper explanation, one that involves more than shifting social systems or structures. Why, for example, are virtually all misogynists troubled by the same dark thoughts of poisoning, of bodily decay and inner corruption? Why are misogynists haunted by the imagery of zoomorphic transformations in which men turn into beasts and women into snakes, spiders, tigresses, lamias, and the like? Why do so many men fear the theft of their vital substances by devilish women and why do they obsess about semen depletion and the drying up of their juices? Why do misogynists the world over quake and quiver about losing control of their bodies and dissolving into some putrid liquid as a consequence of a woman's influence? Why all the hysteria about being pulled down into the murky depths by mermaids, or other ichthymorphs? Why this obsession with wetness with *liquidity*? Why do the malevolent maidens of the male imagination always lurk in the dark and hidden as well as the damp places of the world, and especially in the *underground* concavities (crevices, grottoes, caves, lakes, sandpits, the sea)? What causes the male grievance against "the sulphurous pit": the Pandora's Box, the chthonic gateway to hell, the opening to damnation and also to ecstasy?

To answer any of these questions, as well as those relating to the curious agnatic-aquatic nexus we have unearthed here, we must go beyond time and place to seek a phylogenetic dimension that is shared by all (or nearly all) men everywhere. Only the psychological theories discussed above can address these questions with any pan-species utility. Without a psychological dimension, we can simply make no sense of the striking recurrent nature of the magical beliefs, delusions, and the fantasies that misogyny brings with it, nor can we explain the visceral *horror* that everywhere defines the *horror mulieris*. Since misogyny is so many-layered a phenomenon, no single-sided explanation will work.

What this mass of empirical data does show, though, is that specific and identifiable environmental factors explain the *intensity* of misogyny in any given empirical case. This variation, in turn, requires a complementary materialistic or contextual approach which goes beyond psychology. The exacerbating external stimuli are, first, a specific social order that emphasizes a structural trio associated with a patri-agnatic ideology under preindustrial conditions: these conditions include patrilineal descent, exogamy, and patrilocal residence patterns, as well as the existence of a strongly corporate, cofraternal ideology that devalues the conjugal relationship. Such is the system of belief we discussed above as the idealistic solidarity of brothers. Under such conditions, wives are seen as inimical outsiders who often come from (or are abducted from) antagonistic or outright enemy groups. The men in these patri-agnatic societies are literally "sleeping with the enemy." This is, indeed, a *political* cause, but not in the Marxist sense.

Given the constant pressure under which men live in such beleaguered societies, with war, raiding, and death always on the doorstep, alien women may indeed constitute a potential fifth column in times of war or struggle. And one must assume that the foreign women do indeed maintain loyalties to their kinsmen (how could they not?). The women therefore may take the brunt of intensified male anxieties about invasion and annihilation. This curious situation may help us understand the emphasis on the invasive female scourge in many patrilineal societies: why women are seen as outsiders who can never give undivided loyalty to their husbands. Such an interpretation, even if farfetched or limited to tribal systems, does help us to understand the climactic uxorophobic misogyny of the Melanesians and the Amazonians, which so often emphasizes betrayal and faithlessness.

Conditions of chronic warfare, regardless of what other social factors adhere, also seem to reinforce misogynistic feelings among men. When males bond for purposes of defense against a real or imagined enemy, they tend to cultivate hostility toward a demonized "other" as a means of shoring up a fragile unity. This xenophobic group-binding syndrome may extend to include the scapegoating of women as a kind of by-product of the masculine esprit de corps. As well as warfare, religious fanaticism also seems to play a role when misogyny takes on intensified form. We have seen that most puritanical mysticisms and ascetic sects tend to heighten misogynistic sentiments, largely because such beliefs often use woman as a convenient receptacle for the sins that the men cast out from themselves (especially that of lust) as part of a covenant with God or gods.

Yet, beyond these few vague correlations between the *degree* of misogyny and such factors as warfare, social structure, and ascetic religious doctrine, we cannot really point to any specific situational or material factors that account for the *origin* of this overdetermined male malady. External factors shed light on its degree, its intensity, and perhaps the form it takes, but not its origin. The etiology must lie in the interior recesses of the male psyche.

Dimensions of Male Ambivalence

One other thing is clear about the origins of the male malady, and this will come as no surprise: the material we have presented shows that misogyny is a complex, multilayered phenomenon involving man's deepest wells of feeling about woman, not only as a sexual being, but, as I have emphasized throughout, in all her many different roles, especially her nonsexual nurturing capacity. Still, the first layer of male conflict does relate to woman purely as a sexual object. Unlike the other mammals with whom we share a common evolutionary ancestry, the human male has a superego. He subscribes to some sort of sexual morality which inhibits his libido to some extent. He is therefore inevitably frustrated by the workings of his own mind. In the lower animals sex is cyclical and confined to seasonal matings, which are stimulated by the estrus cycle in females. Human females no longer have estrus cycles, and unlike all other female mammals are receptive (at least theoretically) at all times. This poses a moral dilemma for the males, who, as we have seen, are always interested in sex.

When men decide to be moralistic or ascetic about sex, when they define copulation as dirty or sinful, they cannot help but suffer unremitting inner conflict and "discontent" (i.e., anxiety) which is the price one always pays for the *unrelenting* repression of instinct. This condition of unremitting frustration seems to be one for which the evolutionary process has not adequately prepared human males to cope in any genetic or bioneurological way, for humans are virtually without instinctual repressions; in man, self-control has to be learned. The result of this mismatch between sexual evolution and restraint is a constant inner struggle between impulse and the sense of guilt. This inner struggle is probably sharper, more physiologically driven, in the male than in the female because of the peremptory power of the testosterone-driven male libido. The result is not only unremitting tension, frustration, and the inevitable aggression against the object of desire, but also moral self-doubt and, in the case of puritans, self-hatred. All this leads to the search for a scapegoat to take away the bad feelings, a scapegoat which is, of course, woman, who also serves as a convenient and helpless physical object for the aggression. One may go deeper, and ask why so many men have such rigid prohibitions about sex in the first place. But this question has no answer because all men have culture, and culture presupposes sexual prohibitions, so that some degree of sexual ambivalence in the male is a given. Women suffer in their own way from sexual conflicts, but the result is not antimale hysteria.

Man's sexual ambivalence is also abetted by uniquely masculine intrapsychic processes. All men pass through an Oedipal stage (if Freud is right). At this point in their development, moral and ethical concerns about sex are joined with social prohibitions that further increase self-doubt. Many men, as Freud noted in his papers on the "debasement of the sexual object" (1912), never reconcile their Oedipal conflict and continue to conflate the sexual woman with mother. If this is true, then there may be some unconscious Oedipal contamination in much heterosexual sexuality. The libido itself may be contaminated. Thus the "pollution" of misogynistic discourse may be interpreted as concomitant to the identification of sexual woman and the mother; the pollution may symbolize the stain of incest. If true, then many men will always find sex a two-sided experience, partly gratifying and partly "dirty" and guilt-ridden, and, with particular relevance to the misogynistic imagery we have seen, the bodily liquids of sex evidence then become symbolic of the crime itself, staining and poisoning the transgressor. As a consequence, men who are deeply troubled by this problem of "dirt" will tend to blame women, the object of their conflict, as the cause of their turmoil.

But it has been my contention here that man's conflicted involvement with woman goes beyond sex and its symbolism. Beyond what others have said about sex and the Oedipal complex as the cause of misogyny (Hays 1964; Lederer 1968; Bloch 1991), I want to emphasize that woman is much more than a sexual object to man. He has many other needs that only she can fulfill. These nonsexual needs represent other strata of neediness that challenge his manly self-image and cause unbearable frustration in other walks of life. One of the observations we have made frequently is that men, especially in the androcentric societies, are helplessly dependent upon women for the basics of life, more so than are women upon men. This abject dependency upon women starts in infancy, continues through adolescence, and proliferates in maturity to include abstract social and symbolic cultural needs. The difference between the sexes here is definitive and enormous: girls do not experience such a dependency relationship with their fathers early in life; little girls do not form a symbiotic, feeding dependency on fathers. Fathers do not feed and tenderly comfort their children as do mothers; in particular, again with special relevance for the universal imagery we have seen, fathers cannot, and do not, feed their children *with their bodies*.

This difference seems to be crucial in developmental terms and in the formation of later cross-sex attitudes. Unlike girls also, self-respecting boys, and later men, cannot (or will not) care for themselves. In most cultures, men depend upon their mothers, and later their wives, not only for food preparation and domestic care, but also for the economic labor that will make them rich and powerful (as in New Guinea where women are "the hands of man"). Men also depend upon their wives for procreation and continuity: to bear the sons who will assure them a measure of immortality, protect them in war, care for them in their dotage, validate their masculinity, and assist them in their god-given task of continuing their line.

So man must cling helplessly to woman as a shipwrecked sailor to a lifeboat in choppy seas. He desperately needs her as his salvation from all want and from oblivion; his dependency is total and desperate. But, and here's the rub, man must also separate from woman to achieve anything at all. He must overcome his desire to regress to infantile symbiosis with her if he is to be accountable as a man. He must transcend his need for her, must renounce his dependency upon her. Woman looms the largest of all external objects in the male psyche because she represents the single source of virtually all of man's worldly gratification; yet he must oppose her, renounce her, transcend his need. This coupling of an overdetermined dependency with a developmentally adversarial relationship creates a mental disequilibrium in the male, a psychic imbalance, a supercharged fixation without surcease, as the neo-Freudians like Stoller (1974a, 1974b) and Chodorow (1978, 1989, 1994) have argued for years. And of course this powerful double-sided fixation creates a concomitant fear: the fear of abandonment, loss, withdrawal, disillusionment, and failure in life's most precious endeavors. Fraught with images of defeat, despair, and death, the fear of abandonment leads to regressive depression, panic, guilt, self-doubt, and ultimately to the rage of the thrall. The impotent rage leads to aggression; and aggression, in turn, needs a scapegoat.

The data presented here raise epistemological questions about what is pathological and what is "normal" in the male. I have called misogyny a male *malady,* the assumption throughout being that it represents a widespread form of neurosis or malaise in men. Yet must this lead to the conclusion that all men, or most men, are inherently pathological? To my way of thinking this is a futile question, because it leads to pointless tail-chasing. If we say, as I have above, that most men (or many men) experience severe and irresolvable internal conflicts as a result of experiences with women, and that "irresolvable inner conflict" is technically equivalent to psychopathology, then we may conclude that most men (or many men) are indeed pathological to some degree, since most men retain regressive longings as well as Oedipal guilt. My response to this situation would be to cite the novelist William Golding, who in *The Lord of the Flies* describes human beings as "at once heroic and sick" (1964:96). In the male sex, the sick part includes the misogynistic rage we have witnessed; in women it comes out in other ways, ways that I do not pretend to understand and that are not germane to the present study. Some men, of course, thank goodness, are not misogynists. These lucky men have successfully resolved their inner conflicts over women just as other men have successfully resolved other psychological problems. But the point of this book is that most men have not been so successful.

An Eclectic Approach

Taking all the above into account, my own "theory" of misogyny is not actually a theory at all but rather an eclectic combination of prior propositions with a few additions. First of all, we need to recognize the need for a double-barreled approach. We must explain the virtually universal proclivity of men toward fear and hatred of women. Then we must go on to explain the occasional "outbreaks" of a virulent misogyny in particular times and places.

Avoiding metaphysical and reductionistic traps, we can accomplish the first half of our task most cogently through a combination of four ideas discussed above: Freudian castration anxiety, behaviorist frustration-aggression theory, psychic-dependency theory, and the notion that all men experience regressive impulses.

Castration anxiety best explains universal phobias about menstrual blood. But it also sheds light on the near-universal anxiety of falling into dark and moist cavities in which a man sinks, drowns, is engulfed, devoured, transformed, and destroyed: in other words, the deep-seated fear of the vagina as threatening. Freud's theory most parsimoniously explains all these fantasies as well as the Melanesian form of gynophobia, its strikingly visceral imagery. The vagina seems to embody man's worst fears: mutilation and castration. Given the fact that no other theory so universally accommodates vaginal phobias, it must be afforded primacy of place, if only by default. I simply see no other way of explaining the hysteria involved and the fact of universality.

The second theory, that of frustration-aggression, first proposed by Dollard (1939) and reworked as above to incorporate the male sexual response, brings in man's sexual and evolutionary biology as a mammal and helps us see his hostility to woman as a product of the uniquely human conditions of continual arousal and frustration. The consequent aggression toward women is a displacement of man's anger at the frustrating object, sexual woman. In combination, the final two theories, psychic-dependency and regressive conflict, offer us the most logical, as well as parsimonious, explanation for matriphobia (in full) and uxorophobia (in part). We have seen that a large part of misogyny stems from man's fear of his own regressive longings for the perfect nurturing mother of infancy and his anaclitic dependency upon such a fantasy figure.

Misogynist phobias can be seen from this perspective as reaction-formations against man's abject dependency needs and his desire to return to being an infant at the breast, both of which represent an unacceptable passivity. All the "liquidity" imagery makes better sense if we see it as an overdetermined response to conflicts not only about sexuality, but also about the reproductive functions and fantasies about breastfeeding and returning to the womb. The liquidity of which the female body is capable unites and reifies all these unconscious wish-fears. On all these levels, woman equals wetness and wetness equals life, pleasure, sin, and death. So, from this perspective, misogyny can be seen partly as a reaction against the tidal pull of man's regressive impulses.

Now we can move on to the second question: that of variations in intensity. To explain the plaguelike outbreaks of misogyny in specific cultures and periods (medieval Europe, New Guinea, Sarakatsani, etc.), we need to refer to a combination of the situational, ad hoc theories outlined above, including Marxism, feminism, and structural-functionalism. Each empirical case is different and requires individual analysis. However, I feel that the best and most globally relevant of all these contextual models is the structural model described in Chapter 5, which focuses on patriliny, exogamy, and the agnatic principle of group formation. This "agnatic theory" also accounts for uxorophobia, the hatred and fear of wives. Where agnatic filiation overlaps with chronic warfare and where wives are outsiders, misogyny ends in the persecution of wives and by extension all nubile females.

A final consideration is what might be called existential scapegoating. Men who maintain lofty but unattainable ideals are bound to be disappointed and disillusioned in life. Their inevitable despair leads to frustration and anger. Fanatics who are unwilling to give up or moderate their absolutist beliefs must find a scapegoat to blame. Many men chose an ethnic group, class, race, religious minority, or other outsider group to blame; other men, for reasons that are not altogether clear, choose the sexual "other," women. This would explain why so many of the world's revealed religions have an extremist misogynist strain: the world can never be as perfect as God intended, and therefore some villain (never oneself) must be found to account for the failure of the ideal. This existential scapegoating is one in which sexuality is often present but it is not always the paramount feature. It is curious how the above material seems to show that many men project a fantasy of the all-powerful, all-nurturing mother of infancy onto the world as a dream of utopia, a dream that can only lead to frustration, disillusionment, and rage.

Thus ends our foray into theories of misogyny's causes. As the reader will no doubt have noticed, I am somewhat allergic to pandemic theories that purport to explain everything, and I prefer to leave it to the reader's imagination to choose the best idea or combination of ideas. But clearly, many theories are needed to explain this malady in all its diversity and richness. Misogyny is complex and has many, often unrelated causes. This said, we may now move on to a consideration of possible remedies for this curious and insidious disease.

Prognosis

Misogyny has its origins deep in most men's psyche and can burst into full-blown psychoses under certain conditions. Can the misogynist "bug" ever be cured? Given the fact that all the other prejudices known to humanity since Sophocles immortalized Oedipus are still with us after decades of therapy and "consciousness-raising," the prognosis is not good. Some rather outré cures have been proposed by feminists to combat misogyny, none of which seems promising. For example, literary critic Barbara Dixson offers some "rectifications" for misogyny, which border on science fiction in their degree of relevance to the real world. Like some other activist feminists, Dixson wants men voluntarily to "change their consciousness" and to undergo a "revolution" in self-awareness and agree to become like the fictional hermaphrodites in the feminist fantasy stories she analyzes (1992:392). But how is this miraculous change to be realized? Given the deep roots of misogyny, this desexualizing of consciousness is not likely to occur. As long as men have a sex drive, they will experience the kinds of frustrations and conflicts conducive to misogyny. Hermaphrodism does not seem a feasible solution. This idea also, as well as being slightly repulsive and a little bit stupid, has some discomforting "extinctionalist" implications.

Male feminists also have had their say on this issue. R. W. Connell (1995) and Matthew Gutmann (1997) propose a solution based on men's accepting, or being forced to accept, an androgynist script in life. The problem of woman-hating, they pronounce, is purely culturally created, since in their postmodernistic view sex and gender are themselves entirely culturally constructed. If sexual desire is a product of the cultural "script," ipso facto, misogyny can easily by gotten rid of in the wink of an eye. All we men need to do is to give up masculinity codes and such shallow gender nonsense. If men and women were indistinguishable in behavior and identical in all other things (for example, if men stopped watching football on television and gave up joining fraternities), there would be no sexual "other" to denigrate; thus misogyny would go away because there would be no opposite sex to victimize. The trouble with this is that it is purely wishful thinking, as well as banal and sterile. Men and women are not capable of being the same; men experience a different psychic course through life than women, and androgyny is a pipe dream that few men or women really want. As psychotherapist Adam Jukes astutely puts it: "Gender identity may not be innate, like physical attributes, but the inexorability of anatomical, psychological, and cultural pressures makes it no less certain" (1994:321).

The most androgynous people in the world today, the Semai of the Malay peninsula (Dentan 1979), entertain overtly misogynistic beliefs: they think that menstrual fluid is polluting like fish poison, that the vagina is frightening, and that a woman can turn into a man-eating tiger simply by stepping into a river when menstruating. A repugnant idea to most men and women anyway, androgyny therefore not only will not solve the problem, which is deeper than culture, but can never be imposed upon a resistant population. Is there a better solution than hermaphrodism or androgyny, one that has a better chance of being taken seriously?

There may be no cure for misogyny, but there are ways to mitigate the problem and to facilitate sexual reconciliation. First, as our own American experience with racism has shown, integration helps reduce the sense of danger and alienation that the distancing of human differences promotes. While the jury is still out on the effects of racial desegregation, it does appear that encouraging daily contact can relieve some of the tension between different groups and could thus reduce the sense of the opposite sex as mysterious, frightening, and unattainable. So sexual desegregation may be the first step in ameliorating the worst aspects of misogyny. This has already happened apace in the United States, by choice and by law. In colleges across the land, young men and women are now sharing bathrooms and showering together. Whether misogyny is therefore on the wane in modern America is another question that as yet has no definite answer, but certainly antiwoman institutions, like the exclusion of women from sports, have declined, and women are running successfully for higher political office, which suggests that the male electorate is less misogynistic than previously.

Since we are being speculative, another possibility comes to mind. I have argued throughout that misogyny derives as much from pre-Oedipal fixations and regressive conflicts as from sexual and Oedipal upheaval. Consequently, if the mother's monopoly over infant care were diluted by the father's frequent intervention, it is just possible that the linkage between early dependency needs and the mother as a genderized imago might be reduced somewhat. If fathers fondled and bottle-fed their infants more often than they normally do, especially their boys, the intensity of the maternal fixation might be minimized, as dependency and regressive needs lose an exclusively female focus, which in turn could lead to a reduction in later misogynistic expressions.

On an encouraging note, young fathers do appear to be moving in this direction in many parts of the world, especially in postindustrial societies like ours. But again it is too early to tell if this shift will have any impact upon misogyny. Still, if this kind of routine paternal participation in infant care (rather like a postpartum couvade) were to continue and spread, especially if fathers fed their little boys, the prognosis would be good for a positive impact on the next generations of men. In a sensitive work of comparative synthesis, anthropologist James Taggart has shown that the father-son relationship is indeed a key factor in the development of boys' later attitudes toward women — if not *the* key factor (1997). Comparing Mexican Indian and Spanish ideals of fatherhood, he notes that fathers who take the time to feed their boys "may help their sons separate from the mother with less anger toward women" (240). This seems like a promising lead and a possible antidote to the male malady. But more work on this subject is desperately needed.

Education is another important part of the cure. Naturally, education will help — that is, if people take its message seriously. But any educational program will be counterproductive if men and boys are told that their feelings are shameful and bad. Antimale propaganda will create more antagonism by exacerbating the inner struggle already present and will only lead to more misogyny. The solution, rather, is for elders to alert young men and boys to the nature of their many levels of ambivalence toward women, to raise their consciousness about the duality of their feelings, not only toward women, but toward all things that are important to them. We might call this "ambivalence toleration" or "conflictedness training." Of course we cannot put all growing boys on the couch, but educators could encourage boys, as well as girls, to face the fact that their strongest feelings are often mixed and that dependency needs are not evil, especially when it comes to the opposite sex.

However, sadly, all this is probably wishful thinking. Men are and will always be divided in their feelings about sex and about women. Only self-knowledge and tolerance can help men appreciate the degree of their conflict, and this can only occur at the level of individual awareness. Unfortunately, the degree of sophistication in the man seems not to matter much in reducing misogyny: the most brilliant, urbane, self-reflective, self-analyzed (e.g., Freud, Brahms) sophisticates are as prone to the male disease as are "primitive" tribesmen in New Guinea who believe in foul magic, witchcraft, and vaginal pollution. Furthermore, self-knowledge is not a monopoly of the smart set.

What Is To Be Done?

Simply put: men must get more comfortable with their ambiguous sexuality, their subterranean dependency needs for women's nurturing, their "corrupt" feminine side, and their "poisonous" bisexual self. Only by accepting these supposed weaknesses as normal and not tantamount to emasculation can men learn to love women unambiguously and to appreciate what the dramatist John Webster called the "womanish" in themselves. The need for love, dependency wishes, and the longing for comforting are not character flaws; they are, on the contrary, the very basis of sociability and the path to fulfillment because they push us toward social contact and commitment. Only self-knowledge can free men from fear of women, and self-knowledge in this case means the acceptance of the divided self within and an imperfect universe without. And only through such an acceptance of wholeness can men appreciate the loveliness, gentleness, and beauty of women. The key lies in forging a primary alliance with the self and an acceptance of the incongruities of human existence. The demon within thus neutralized by self-forgiveness, one can then go on to form an alliance with the Other against the darkness. Only through such a therapeutic gender alliance can men and women be happy together. As Robert Meagher writes, "A species divided against itself cannot stand" (1995:5). Men and women thus united, misogyny will wither away of its own accord. And on that ambiguous note, we end.

Glossary of Kinship Terminology

Affine, affinal. Kinship relation through marriage, in-law(s).

Agnate, agnatic. A kinship relationship traced through the male line.

Bilateral. Rule of descent or inheritance recognizing both father's and mother's sides.

Cognate, cognatic. Kinship relation traced through either mother or father.

Collateral. A relation of the same generation as individual, e.g., siblings, cousins; in contrast to *lineal* (ancestors and descendants).

Consanguine, consanguineal. Blood relation.

Corporate, corporacy. Refers to any group in which property is owned jointly and social identity is merged.

Exogamous. Out-marrying; in contrast to *endogamous* (in-marrying).

Gynophobia. Fear or hatred of women's bodies or biological functions, especially of the sexual organs.

Horror mulieris. Horror of women; misogyny.

Kindred. Ego-based extended family, usually including siblings, cousins, and their descendants.

Matrilineal. Rule of descent or inheritance through the mother's side.

Matrilocal. Postmarital residence with the wife's kin.

Matriphobia. Fear or hatred of mothers.

Misogamy. Fear or hatred of marriage.

Patrilineal. Rule of descent or inheritance through the father's side.

Patrilocal. Postmarital residence with the husband's kin.

Uterine. Kinship relationship traced through women.

Uxorophobia. Fear or hatred of wives.

References

Abbey, Ruth. 1996. Beyond misogyny and metaphor: women in Nietzsche's middle period. *Journal of the History of Philosophy* 34: 233–56.

Abu-Lughod, Lila. 1986. *Veiled Sentiments: Honor and Poetry in a Bedouin Society.* Berkeley: University of California Press.

Ackley, Katherine A., ed. 1992. *Misogyny in Literature: An Essay Collection.* New York: Garland.

Ahern, Emily M. 1978. The power and pollution of Chinese women. In *Studies in Chinese Society,* ed. Arthur P. Wolf, pp. 269–90. Stanford, Calif.: Stanford University Press.

Ahmed, Leila. 1992. *Women and Gender in Islam.* New Haven, Conn.: Yale University Press.

Almeida, Miguel Vale de. 1996. *The Hegemonic Male: Masculinity in a Portuguese Town.* Providence, R.I.: Berghahn Books.

Alter, Joseph. 1996. Seminal truth: a modern science of male celibacy in north India. *Medical Anthropology Quarterly* 11: 275–98.

Antoun, Richard T. 1968. On the modesty of women in Arab villages. *American Anthropologist* 70: 671–97.

Ardener, Shirley. 1978. Introduction: the nature of women in society. In *Defining Females: The Nature of Woman in Society,* ed. Shirley Ardener, pp. 9–48. New York: John Wiley and Sons.

Århem, Kaj. 1987. Wives for sisters: the management of marriage exchange in northwest Amazonia. In *Natives and Neighbors in South America: Anthropological Essays,* ed. Harald Sklar and Frank Salomon, pp. 130–201. Goteborg, Sweden: Etynologiska Studier, 38.

Auerbach, Nina. 1982. *Woman and the Demon: The Life of a Victorian Myth.* Cambridge, Mass.: Harvard University Press.

Bachofen, Johann. 1861 (1948). *Das Mutterrecht.* Basel: B. Schwabel.

Bailey, F. G. 1971. Gifts and poison. In *Gifts and Poison: The Politics of Reputation,* ed. F. G. Bailey, pp. 1–25. Oxford: Basil Blackwell.

Bakhtin, Mikhail. 1984. *Rabelais and His World.* Trans. Hélène Iswolsky. Bloomington: Indiana University Press.

Bamberger, Joan. 1974. The myth of matriarchy: why men rule in primitive society. In *Women, Culture, and Society,* ed. Michelle Zimbalist Rosaldo and Louise Lamphere, pp. 263–80. Stanford, Calif.: Stanford University Press.

Baraheni, Reza. 1977. *The Crowned Cannibals.* New York: Vintage Books.

Barnes, J. A. 1962. African models in the New Guinea Highlands. *Man* 62: 5–9.

Barnouw, Victor. 1985. *Culture and Personality.* 4th ed. Homewood, Ill.: Dorsey Press.

Basso, Ellen. 1973. *The Kalapalo Indians of Central Brazil.* New York: Holt, Rinehart, Winston.

Bates, Daniel G. 1974. Normative and alternative systems of marriage among the Yörük of southeastern Turkey. *Anthropological Quarterly* 47: 270–87.

Bates, Daniel G., Francis P. Conant, and Ayse Kudat, eds. 1974a. *Kidnapping and Elopement as Alternative Systems of Marriage*. Special Issue. *Anthropological Quarterly* 47, no. 3.

———. 1974b. Introduction. In *Kidnapping and Elopement as Alternative Systems of Marriage,* ed. Bates, Conant, and Kudat. Special Issue. *Anthropological Quarterly* 47, no. 3: 233–37.

Bennett, Lynn. 1983. *Dangerous Wives, Sacred Sisters*. New York: Columbia University Press.

Berndt, Ronald M. 1962. *Excess and Restraint: Social Control Among a New Guinea Mountain People*. Chicago: University of Chicago Press.

———. 1964. Warfare in the New Guinea highlands. *American Anthropologist* 66 part II: 183–203.

Bettelheim, Bruno. 1954. *Symbolic Wounds*. London: Thames and Hudson.

Blamires, Alcuin, ed. 1992. *Woman Defamed and Women Defended: An Anthology of Medieval Texts*. Oxford: Clarendon Press.

Bloch, R. Howard. 1989. Medieval misogyny. In *Misogyny, Misandry, and Misanthropy,* ed. R. Howard Bloch and Frances Ferguson, pp. 1–24. Berkeley: University of California Press.

———. 1991. *Medieval Misogyny and the Invention of Romantic Love*. Chicago: University of Chicago Press.

Bloch, R. Howard and Frances Ferguson. 1989a. Introduction. In *Misogyny, Misandry, and Misanthropy,* ed. Bloch and Ferguson, pp. vii–xvii. Berkeley: University of California Press.

———, eds. 1989b. *Misogyny, Misandry, and Misanthropy*. Berkeley: University of California Press.

Bloom, Harold. 1998. *Shakespeare: The Invention of the Human*. New York: Riverhead Books.

Blum, Richard and Eva Blum. 1965. *Health and Healing in Rural Greece: A Study of Three Communities*. Stanford, Calif.: Stanford University Press.

———. 1970. *The Dangerous Hour: The Lore and Culture of Crisis and Mystery in Rural Greece*. London: Chatto and Windus.

Bottigheimer, Ruth. 1987. *Grimm's Bad Girls and Bold Boys: The Moral and Social Vision of the Tales*. New Haven, Conn.: Yale University Press.

Bouhdiba, Abdelwahab. 1985. *Sexuality in Islam*. Trans. Alan Sheridan. London: Routledge and Kegan Paul.

Bourdieu, Pierre. 1966. The sentiment of honour in Kabyle society. In *Honour and Shame: The Values of Mediterranean Society,* ed. J. G. Péristiany, pp. 191–242. Chicago: University of Chicago Press.

Brain, James L. 1988. Male menstruation: further thoughts. *Journal of Psychohistory* 15: 311–23.

———. 1996. Witches and wizards: a male/female dichotomy? In *Denying Biology: Essays on Gender and Pseudo-Procreation,* ed. Warren Shapiro and Uli Linke, pp. 75–88. Lanham, Md.: University Press of America.

Brandes, Stanley H. 1980. *Metaphors of Masculinity: Sex and Status in Andalusian Folklore.* Philadelphia: University of Pennsylvania Press.

Brenner, Charles. 1974. *An Elementary Textbook of Psychoanalysis.* New York: Doubleday.

Breuner, Nancy F. 1992. The cult of the Virgin Mary in southern Italy and Spain. *Ethos* 20: 66–95.

Brown, Norman O. 1966. *Love's Body.* New York: Random House.

Brown, Paula. 1964. Enemies and affines. *Ethnology* 3: 335–56.

———. 1978. *Highland Peoples of New Guinea.* New York: Cambridge University Press.

Brown, Paula and Georgeda Buchbinder. 1976. Introduction. In *Man and Woman in the New Guinea Highlands,* ed. Brown and Buchbinder, pp. 1–12. Special Publications 8. Washington, D.C.: American Anthropological Association.

Brown, Peter. 1988. *The Body and Society: Men, Women, and Sexual Renunciation in Early Christianity.* New York: Columbia University Press.

Bruckman, Jan. 1974. Stealing women among the Koya of south India. *Anthropological Quarterly* 47: 304–13.

Buchbinder, Georgeda and Roy A. Rappaport. 1976. Fertility and death among the Maring. In *Man and Woman in the New Guinea Highlands,* ed. Paula Brown and Buchbinder, pp. 13–35. Special Publications 8. Washington, D.C.: American Anthropological Association.

Buckley, Thomas. 1982. Menstruation and the power of Yurok women: methods of cultural reconstruction. *American Ethnologist* 9: 47–60.

Buckley, Thomas and Alma Gottlieb, eds. 1988a. *Blood Magic: The Anthropology of Menstruation.* Berkeley: University of California Press.

———. 1988b. A critical appraisal of theories of menstrual symbolism. In *Blood Magic: The Anthropology of Menstruation,* ed. Buckley and Gottlieb, pp. 2–50. Berkeley: University of California Press.

Callaghan, Dympna. 1989. *Women and Gender in Renaissance Tragedy: A Study of* King Lear, Othello, The Duchess of Malfi, *and* The White Devil. New York: Harvester Wheatsheaf.

Campbell, John K. 1964. *Honour, Family, and Patronage.* Oxford: Oxford University Press.

Caro Baroja, Julio. 1965. *El Carnaval: Análisis histórica cultural.* Madrid: Taurus.

Carroll, Michael. 1986. *The Cult of the Virgin Mary.* Princeton, N.J.: Princeton University Press.

Carstairs, G. Morris. 1958. *The Twice Born.* Bloomington: Indiana University Press.

Chagnon, Napoleon. 1997. *Yanomamo.* 5th ed. New York: Harcourt, Brace, Jovanovich.

Chandos, John. 1984. *Boys Together: English Public Schools, 1800–1864.* New Haven, Conn.: Yale University Press.

Chasseguet-Smirgel, Janine. 1986. *Sexuality and Mind: The Role of the Father and the Mother in the Psyche.* New York: New York University Press.

Chodorow, Nancy. 1978. *The Reproduction of Mothering: Psychoanalysis and the Sociology of Gender.* Berkeley: University of California Press.

———. 1989. *Feminism and Psychoanalytic Theory.* New Haven, Conn.: Yale University Press.

————. 1994. *Femininities, Masculinities, and Sexualities*. Lexington: University Press of Kentucky.

Christensen, Peter G. 1997. Clive Sinclair's *Augustus Rex*: Misogyny, megalomania, and anti-semitism in the life of August Strindberg. In *Nordic Experiences: Exploration of Scandinavian Cultures,* ed. Berit I. Brown, pp. 27–38. Westport Conn.: Greenwood Press.

Collins, Randall. 1975. *Conflict Theory: Toward an Explanatory Social Science*. New York: Academic Press.

Connell, R. W. 1995. *Masculinities*. Berkeley: University of California Press.

Conrad, Joseph. 1902 (1983). *Heart of Darkness*. Ed. Paul O'Prey. New York: Penguin Books.

Coole, Linda. 1988. *Women in Political Theory: From Ancient Misogyny to Contemporary Feminism*. Sussex: Wheatsheaf.

Counihan, Carole M. 1985. Transvestism and gender in a Sardinian carnival. *Anthropology* 9: 11–24.

Cravalho, Mark A. 1999. Shameless creatures: an ethnozoology of the Amazon River Dolphin. *Ethnology* 38: 47–58.

Danforth, Loring M. 1989. *Firewalking and Religious Healing: The Anastenaria of Greece and the American Firewalking Movement*. Princeton, N.J.: Princeton University Press.

Darwin, Charles. 1871. *The Descent of Man, and Selection in Relation to Sex*. New York: D. Appleton.

Davis, John. 1973. *Land and Family in Pisticci*. London: Athlone Press.

Davis, Natalie Z. 1978. Women on top: symbolic sexual inversion and political disorder in early modern Europe. In *The Reversible World: Symbolic Inversion in Art and Society,* ed. Barbara H. Babcock, pp. 147–90. Ithaca, N.Y.: Cornell University Press.

Delaney, Carol. 1987. Seeds of honor, fields of shame. In *Honor and Shame and the Unity of the Mediterranean,* ed. David D. Gilmore, pp. 35–48. Special Publications 22. Washington, D.C.: American Anthropological Association.

————. 1988. Mortal flow: menstruation in Turkish village society. In *Blood Magic: The Anthropology of Menstruation,* ed. Thomas Buckley and Alma Gottlieb, pp. 75–93. Berkeley: University of California Press.

Delaney, Janice, Mary Jane Lupton, and Emily Toth. 1988. *The Curse: A Cultural History of Menstruation*. New York: E. P. Dutton.

Demos, John. 1982. *Entertaining Satan: Witchcraft and the Culture of Early New England*. New York: Oxford University Press.

Dentan, Robert. 1979. *The Semai: A Non-violent People of Malaya*. New York: Holt, Rinehart, Winston.

Derné, Steven. 1994. Hindu men talk about controlling women: cultural ideas as a tool of the powerful. *Sociological Perspectives* 37: 203–27.

————. 1995. *Culture in Action: Family Life, Emotion, and Male Dominance in Banaras, India*. Albany: State University of New York Press.

Detwiler, Bruce. 1990. *Nietzsche and the Politics of Aristocratic Radicalism*. Chicago: University of Chicago Press.

Dijkstra, Bram. 1986. *Idols of Perversity: Fantasies of Feminine Evil in Fin-de-Siècle Culture*. New York: Oxford University Press.

———. 1996. *Evil Sisters: The Threat of Female Sexuality and the Cult of Manhood.* New York: Knopf.

Dinnerstein, Dorothy. 1976. *The Mermaid and the Minotaur.* New York: Harper and Row.

Dixson, Barbara. 1992. What to do about misogyny? Three science fiction writers. In *Misogyny in Literature: An Essay Collection,* ed. Katherine A. Ackley, pp. 379–93. New York: Garland.

Dollard, John, Neal E. Miller, Orval H. Mowrer, and Robert R. Sears. 1939. *Frustration and Aggression.* New Haven, Conn.: Yale University Press.

Doniger, Wendy O'Flaherty. 1973. *Asceticism and Eroticism in the Mythology of Siva.* London: Oxford University Press.

———. 1976. *The Origins of Evil in Hindu Mythology.* Berkeley: University of California Press.

———. 1980. *Women, Androgynes, and Other Mythical Beasts.* Chicago: University of Chicago Press.

Dundes, Alan. 1962. Earth-diver: creation of the mythopoeic male. *American Anthropologist* 64: 1032–51.

Durand, Gilbert. 1969. *Les structures antropologiques de l'imaginaire: Introduction à l'archétypologie générale.* Paris: Bordas, Collection Etudes Supérieures.

Durkheim, Emile. 1893 (1933). *The Division of Labor in Society.* Trans. George Simpson. New York: Macmillan.

———. 1938. *The Rules of the Sociological Method.* Trans. Sarah A. Solovay and John Mueller. Chicago: University of Chicago Press.

Dwyer, Daisy. 1978. *Images and Self Images.* New York: Columbia University Press.

Elshtain, Jean Bethke. 1981. *Public Man, Private Woman: Women in Social and Political Thought.* Princeton, N.J.: Princeton University Press.

Elwin, Verrier. 1968. *The Kingdom of the Young.* London: Oxford University Press.

Epstein, Scarlett. 1967. A sociological analysis of witch beliefs in a Mysore village. In *Magic, Witchcraft, and Curing,* ed. John Middleton, pp. 135–54. Austin: University of Texas Press.

Erikson, Erik. 1950. *Childhood and Society.* New York: Norton.

Evans-Pritchard. E. E. 1940. *The Nuer.* Oxford: Clarendon Press.

———. 1965. *Witchcraft, Oracles, and Magic Among the Azande.* Oxford: Clarendon Press.

Faithorn, Elizabeth D. 1975. The concept of pollution among the Kafe of the Papua New Guinea highlands. In *Toward an Anthropology of Women,* ed. Rayna R. Rapp, pp. 127–40. New York: Monthly Review Press.

———. 1976. Women as persons: aspects of female life and male-female relations among the Kafe. In *Man and Woman in the New Guinea Highlands,* ed. Paula Brown and Georgeda Buchbinder, pp. 86–95. Special Publications 8. Washington, D.C.: American Anthropological Association.

Fallers, Lloyd and Margaret C. Fallers. 1976. Sex roles in Edremit. In *Mediterranean Family Structures,* ed. J. G. Péristiany, pp. 243–60. Cambridge: Cambridge University Press.

Favret-Saada, Jeanne. 1980. *Deadly Words: Witchcraft in the Bocage.* Cambridge: Cambridge University Press.

Fenichel, Otto. 1945. *The Psychoanalytic Theory of Neuroses*. New York: Norton.

Fischer, Michael M. 1978. On changing the concept and position of Persian women. In *Women in the Muslim World*, ed. Lois Beck and Nikki Keddie, pp. 189–215. Cambridge: Cambridge University Press.

Fogelson, Raymond D. 1980. Windigo goes south: Stoneclad among the Cherokees. In *Manlike Monsters on Trial: Early Accounts and Modern Evidence*, ed. Marjorie M. Halpin and Michael M. Ames, pp. 132–51. Vancouver: University of British Columbia Press.

Fortes, Meyer. 1959. Descent, filiation, and affinity. *Man* 59: 206–12.

Fortune, Reo. 1932. *Sorcerers of Dobu: The Social Anthropology of the Dobu Islanders of the Western Pacific*. New York: E. P. Dutton.

Fox, Robin. 1983. *Kinship and Marriage: An Anthropological Perspective*. 2nd ed. Cambridge: Cambridge University Press.

Francus, Marilyn. 1994. The monstrous mother: reproductive anxiety in Swift and Pope. *English Literary History* 61: 829–51.

Frazer, Sir James. 1890 (1951). *The Golden Bough*. New York: Macmillan.

Freud, Sigmund. 1910. A special type of choice of object made by men. *Standard Edition* (1975), ed. Lytton Strachey, vol. 11, pp. 165–75. London: Hogarth Press.

———. 1912. On the universal tendency to debasement in the sphere of love. *Standard Edition* (1975), ed. James Strachey, vol. 11, pp. 177–90. London: Hogarth Press.

———. 1931a. *Civilization and Its Discontents*. Trans. James Strachey. New York: Norton.

———. 1931b. Female sexuality. *Standard Edition* (1975), ed. James Strachey, vol. 21, pp. 225–43. London: Hogarth Press.

———. 1937. Analysis terminable and interminable. *Standard Edition* (1975), ed. James Strachey, vol. 23, pp. 209–53. London: Hogarth Press.

———. 1922 (1940). Medusa's head. *Standard Edition* (1975), ed. James Strachey, vol. 18, pp. 273–74. London: Hogarth Press.

Gage, Nicholas. 1989. *A Place for Us*. Boston: Houghton Mifflin.

Gallagher, Philip. 1987. *Milton, the Bible, and Misogyny*. Ed. Eugene R. Cunnar and Gail L. Mortimer. Columbia: University of Missouri Press.

Garber, Marjorie. 1991. *Vested Interests: Cross-Dressing and Cultural Anxiety*. New York: Routledge.

Geertz, Hildred. 1979. The meanings of family ties. In *Meaning and Order in Moroccan Society*, ed. Clifford Geertz, Hildred Geertz, and Lawrence Rosen, pp. 315–86. New York: Cambridge University Press.

Gelber, Marilyn G. 1986. *Gender and Society in the New Guinea Highlands*. Boulder, Colo.: Westview Press.

Gewertz, Deborah B. 1982. The father who bore me: the role of *Tsambunwuro* during Chambiri initiation ceremonies In *Rituals of Manhood: Male Initiation in Papua New Guinea*, ed. Gilbert H. Herdt, pp. 286–320. Berkeley: University of California Press.

Gillison, Gillian. 1993. *Between Culture and Fantasy: A New Guinea Mythology*. Chicago: University of Chicago Press.

Gilman, Sander. 1988. *Disease and Representations: Images of Illness from Madness to AIDS*. Ithaca, N.Y.: Cornell University Press.

Gilmore, David D. 1978. Varieties of gossip in a Spanish town. *Ethnology* 17: 89–100.

———. 1987. Introduction: the shame of dishonor. In *Honor and Shame and the Unity of the Mediterranean,* ed. Gilmore, pp. 2–21. Special Publications 22. Washington, D.C.: American Anthropological Association.

———. 1990. *Manhood in the Making: Cultural Concepts of Masculinity.* New Haven, Conn.: Yale University Press.

———. 1996. Sexual imagery in Spanish carnival. In *Denying Biology: Essays on Gender and Pseudo-Procreation,* ed. Warren Shapiro and Uli Linke, pp. 27–50. Lanham, Md.: University Press of America.

———. 1997. Review of Miguel Vale de Almeida, *The Hegemonic Male. American Anthropologist* 99: 434–35.

———. 1998. *Carnival and Culture: Sex, Symbol and Status in Spain.* New Haven, Conn.: Yale University Press.

Glenn, Kathleen M. 1992. Textual and social authority in the fiction of Ignacio Martínez de Pisón. In *Misogyny in Literature: An Essay Collection,* ed. Katherine A. Ackley, pp. 363–77. New York: Garland.

Godelier, Maurice. 1986. *The Making of Great Men: Male Dominance and Power Among the New Guinea Baruya.* Cambridge: Cambridge University Press.

Golding, William. 1964. *The Lord of the Flies: Casebook Edition.* Ed. James R. Baker and Arthur P. Ziegler. New York: Putnam.

Goodenough, Ward. 1996. Procreation, gender, and pollution. In *Denying Biology: Essays on Gender and Pseudo-Procreation,* ed. Warren Shapiro and Uli Linke, pp. 191–208. Lanham, Md.: University Press of America.

Goody, Jack. 1983. *The Development of the Family and Marriage in Europe.* Cambridge: Cambridge University Press.

Greenson, Ralph R. 1968 (1978). Disidentifying from the mother: its special importance for the boy. In *Explorations in Psychoanalysis* (Collected Papers of Ralph R. Greenson), pp. 305–12. New York: International University Press.

Gregor, Thomas. 1985. *Anxious Pleasures: The Sexual Life of an Amazonian People.* Chicago: University of Chicago Press.

Gubar, Susan. 1977. The female monster. *Signs* 3: 380–94.

Gutmann, Matthew. 1997. Trafficking in men: the anthropology of masculinity. *Annual Review of Anthropology* 26: 385–409.

Guttentag, Marcia and Paul F. Secord. 1983. *Too Many Women? The Sex Ratio Question.* Beverly Hills, Calif.: Sage Publications

Haeri, Shahla. 1989. *Law of Desire: Temporary Marriage in Shi'i Iran.* Syracuse, N.Y.: Syracuse University Press.

Haggard, H. Rider. 1887 (1976). *She.* New York: Hart.

Harding, M. Esther. 1971. *Women's Mysteries: Ancient and Modern.* New York: Harper and Row.

Harding, Susan. 1975. Woman and words in a Spanish village. In *Toward an Anthropology of Women,* ed. Rayna R. Reiter, pp. 283–308. New York: Monthly Review Press.

Harrowitz, Nancy A. 1994. *Antisemitism, Misogyny, and the Logic of Cultural Difference: Cesare Lombroso and Matilde Serao.* Lincoln: University of Nebraska Press.

Hattaway, Michael. 1993. Fleshing his will in the spoil of her honour: desire, misogyny, and the perils of chivalry. *Shakespearean Survey* 46: 121–35.

Hayano, David. 1974. Misfortune and traditional political leadership among the Tauna Awa of New Guinea. *Oceania* 45: 18–26.

Hays, Hoffman R. 1964. *The Dangerous Sex: The Myth of Feminine Evil.* New York: Putnam.

Hays, Terence and Patricia H. Hays. 1982. Opposition and complementarity of the sexes in Ndumba initiation. In *Rituals of Manhood: Male Initiation in Papua New Guinea,* ed. Gilbert H. Herdt, pp. 201–38. Berkeley: University of California Press.

Herdt, Gilbert H. 1981. *Guardians of the Flutes: Idioms of Masculinity.* New York: McGraw-Hill.

———. 1982a. Fetish and fantasy in Sambia initiation. In *Rituals of Manhood: Male Initiation in Papua New Guinea,* ed. Herdt, pp. 44–98. Berkeley: University of California Press.

———, ed. 1982b. *Rituals of Manhood: Male Initiation in Papua New Guinea.* Berkeley: University of California Press.

———. 1986. *The Sambia: Ritual and Gender in New Guinea.* New York: Holt, Rinehart, Winston.

Herzfeld, Michael. 1985. *The Poetics of Manhood: Contest and Identity in a Cretan Mountain Village.* Princeton, N.J.: Princeton University Press.

Hirschon, Renée. 1978. Open body/closed space: the transformation of female sexuality. In *Defining Female: The Nature of Women in Society,* ed. Shirley Ardener, pp. 66–88. New York: John Wiley.

Hogbin, Ian. 1970. *The Island of Menstruating Men: Religion in Wogeo, New Guinea.* Scranton, Pa.: Chandler.

Holmberg, Allan R. 1950. *Nomads of the Long Bow: The Siriono of Eastern Bolivia.* Washington, D.C.: Smithsonian Institution Press.

Hoover, Claudette. 1989. Women, centaurs, and devils in *King Lear. Women's Studies* 16: 349–59.

Horney, Karen. 1926. The flight from womanhood: the masculinity complex in women as viewed by men and women. *International Journal of Psycho-Analysis* 7: 324–39.

———. 1932. The dread of women. *International Journal of Psycho-Analysis* 13:358–60.

Htin Aung, U. 1937. *Burmese Drama.* Oxford: Oxford University Press.

Hugh-Jones, Christine. 1979. *From the Milk River: Spatial and Temporal Processes in Northwest Amazonia.* Cambridge: Cambridge University Press.

Hugh-Jones, Stephen. 1979. *The Palm and the Pleiades: Initiation and Cosmology in Northwest Amazonia.* Cambridge: Cambridge University Press.

Jackson, Jean E. 1992. The meaning and message of symbolic sexual violence in Tukanoan ritual. *Anthropological Quarterly* 65: 1–18.

———. 1996. Coping with the dilemmas of affinity and female sexuality: male rebirth in the central northwest Amazon. In *Denying Biology: Essays on Gender and Pseudo-Procreation,* ed. Warren Shapiro and Uli Linke, pp. 89–127. Lanham, Md.: University Press of America.

Jacobsen, Edith. 1950. The development of the wish for a child in boys. *Psychoanalytic Study of the Child* 5: 139–52.

Jukes, Adam. 1994. *Why Men Hate Women.* London: Free Association Books.

Kakar, Sudhir. 1981. *The Inner World: A Psychoanalytic Study of Childhood and Society in India.* Delhi: Oxford University Press.

Kaufmann, Walter. 1950. *Nietzsche: Philosopher, Psychologist, Antichrist.* Princeton, N.J.: Princeton University Press.

Keesing, Roger M. 1975. *Kin Groups and Social Structure.* New York: Harcourt, Brace, Jovanovich.

Kelly, Raymond C. 1976. Witchcraft and sexual relations: an exploration in the social and semantic implications of the structure of belief. In *Man and Woman in the New Guinea Highlands,* ed. Paula Brown and Georgeda Buchbinder, pp. 36–54. Special Publications 8. Washington, D.C.: American Anthropological Association.

Kestner, Joseph A. 1989. *Mythology and Misogyny: The Social Discourse of Nineteenth-Century British Classical-Subject Painting.* Madison: University of Wisconsin Press.

Konner, Melvin. 1982. *The Tangled Wing: Biological Constraints on the Human Spirit.* New York: Holt, Rinehart, Winston.

Kramer, Heinrich and Jacob Sprenger. 1487 (1971). *The Malleus Maleficarum of Heinrich Kramer and James Sprenger.* Trans. Montague Summers. New York: Dover.

Kudat, Ayse. 1974. Institutional rigidity and individual initiative in marriages of Turkish peasants. *Anthropological Quarterly* 47: 288–303.

Kuper, Hilda. 1947. *An African Aristocracy: Rank Among the Swazi of Bechuanaland.* London: Oxford University Press.

La Fontaine, Jean S. 1972. Ritualization of women's life-crises in Bugisu. In *The Interpretation of Ritual: Essays in Honour of I. A. Richards,* ed. Jean S. La Fontaine, pp. 159–86. London: Tavistock.

———. 1985. *Initiation.* Harmondsworth: Penguin.

Lakoff, George. 1987. *Women, Fire, and Dangerous Things: What Categories Reveal About the Mind.* Chicago: University of Chicago Press.

Lamphere, Louise. 1974. Strategies, cooperation, and conflict among women in domestic groups. In *Woman, Culture, and Society,* ed. Michelle Zimbalist Rosaldo and Lamphere, pp. 97–112. Stanford, Calif.: Stanford University Press.

Langness, Lewis L. 1967. Sexual antagonism in the New Guinea highlands: a Bena Bena example. *Oceania* 37: 161–77.

———. 1974. Ritual power and male dominance in the New Guinea highlands. *Ethos* 2: 189–212.

———. 1976. Discussion. In *Man and Woman in the New Guinea Highlands,* ed. Paula Brown and Georgeda Buchbinder, pp. 96–106. Special Publications 8. Washington, D.C.: American Anthropological Association.

———. 1999. *Men and "Woman" in New Guinea.* Novato, Calif.: Chandler and Sharpe.

Lassner, Jacob. 1993. *Demonizing the Queen of Sheba: Boundaries of Gender and Culture in Postbiblical Judaism and Medieval Islam.* Chicago: University of Chicago Press.

Lawrence, D. H. 1930. *Aaron's Rod.* New York: Albert and Charles Boni.

Lawrence, Denise L. 1982. Reconsidering the menstrual taboo: a Portuguese case. *Anthropological Quarterly* 55: 84–89.

Lederer, Wolfgang. 1968. *The Fear of Women*. New York: Grune and Stratton.

Lee, Richard B. 1979. *The !Kung San: Men, Women, and Work in a Foraging Society*. Cambridge: Cambridge University Press.

Lehman, Arthur C. and James E. Myers. 1993. *Magic, Witchcraft, and Religion: An Anthropological Study of the Supernatural*. 3rd ed. Mountain View, Calif.: Mayfield.

Lévi-Strauss, Claude. 1961. *Tristes tropiques*. Trans. John Russell. New York: Criterion Books.

——. 1949 (1969). *The Elementary Structures of Kinship*. Trans. James Harle Bell, John Richard von Sturmer, and Rodney Needham. Boston: Beacon Press.

Levy, Robert I. 1973. *Tahitians: Mind and Experience in the Society Islands*. Chicago: University of Chicago Press.

Lidz, Theodore and Ruth Lidz. 1989. *Oedipus in the Stone Age*. New York: International University Press.

Lindenbaum, Shirley. 1972. Sorcerers, ghosts, and polluting women: an analysis of religious belief and population control. *Ethnology* 11: 241–53.

——. 1976. A wife is the hand of man. In *Man and Woman in the New Guinea Highlands*, ed. Paula Brown and Georgeda Buchbinder, pp. 54–62. Special Publications 8. Washington, D.C.: American Anthropological Association.

——. 1979. *Kuru Sorcery: Disease and Danger in the New Guinea Highlands*. Palo Alto, Calif.: Mayfield.

Linke, Uli. 1996. The origin of poetry: narratives of masculinity and female empowerment in Icelandic mythology. In *Denying Biology: Essays on Gender and Pseudo-Procreation*, ed. Warren Shapiro and Uli Linke, pp. 129–65. Lanham, Md.: University Press of America.

——. 1997. Gendered differences, violent imagination: blood, race, nation. *American Anthropologist* 99: 559–73.

Lipkin, Mack, Jr. and Gerri S. Lamb. 1982. Couvade symptoms in a primary care practice: use of an illness without disease to examine health care behavior. In *The Use and Misuse of Medicine*, ed. Marten W. de Vries, Robert L. Berg, and Mack Lipkin, Jr., pp. 96–117. New York: Praeger Scientific.

Lloyd-Jones, Hugh. 1975. *Females of the Species: Semonides on Women*. Park Ridge, N.J.: Noyes Press.

Lockridge, Kenneth A. 1992. *On the Sources of Patriarchal Rage: The Commonplace Books of William Byrd and Thomas Jefferson and the Gendering of Power in the Eighteenth Century*. New York: New York University Press.

Lockwood, William G. 1974. Bride theft and social maneuverability in western Bosnia. *Anthropological Quarterly* 47: 253–70.

Loewald, Hans W. 1980. Ego and reality. In Loewald, *Papers on Psychoanalysis*. New Haven, Conn.: Yale University Press.

Lombroso, Cesare and Guglielmo Ferrero. 1890. *The Female Offender*. Trans. W. Douglass Morrison. New York: D. Appleton.

Lowie, Robert H. 1956. *The Crow Indians*. New York: Holt, Rinehart, Winston.

Lu, Tonglin, ed. 1993. *Gender and Sexuality in Twentieth-Century Chinese Literature and Society*. Albany: State University of New York Press.

——. 1995. *Misogyny, Cultural Nihilism and Oppositional Politics: Contemporary Chinese Experimental Fiction*. Stanford, Calif.: Stanford University Press.

Maher, Vanessa. 1978. Women and social change in Morocco. In *Woman in the Muslim World,* ed. Louise Beck and Nikki Keddie, pp. 100–123. Cambridge, Mass.: Harvard University Press.

Mahler, Margaret S., Fred Pine, and Anni Bergman. 1975. *The Psychological Birth of the Human Infant.* New York: Basic Books.

Malinowski, Bronislaw. 1922 (1961). *Argonauts of the Western: An Account of Native Enterprise and Adventure in the Archipelagoes of Melanesian New Guinea.* Prospect Heights, Ill.: Waveland Press.

Mannheim, Karl. 1964. *Ideology and Utopia.* Trans. Louis Wirth and Edward Shils. New York: Harvest Books.

Marx, Karl and Frederick Engels. 1970 (1845–46). *The German Ideology, Part One.* New York: International Publishers.

Mason, John P. 1975. Sex and symbol in the treatment of women: the wedding rite in a Libyan oasis community. *American Ethnologist* 2: 649–61.

McLennan, John. 1865 (1965). *Primitive Marriage: An Inquiry into the Origin of the Form of Capture in Marriage Ceremonies.* Chicago: University of Chicago Press.
——. 1896 (1976). *Studies in Ancient Society.* New York: Macmillan.

Mead, Margaret. 1940. *The Mountain Arapesh.* Vol. 2. New York: Natural History Press.

Meagher, Robert E. 1995. *Helen: Myth, Legend, and the Culture of Misogyny.* New York: Continuum.

Meggitt, Mervyn J. 1958. The Enga of the New Guinea Highlands. *Oceania* 28: 253–330.
——. 1964. Male-female relationships in the highlands of Australian New Guinea. *American Anthropologist* 66, Part II: 204–24.
——. 1976. A duplicity of demons: sexual and familial roles expressed in western Enga stories. In *Man and Woman in the New Guinea Highlands,* ed. Paula Brown and Georgeda Buchbinder, pp. 63–85. Special Publications 8. Washington, D.C.: American Anthropological Association.

Meigs, Anna S. 1984. *Food, Sex, and Pollution: A New Guinea Religion.* New Brunswick, N.J.: Rutgers University Press.

Menninger, Karl A. 1941. Psychogenic influences on the appearance of the menstrual period. *International Journal of Psychoanalysis* 22: 60–64.

Mernissi, Fatima. 1987. *Beyond the Veil: Female Dynamics in a Modern Muslim Society.* Rev. ed. Bloomington: Indiana University Press.

Mettler, Cecilia Charlotte. 1947. *History of Medicine: A Correlative Text.* Philadelphia: Blakiston.

Mitchell, Timothy. 1998. *Betrayal of the Innocents: Desire, Power, and the Catholic Church in Spain.* Philadelphia: University of Pennsylvania Press.

Momoko, Takemi. 1983. "Menstruation sutra" belief in Japan. *Japanese Journal of Religious Studies* 10: 229–46.

Montherlant, Henry de. 1939. *Les Leprouses.* Paris: Gallimard.

Muir, Edward. 1997. *Ritual in Early Modern Europe.* Cambridge: Cambridge University Press.

Munroe, Robert L., Ruth H. Munroe, and John W. M. Whiting. 1973. The couvade: a psychological analysis. *Ethos* 1: 28–74.
——. 1981. Male sex-role resolutions. In *Handbook of Cross-Cultural Human De-*

velopment, ed. Munroe, Munroe, and Whiting, pp. 611–32. New York: Garland STPM Press.

Murdock, George P. 1949. *Social Structure.* New York: Macmillan.

Murphy, Robert F. 1977. Man's culture and woman's nature. *Annals of the New York Academy of Science* 293: 15–24.

———. 1978. *Headhunter's Heritage.* New York: Octagon Books.

Murphy, Yolanda and Robert F. Murphy. 1974. *Women of the Forest.* New York: Columbia University Press.

Newman, Philip L. 1965. *Knowing the Gururumba.* New York: Holt, Rinehart, Winston.

Newman, Philip L. and David J. Boyd. 1982. The making of men: ritual and meaning in Awa male initiation. In *Rituals of Manhood: Male Initiation in Papua New Guinea,* ed. Gilbert H. Herdt, pp. 239–85. Berkeley: University of California Press.

Nietzsche, Friedrich W. 1967. *On the Genealogy of Morals.* Trans. Walter Kaufmann and R. J. Hollingdale. *Ecce Homo.* Ed. and trans. Walter Kaufmann. New York: Vintage.

———. 1969 (1886). *Beyond Good and Evil.* Trans. R. J. Hollingdale. Great Books of the Western World 43, pp. 463–545. Chicago: Encyclopaedia Britannica.

Nikhilananda, Swami. 1962. *Holy Mother.* New York: Ramakrishna-Vivekananda Center.

Nixon, Cornelia. 1986. *Lawrence's Leadership: Politics and the Turn Against Women.* Berkeley: University of California Press.

Noddings, Nel. 1989. *Women and Evil.* Berkeley: University of California Press.

Ortner, Sherry B. 1974. Is female to male as nature is to culture? In *Women, Culture, and Society,* ed. Michelle Zimbalist Rosaldo and Louise Lamphere, pp. 67–88. Stanford, Calif.: Stanford University Press.

Pagels, Elaine. 1988. *Adam, Eve, and the Serpent.* New York: Random House.

Paige, Karen F. 1977. Sexual pollution: reproductive sex taboos in American Society. *Journal of Social Issues* 33: 144–65.

Pater, Walter. 1873 (1971). *The Renaissance: Studies in Art and Poetry.* London: Phaidon.

Paul, Robert A. 1996. Symbolic reproduction and Sherpa monasticism. In *Denying Biology: Essays on Gender and Pseudo-Procreation,* ed. Warren Shapiro and Uli Linke, pp. 51–73. Lanham, Md.: University Press of America.

Péristiany, J. G., ed. 1966. *Honour and Shame: The Values of Mediterranean Society.* Chicago: University of Chicago Press.

Pitt-Rivers, Julian A. 1961. *The People of the Sierra.* Chicago: Chicago University Press.

———. 1977. *The Fate of Schechem.* Cambridge: Cambridge University Press.

Pizan, Christine de. 1405 (1982). *The Book of the City of Ladies.* Trans. Earl J. Richards. New York: Persea Books.

Podhoretz, Norman. 1999. *Ex-Friends: Falling Out with Allen Ginsberg, Lionel and Diana Trilling, Lillian Hellman, Hannah Arendt, and Norman Mailer.* New York: Free Press.

Poole, Fitz John Porter. 1982a. Couvade and clinic in a New Guinea society: birth among the Bimin-Kuskusmin. In *The Use and Abuse of Medicine,* ed. Marten W.

de Vries, Robert L. Berg, and Mack Lipkin, Jr., pp. 54–95. New York: Praeger Scientific.

———. 1982b. The ritual forging of identity: aspects of self in Bimin-Kuskusmin male initiation. In *Rituals of Manhood: Male Initiation in Papua New Guinea,* ed. Gilbert H. Herdt, pp. 99–156. Berkeley: University of California Press.

Quinn, Naomi. 1977. Anthropological studies on women's status. *Annual Review of Anthropology* 6: 185–222.

Racine, Jean. (1998). *Phèdre.* A New Translation by Ted Hughes. New York: Farrar, Straus, Giroux.

Rancour-Laferriere, Daniel. 1998. *Tolstoy on the Couch: Misogyny, Masochism, and the Absent Mother.* New York: New York University Press.

Read, Kenneth E. 1952. *Nama* cult of the central highlands, New Guinea. *Oceania* 23: 1–25.

———. 1954. Marriage among the Gahuku-Gama of the eastern central highlands, New Guinea. *South Pacific* 7: 864–71.

———. 1965. *The High Valley.* New York: Scribner.

Reed, Barbara E. 1992. The gender symbolism of Kuan-yin Bodhisattva. In *Buddhism, Sexuality, and Gender,* ed. José Ignacio Cabezón, pp. 159–65. Albany: State University of New York Press.

Richards, Audrey I. 1956. *Chisung: A Girl's Initiation Ceremony.* London: Faber and Faber.

Rival, Laura. 1998. Androgynous parents and guest children: the Huaorani couvade. *Journal of the Royal Anthropological Institute* 4: 619–42.

Rodriguez, Sylvia. 1991. The Taos Pueblo *matachines*: ritual symbolism and interethnic relations. *American Ethnologist* 18: 234–56.

Rogers, Katherine M. 1966. *The Troublesome Helpmate: A History of Misogyny in Literature.* Seattle: University of Washington Press.

Roheim, Geza. 1949. The symbolism of subincision. *American Imago* 6: 321–25.

———. 1950. *Psychoanalysis and Anthropology.* New York: International University Press.

Rosen, Lawrence. 1979. The negotiation of reality: male-female relations in Sefrou, Morocco. In *Meaning and Order in Moroccan Society,* ed. Clifford Geertz, pp. 19–111. New York: Cambridge University. Press.

Salisbury, Richard F. 1962. *From Stone to Steel: Economic Consequences of Technological Change in New Guinea.* Melbourne: Australian National University Press.

———. 1965. The Siane of the eastern highlands. In *Gods, Ghosts and Men in Melanesia: Some Religions of Australian New Guinea and the New Hebrides,* ed. Peter Lawrence and Mervyn J. Meggitt, pp. 50–77. New York: Oxford University Press.

Schneider, David Murray. 1965. Some muddles in the models: the relevance of models for social anthropology. ASA Monographs 1, pp. 25–85. London: Tavistock.

———. 1984. *A Critique of the Study of Kinship.* Ann Arbor: University of Michigan Press.

Schneider, Jane. 1971. Of vigilance and virgins. *Ethnology* 9: 1–24.

Schopenhauer, Arthur. 1970. *Essays and Aphorisms.* Trans. R. J. Hollingdale. Harmondsworth: Penguin.

Sein Tu. 1964. The psychodynamics of Burmese personality. *Journal of the Burmese Research Society* 47: 263–86.

Shapiro, Warren. 1989. The theoretical importance of pseudo-procreative symbolism. *Psychoanalytic Study of Society* 14: 71–88.

———. 1996. Introduction. In *Denying Biology: Essays on Gender and Pseudo-Procreation,* ed. Shapiro and Uli Linke, pp. 1–26. Lanham, Md.: University Press of America.

Shapiro, Warren and Uli Linke, eds. 1996. *Denying Biology: Essays on Gender and Pseudo-Procreation.* Lanham, Md.: University Press of America.

Sheehy, Michael. 1968. *Is Ireland Dying?* New York: Taplinger.

Shklar, Judith. 1984. *Ordinary Vices.* Cambridge, Mass.: Harvard University Press.

Shostak, Marjorie. 1983. *Nisa: The Life and Work of a !Kung Woman.* New York: Random House.

Shweder, Richard A. 1991. Menstrual pollution and soul loss and the comparative study of emotions. In *Thinking Through Cultures: Expeditions in Cultural Psychology,* pp. 241–68. Cambridge, Mass.: Harvard University Press.

Slater, Michael. 1983. *Dickens and Women.* Stanford, Calif.: Stanford University Press.

Slipp, Samuel. 1993. *The Freudian Mystique: Freud, Women, and Feminism.* New York: New York University Press.

Small, Meredith F. 1999. A woman's curse? *The Sciences* 39: 24–29.

Smyers, Karen A. 1983. Women and Shinto: the relation between purity and pollution. *Japanese Religions* 12: 7–18.

Solomon, Michael. 1997. *The Literature of Misogyny in Medieval Spain: The* Arcipreste de Talavera *and the* Spill. Cambridge: Cambridge University Press.

Spacks, Patricia A. M. 1985. *Gossip.* New York: Knopf.

Spiro, Melford. 1982. *Oedipus in the Trobriands.* Chicago: University of Chicago Press.

———. 1997. *Gender Ideology and Psychological Reality: An Essay on Cultural Reproduction.* New Haven, Conn.: Yale University Press.

Sponberg, Alan. 1992. Attitudes toward women and the feminine in early Buddhism. In *Buddhism, Sexuality, and Gender,* ed. José Ignacio Cabezón, pp. 3–36. Albany: State University of New York Press.

Stephens, William N. 1962. *The Oedipus Complex: Cross-Cultural Evidence.* New York: Free Press.

———. 1967. A cross-cultural study of menstrual taboos. In *Cross-Cultural Approaches: Readings in Comparative Research,* ed. Clellan S. Ford, pp. 67–94. New Haven, Conn.: HRAF Press.

Stewart, Frank H. 1994. *Honor.* Chicago: University of Chicago Press.

Stoll, Anita K. and Dawn L. Smith. 1991. *The Perception of Women in Spanish Theater of the Golden Age.* Lewisburg, Pa.: Bucknell University Press.

Stoller, Robert. 1974a. Facts and fancies: an examination of Freud's concept of bisexuality. In *Women and Analysis,* ed. Jean Strouse, pp. 343–64. New York: Dell.

———. 1974b. Symbiosis anxiety and the development of gender identity. *Archives of General Psychiatry* 30: 163–72.

Stowasser, Barbara F. 1993. Women's issues in modern Islamic thought. In *Arab Women: Old Boundaries, New Frontiers,* ed. Judith E. Tucker, pp. 3–28. Bloomington: Indiana University Press.

———. 1994. *Women in the Qur'an: Traditions, and Interpretations.* Oxford: Oxford University Press.

Stross, Brian. 1974. Tzeltal marriage by capture. *Anthropological Quarterly* 47: 328–46.

Swafford, Jan. 1997. *Johannes Brahms: A Biography.* New York: Knopf.

Symons, Donald. 1979. *The Evolution of Human Sexuality.* New York: Oxford University Press.

Taggart, James M. 1997. *The Bear and His Sons: Masculinity in Spanish and Mexican Folktales.* Austin: University of Texas Press.

Taylor, Edward B. 1888. On a method of investigating the development of institutions, applied to laws of marriage and descent. *Journal of the Royal Anthropological Institute* 17: 245–72.

Theweleit, Klaus. 1987. *Male Fantasies.* Trans. Stephan Conway, Erica Carter, and Chris Turner. Minneapolis: University of Minnesota Press.

Thompson, Stith. 1956. *Motif-Index of Folk Culture.* 6 vols. Bloomington: Indiana University Press.

Thweatt, Vivien. 1980. *La Rochefoucauld and the Seventeenth-Century Concept of the Self.* Geneva: Droz.

Tinder, Glenn. 1997. *Political Thinking: The Perennial Questions.* 6th ed. New York: HarperCollins.

Torgovnick, Marianna. 1990. *Gone Primitive: Savage Intellects, Modern Lives.* Chicago: University of Chicago Press.

Trethowan, William H. 1972. The couvade syndrome. In *Modern Perspectives in Psycho-Obstetrics,* ed. John G. Howells, pp. 68–93. New York: Brunner/Mazel.

Tucker, Judith E., ed. 1993. *Arab Women: Old Boundaries, New Frontiers.* Bloomington: Indiana University Press.

———. 1998. *In the House of the Law: Gender and Islamic Law in Ottoman Syria and Palestine.* Berkeley: University of California Press.

Turner, Victor. 1967. *The Forest of Symbols.* Ithaca, N.Y.: Cornell University Press.

Tuzin, Donald F. 1980. *The Voice of the Tambaran: Truth and Illusion in Ilahita Arapesh Religion.* Berkeley: University of California Press.

———. 1982. Ritual violence among the Ilahita Arapesh: the dynamics of moral and religious uncertainty. In *Rituals of Manhood: Male Initiation in Papua New Guinea,* ed. Gilbert H. Herdt, pp. 321–56. Berkeley: University of California Press.

———. 1997. *The Cassowary's Revenge.* Chicago: University of Chicago Press.

Varisco, Daniel M. 1995. Gendering Islam: orientalists, believers, and feminists at play in the bed of the prophet. Paper read at the Annual Meeting of the American Anthropological Association, Washington, D.C., December 3.

Vogt, Carl. 1864. *Lectures on Man: His Place in Creation, and in the History of the Earth.* Ed. James Hunt. London: Longman, Green.

Warner, Marina. 1998. *No Go the Bogeyman: Scaring, Lulling, and Making Mock.* New York: Farrar, Straus and Giroux.

Waterman, T. T. and A. L. Kroeber. 1965 (1934). Yurok marriages. *American Archaeology and Ethnology* 35: 1–15. New York: Kraus Reprints.

Watson, Patricia A. 1995. *Ancient Stepmothers: Myth, Misogyny, and Reality.* Leiden: E. J. Brill.

Wedekind, Frank. 1972. *The Lulu Plays and Other Tragedies*. Trans. Stephen Spender. London: Calder Books.

Weideger, Paula. 1976. *Menstruation and Menopause: The Physiology and Psychology, the Myth and the Reality*. New York: Knopf.

Weigert, Andrew. 1991. *Mixed Emotions: Certain Steps Toward Understanding Ambivalence*. Albany: State University of New York Press.

Weininger, Otto. 1906. *Sex and Character*. Authorized trans. New York: W. Heinemann.

White, David Gordon. 1991. *Myths of the Dog-Man*. Chicago: University of Chicago Press.

Whiting, John M. W., R. K. Kluckhohn, and A. Anthony. 1958. The function of male initiation ceremonies at puberty. In *Readings in Social Psychology,* ed. Eleanor Maccoby, T. M. Newcomb, and E. L. Hartley, pp. 359–70. New York: Holt, Rinehart, Winston.

Williams, David. 1996. *Deformed Discourse: The Function of the Monster in Medieval Thought and Literature*. Montreal: McGill-Queen's University Press.

Williams, Francis E. 1969 (1936). *Papuans of the Trans-Fly*. Oxford: Clarendon Press.

Williams, Thomas R. 1965. *The Dusun: A North Borneo Society*. New York: Holt, Rinehart, Winston.

Wilson, Katharina M. and Elizabeth M. Makowski. 1990. *Wykked Wives and Woes of Marriage: Misogamous Literature from Juvenal to Chaucer*. Albany: State University of New York Press.

Wycherley, William. (1979). *The Plays of William Wycherley*. Ed. Arthur Friedman. Oxford: Clarendon Press.

Wylie, Philip. 1942 (1959). *Generation of Vipers*. New York: Pocket Books.

Yalman, Nur. 1963. On the purity of women in the castes of Ceylon and Malabar. *Journal of the Royal Anthropological Institute* 93: 25–58.

Zapperi, Roberto. 1991. *The Pregnant Man*. Trans. Brian Williams. 4th ed. New York: Harwood Academic.

Zilboorg, Gregory. 1944. Masculine and feminine: some biological and cultural aspects. *Psychiatry* 7: 289–301.

Index